C000006248

Eyewitness on the
Somme
1916

Eyewitness on the
Somme

1916

Matthew Richardson

Foreword by
Professor Gary Sheffield

Pen & Sword
MILITARY

First published in Great Britain in 2015 by
Pen & Sword Military
an imprint of
Pen & Sword Books Ltd
47 Church Street
Barnsley
South Yorkshire
S70 2AS

Copyright © Matthew Richardson 2015

ISBN 978 1 78159 299 1

The right of Matthew Richardson to be identified as the Author of this Work
has been asserted by him in accordance with the Copyright, Designs and
Patents Act 1988.

A CIP catalogue record for this book is available from the British Library

All rights reserved. No part of this book may be reproduced or transmitted in
any form or by any means, electronic or mechanical including photocopying,
recording or by any information storage and retrieval system, without
permission from the Publisher in writing.

Typeset in Ehrhardt by
Mac Style Ltd, Bridlington, East Yorkshire
Printed and bound in the UK by CPI Group (UK) Ltd,
Croydon, CR0 4YY

Pen & Sword Books Ltd incorporates the imprints of Pen & Sword
Archaeology, Atlas, Aviation, Battleground, Discovery, Family History,
History, Maritime, Military, Naval, Politics, Railways, Select, Transport, True
Crime, and Fiction, Frontline Books, Leo Cooper, Praetorian Press, Seaforth
Publishing and Wharncliffe.

For a complete list of Pen & Sword titles please contact
PEN & SWORD BOOKS LIMITED
47 Church Street, Barnsley, South Yorkshire, S70 2AS, England
E-mail: enquiries@pen-and-sword.co.uk
Website: www.pen-and-sword.co.uk

Contents

Foreword

by Professor Gary Sheffield

During my career as a professional military historian, the Battle of the Somme, July to November 1916, has never been very far away. As I've related elsewhere, reading Martin Middlebrook's *The First Day on the Somme* (1971) fired my imagination in my early teens. The battalion that I studied for my MA thesis [22nd Royal Fusiliers (Kensington)] fought on the Somme, and I made the first of very many visits to the Somme battlefield in 1986. Over the years I have lectured about the Somme, written about it, and on many occasions taken civilian and military groups over the ground. One might be forgiven for thinking that after all this time there is nothing fresh to say about this battle, but this is far from true. The Battle of the Somme remains intensely controversial among historians, and the popular media returns to the subject again and again. Interestingly, it now occupies the place once reserved for 'Passchendaele', the Third Battle of Ypres, as the totemic ghastliest British battle of the First World War. Or, at least, the first day of the battle has; the other 141 days of the battle, with the possible exception of 15 September 1916, the first time that tanks were used in combat, have almost entirely disappeared from collective British memory.

One of the many virtues of Matthew Richardson's new account of the Somme is that he does not lose sight of the fact that the battle lasted for four months, not a single day. He also looks far beyond the British contribution to examine the perspective of German and French participants in the battle, and, significantly, acknowledges the Imperial dimension. Rarely is the voice of a Black African soldier from France's colonies heard in the context of the Somme, but the memories of Nar Diouf, a Senegalese tirailleur, appear here. Collections of first-hand accounts tend to focus on the conditions experienced by soldiers, but those quoted here sometimes move beyond the small change of soldiering. Thus Sous Lieutenant Louis Mairet reflected on the way his motivation for fighting had changed, while Lieutenant Adrian Stephen of the Royal Field Artillery gave valuable contemporary evidence on the evolution of British infantry tactics.

Next year, 2016, marks the centenary of the Battle of the Somme, and I can safely predict that media interest will be significant, and much of the reporting will be hackneyed and ill-informed. The new perspectives in Matthew Richardson's excellent book are therefore very timely. *Eyewitness on the Somme* deserves a wide audience.

Gary Sheffield MA Ph D FRHistS FRSA
Professor of War Studies
University of Wolverhampton

Acknowledgements

No book such as this could reach print without the assistance of a great number of people. The first and most obvious acknowledgement which I must make is to Gary Sheffield for providing the Foreword. Although our paths have crossed directly only a handful of times, I have always been something of a 'fan' of his work and more importantly a great respecter of his scholarship. I am immensely grateful to him for finding the time to do me this honour. Over the years my knowledge and understanding of the Battle of the Somme were shaped by contact and conversation with numerous people, both in Britain and in France. First and foremost of these are undoubtedly Dr Peter Liddle, friend and former colleague, whose personal contribution to preserving the documentary record of the battle at an individual level is unrivalled, and Paul Reed, who has spent many years walking and studying the battlefield. Both of these men were kind enough to share their thoughts with me over the years. Naturally, any errors of fact or interpretation within this book remain solely my own responsibility.

Once again I would like to thank Margaret Holmes for permission to quote from her father Frank Richards' wonderful memoir *Old Soldiers Never Die*. I read this book for the first time when my interest in the First World War was just awakening. It made a profound impact upon me, and a few years later I was able to realise an ambition when I stood at the spot from which Richards had observed the attack on High Wood. Jo Edkins was likewise extremely helpful in allowing me to quote from her father's memoir. Frédéric Henry allowed me to use extracts from his grandfather's book *Un Meusien au Coeur des Deux Guerres*. Andrew Jackson generously allowed me to use material from his website, for which I thank him. Christian Griesinger again helped me with German material. John Davies kindly loaned to me paperwork relating to his grandfather's service on the Somme. Guy Brocklebank allowed me once again to quote from the memoirs of his great uncle Major Richard Archer-Houblon, whilst Dr Robert Murray granted my request to quote from the diary of his grandfather C.M. Murray. Similar kindness was shown to me by Mrs Mavis Cripps in regard to her late husband Brigadier B.U.S. Cripps, and many years ago by the late Chester Read, who so generously allowed me to use the material of his father, I.L. Read. Richard Davies at the University of Leeds was of great help to me in my research once again. Special mention must also be made of Professor Joe Lunn of the University of Michigan. Despite the pressing responsibilities of his academic position, Professor Lunn found time to source for me from his own oral history archive first-hand testimony from Senegalese veterans of the Somme, and generously allowed me to use this material. I thank him warmly, and recommend his book *Memoirs of the Maelstrom: A Senegalese Oral History of the First World War*.

Ron Austin's books *Forward Undeterred* and *Cobbers in Khaki* are a marvellous resource, being generously leavened with first-hand accounts, and are a fitting tribute to the two Australian battalions which they document. I first came across these books in Australia in 2001, and I still refer to them often. Likewise Ian Uys's *Rollcall* is to be commended.

Others who helped me in Germany were Lars Fischer at the Staatsarchiv in Bremen, and Sylvia Schönwald at the Deutsche Nationalbibliothek, Leipzig. I would like to pay special tribute to my friend and colleague John Caley, who prepared so many of the photographs in this book; Jori Wiegmans also deserves great credit once again for his assistance with illustrations. Rupert Harding and the team at Pen & Sword have shown consistent support for my research over a number of years, which I gratefully acknowledge. Finally, as always, I thank my family for their forbearance and patience whilst this book was in preparation.

Matthew Richardson
Douglas, Isle of Man
2015

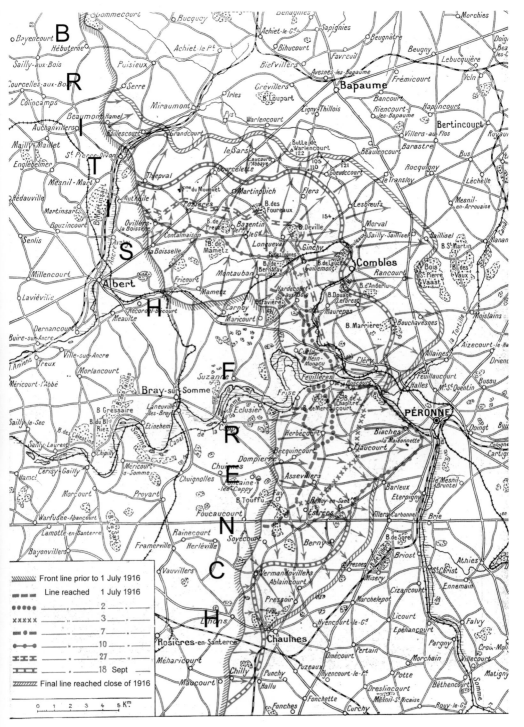

The Battle of the Somme, July–November 1916.

Introduction

The Battle of the Somme, fought in the summer of 1916 across a tract of land in north-eastern France, was a compromise. It was born out of the realities of coalition warfare. The British and French were allies in the First World War, but not necessarily always equal partners. Britain was a sea power, and her peacetime army was relatively small. If the British were the senior partner at sea, on land the French, with a mass army based on conscription, called the tune. The French had borne much of the burden of the fighting on the Western Front up to 1916, and were anxious that, as the newly raised divisions of 'Kitchener's Army' began to arrive on the Western Front, so the British should now pull their weight in the effort to drive the Germans out of France. With all of the allied nations committed to offensives that summer, there was widespread hope that the tide of the war could finally be turned against the Central Powers. On the Western Front, the French commander Joffre suggested that the British and French armies attack where their two sectors adjoined, on the Somme. The British Commander-in-Chief, Sir Douglas Haig, conscious of his status as the junior partner, acquiesced, even though he would have preferred to attack in Flanders, where at that time the enemy defences were weaker. Haig was also aware that whilst an attack in Flanders would have a strategic dimension in that it might force the enemy to give up part of the Belgian coast, an offensive on the Somme offered no objective of significant strategic value, beyond perhaps the railway junction of Bapaume.

When the Verdun offensive was launched by the Germans in February 1916, it drew more and more French troops into its jaws. The effect of this was twofold. Firstly, the French contribution to the Battle of the Somme was reduced as less manpower was available (thus leaving the control and direction of the battle more firmly in the hands of Haig and his subordinates). Secondly, the political pressure from the French to launch the battle sooner rather than later, in order to draw German troops away from Verdun and thus relieve the hard-pressed French troops in that sector, became almost irresistible.

The battle was launched on 1 July 1916 with high hopes that Bapaume would be taken within days. However, sturdy belts of barbed wire, relatively undamaged by the British bombardment and stoutly defended by the enemy, put paid to any ideas of opening up the German lines and letting the cavalry through. When the realistic prospect of an allied breakthrough on the Somme began to recede, then even this limited objective was eschewed. The objective of the allies here became instead simply the destruction of the German army. The Germans for their part had had two years of relative peace on the Somme to construct their defences, but as the battle wore on they to no small extent also contributed towards achieving Haig's objective by their relentless policy of counter-attacking.

In sitting down to write this book, I was conscious of the fact that acres of paper and gallons of ink had already been expended on the Battle of the Somme. What could I possibly say about it that was new and original? Well, for many previous authors, from the United Kingdom at least, the Somme has been perceived exclusively as a British (or at best a Commonwealth) battle. Yes, it was a British battle, but it was also a German battle, a French battle, a Senegalese battle and even an American battle, for many citizens of the USA served in the British and French ranks, even though their country was still neutral. How many British readers know, for example, that a much-respected American war poet called Alan Seeger died on the Somme in a French uniform? Thus this book tries as far as possible to include testimony from a wide range of sources, reflecting experiences on both sides of the front line, and from both allied partners. There is also a tendency among British authors either to treat the air battle on the Somme as a separate entity, or in some cases to disregard it altogether. This book attempts to integrate both the land and air campaigns.

Finally, I felt that it was time for a return to first principles, and this book, as the title suggests, has been put together using often long-forgotten first-hand eyewitness accounts. Many of these have never before appeared in English, whilst those that have are often now many years out of print and known only to those with a specialist knowledge of the subject. I have long been fascinated by the First World War as it was experienced by ordinary soldiers, and have spent most of my adult life engaged in a study of what that war was really like for British infantrymen. Yet the research for this book has brought me into contact with many new authors and diarists with whom I was previously unfamiliar, men in *feldgrau* or *horizon bleu*, and if this book achieves nothing else then I hope at the very least to have introduced English-speaking readers to some protagonists in the Battle of the Somme whose words have never previously appeared in their language. If I could wish to go further than this, then the objective of this book would be to chart the hopes and aspirations of the men (and women) involved, and their attitudes towards themselves, towards their cause, and towards their enemies. It will examine the rising and falling barometer of morale in the three armies involved as the battle ground on and fatigue and ultimately the weather took their toll, as well as offering some insight into what the experience of combat was truly like, and what enabled men to endure this hardship.

And there are other eyewitnesses, not necessarily human, that can tell us something about this battle. The colour plates of this book contain photographs of objects which one hundred years later remain as silent witnesses to the ferocity of the fighting on the Somme. These objects may speak softly, but they have much to tell us if we choose to listen. The equipment or rifle dropped by a soldier many years ago speaks of a moment of individual tragedy; the bullet-holed mess tin or twisted shell fragment tell us of the sheer fury of the onslaughts which collectively made up the battle. Mundane items such as food tins tell us of the everyday life of the combatants. Many of the objects featured also have personal significance, as they were found by me, over many years of field walking, whilst seeking to understand the topography of the Somme battlefield. If you have never walked the ground, and the opportunity presents itself, then I would unhesitatingly recommend that you should take it. Viewing the battlefield from the German positions, one is often left with a sense of awe. The Germans could see for miles, and the question often becomes not 'how were so many casualties caused?' but one of wonder that the British and French ever turned the Germans out of these positions at all.

Chapter One

An Atmosphere Inimical to Anxiety

The Battle of the Somme was born at the Chantilly inter-allied conference in December 1915. The First World War was then just short of eighteen months old, and the Germans remained resolutely entrenched along a line from the Channel to the Swiss frontier, behind which lay much of Belgium and a considerable stretch of French territory. The political imperative to drive them back and to free these lands was felt acutely at both British and French general headquarters. It was at Chantilly that the French Commander in Chief, Joseph Joffre, had outlined his strategic ambitions for the coming year, which amounted to a series of co-ordinated offensives on all of the major battlefronts, to be launched as soon as practicably possible, in order to apply simultaneous pressure to the Central Powers. In particular, he wanted a joint Anglo-French offensive to be launched on the Western Front. At this point in the war the British were still very much the junior partner in this theatre of operations, the French having more than twice the number of divisions as the British. Thus it was Joffre's view which carried the day,

Sir Douglas Haig arrives at a conference with his French counterparts. (*Library of Congress*)

despite the fact that his British opposite number, Sir Douglas Haig, believed that Flanders offered better scope for an offensive. Haig's weakness was further underlined by a set of instructions given to him at the end of December by the British Secretary of State for War, Lord Kitchener, which stated that Haig was to co-operate in as full a manner as possible with the French.

Later conferences fixed the location and date of the offensive as the Somme sector, in the countryside of Picardy, in the early summer of 1916 – also matters of Joffre's choosing. Two subsequent elements also influenced the planning of the battle. The first was the growing strength of the British Expeditionary Force (BEF), with the arrival in France in late 1915 of numbers of divisions raised the previous year as Kitchener's New Army. The second factor was the launch on 21 February 1916 of the German offensive against the French army at Verdun, which meant that the need for the battle took on renewed urgency in order to relieve the pressure on the French. These two developments combined to ensure that even though the choice of ground and timing were of French origin, ironically the bulk of the effort on the Somme would be made by the British.

Units of the British army began to arrive in the Somme region in the late autumn of 1915. They found it a quieter sector than those from which many of these British battalions had come, particularly around Ypres or La Bassée for example. With gently undulating fields, and woods and villages largely intact and undamaged by shellfire, and birdsong coming from the trees, it offered to many a vision of tranquillity. The German and French units in the area had in most cases been there since the autumn of 1914. Although there had been skirmishes around then, the sector had remained largely peaceful ever since. British officer G.C.N. Webb was typical of many when he wrote in a letter home:

> The country is simply superb. I have never seen anything in England to compare with the valley of the Somme. It is one mass of lakes and ponds in a broad valley for miles and miles and the woods are beyond description.[1]

Even the simple beauty of the Somme country was by itself enough to inspire fresh hope, and to buoy the morale of those who arrived there from further north. British Royal Horse Artillery officer Major R. Archer-Houblon wrote in his memoirs:

> The troops destined to open the battle of the Somme assembled in the highest spirits. Everything was in their favour. The broad plains of Picardy basked in the generous rays of a warm sun; for days a cloudless sky vaulted the smiling landscape; the birds sang, and rooks ranged lazily over the slumbering fields; and on every side the rich crops promised an ample harvest.

> To numbers of men the Somme country proved deeply attractive. Several divisions hailed from the dreary waterlogged levels of Flanders, where at best a few flat fields of muddy ploughland, wearying to the eye and depressing to the soul, had formed their outlook; others had bade glad farewell to the nightmare horrors of the Salient, where the shadow of doom had always hung over them so closely. Now, however, they had come to a country which was not only pleasant to look upon, but which seemed to promise every prospect of victory. It was a land of mile upon mile of rolling plain; of sheltered sun-warmed valleys; and of shady roads bordered by rows of tall and noble poplars. Here lay displayed the rich foliage of a densely timbered wood; there, nestling

in trees, stood the grey church tower and clustering houses of a village. It was a land of great distances, where all the far hills and shadowed woods were bathed in deepest blue. To the east the landscape grew wilder, till near the line the abandoned fields grew self-sown crops in wanton profusion, and great blazes of scarlet poppies, yellow mustard, blue cornflowers, and rich crimson clover ran riot on the sun-bathed slopes.[2]

The bulk of the fighting here would be taken on by General Sir Henry Rawlinson's Fourth Army. Much has been made of the fact that Rawlinson's army contained a high proportion of New Army recruits, in whom their commander allegedly had little faith. Be that as it may, the fact is that his army also contained a good leavening of Regular units. Indeed, of the twenty-five divisions which began the battle, six were Regular in origin. As the battle developed, General Sir Hubert Gough's Reserve Army would grow in strength to become the Fifth Army. To the south, the French Sixth Army held positions astride the River Somme itself.

The Germans in particular had put their time to good use during the months of peace on the Somme, in fortifying their positions. They had constructed deep dugouts, in some cases thirty feet below the surface, in which their men could shelter from bombardment. Each village on their front line had been turned into a fortress, with loopholed walls and concrete reinforcement. Where a sizeable distance existed between these fortress villages, the Germans had constructed redoubts. In the months leading up to the battle, activity intensified behind the British lines as well. At several positions along the front line British engineers constructed tunnels beneath No Man's Land for the purpose of placing explosive charges under German strongpoints. Eight of these mines were set to explode before zero hour at 7.20am on the first morning of the battle. New railway lines and sidings

A German postcard from 1915 showing the ruins of Fricourt château. The village was to be built into the German front-line defences, and all trace of the château would soon be gone.

were constructed for the movement of men and ammunition, and training of the troops who were to undertake the assault intensified. For example, Private Charles Barton of the RAMC, writing in the summer of 1916, stated:

> The preparations were magnificent in every detail. Here is one instance: We had a model of the German lines, roads, trenches, and all units of our division concerned in this great attack received lectures at it. Our people meant to have no mistakes this time … Before the attack we were all ready …[3]

Other preparations were being undertaken by the men and machines of the Royal Flying Corps (RFC). The strength of the RFC on the Somme front had grown progressively during June 1916, and the British Fourth Army now had some 109 aircraft directly in its support, plus a further 70 upon which it could call for reinforcement. Opposing them were 129 German aircraft of various types. Allied aerial observation of the German positions was hampered by bad weather that month – on 23 June lightning destroyed the kite balloons of No. 1 and No. 14 sections, and damaged another. On 24 June, in low cloud and rain, the preparatory bombardment for the attack began. Despite the difficulties imposed by the weather, RFC pilots flew low and directed fire onto forty enemy targets. Two days later British aviators made a concerted effort to cripple the enemy's observation capability by attacking German observation balloons along the entire front. Five were destroyed, followed by another three on 26 June.

Captain George F. Campbell was a Royal Flying Corps pilot with 32 Squadron. During the final weeks before the battle he and his comrades were engaged in the vital task of securing aerial supremacy over the battlefield:

> France is beautiful in summer anyway, though we found the heat intense during the last days of June and the first of July, the period of the greatest air battles of history up to that time. It was up to us of the air service to prepare for the 'big push' by blinding the 'eyes' of the Boche, if we could. His observers must be driven from the air. We knew that we had our work cut out for us, because at the outset we were getting pretty well outnumbered in the air, and air supremacy meant much to the boys of the Army in general. But all of our pilots kept a stiff upper lip, said little or nothing, and looked forward keenly to our coming engagements. There was a little uncertainty about everything, and this was far from cheering, because it looked for a while as if we were about to make a last stand against the enemy. Up to this time our Squadron had been fairly lucky, having lost only three missing and two killed of the combatant quota, that is, the pilots. But we knew our time was coming, for stern work was ahead of us. We felt it in the air.[4]

Yet the British commanders also faced a conundrum. Experience, particularly at the Battle of Loos the previous year, had taught them that if an offensive were to stand any chance of success, then ammunition dumps must be created within easy reach of the front line, and camps must be established in similar proximity in which to hold reinforcements, ready to quickly exploit any breakthrough. The trouble was that these thorough preparations, necessary though they were, also signalled like a beacon to the enemy the probable location of a forthcoming attack. The Germans for their part could be in no doubt that something was afoot on the Somme front. In spite of British efforts to restrict aerial observation, their pilots could still see and report the developments below them. The only question as far as the Germans were concerned was what to make of all this activity. Indeed, to them the British and French preparations seemed so obvious as to constitute a deliberate feint, at least as far as the army was concerned. German airmen, however, repeatedly tried to warn their infantry counterparts that a major Anglo–French attack on the Somme was imminent. A senior German air officer wrote of this at the end of the war, stating that:

In March 1916, our airmen reported the movement of large masses of troops of the French Arras group to the south, numerous new tented camps north of the Somme, and attempts by the enemy airmen to block us and deny us this insight. Thus, for example, the Bavarian Flying Section Nr 1 found on 23 April, to the east of Villers Brettoneux, two new enemy airfields, also a large practice works at Corbie, likewise large new factory-like buildings in the same area. By mid–May, the two aforementioned airfields had increased to four, with thirteen sheds for about 50 aircraft, also reported was the emergence of tented and hutted camps between the Ancre and the Somme. Military training areas and railway facilities at Vecquemont were visible in the photos. In the reports the view was also expressed that the camps north of the Somme could be regarded as English and those south of the Somme as of French origin. In May, similar findings were made by Flying Sections 23, 32 and 59. Already by then there could be little doubt about the area and direction of the attack.

In the first half of June, pictures from the area of Hammerwald showed new attack trenches, leading far back from the front to the north. The leader of the Bavarian Flying Section Nr 1 brought this information to the responsible staff officer of the XIV Reserve Armee Korps for discussion, stressing that together with lively and aggressive enemy air activity in this area, it meant that an attack from that direction must be likely. He was dismissed with the decision that nothing was going on down there, an attack could be achieved only further north and was anticipated at Serre and Hebuterne. His view that the probability of an attack could be expected on the weak projecting salient of Fricourt was not heeded. The request of the section to General Headquarters for permission to make a daily report on the position was rejected in writing. A flight by the same unit on 17 June showed with complete clarity a massive proliferation of battery positions, dugout constructions, proximity, assembly and cable trenches, especially south and east of Hammerwald. All photographic images were rushed to General Headquarters and to the AOK 2 and to the troops concerned. On 19 June the findings made so far were confirmed by further aerial reconnaissances, especially the construction of a honeycomb of trenches in the park and to the south of Maricourt.

On 20 June General Headquarters was presented with a new sketch showing the position of the recently constructed works. On 17 July, on the occasion of my presence at the Bavarian Flying Section Nr 1, I personally had sight of a copy of an aviator's message dated 22 June, 10.30am to the General Headquarters XIV Reserve Armee Korps, endorsed with the following wording:

'*The enemy attack – when he attacks – will have Maricourt as the centre of the right wing, not only the area around Gommecourt. He will not miss the Fricourt salient which is tactically favourable to him.*'

Flying Section Nr 32 presented photographs which identified Gommecourt as the place against which earthworks for an attack were most advanced, and south of the Somme

A close-up view of a German aircraft-mounted camera, used for observation of enemy positions on the Somme. (*Library of Congress*)

A German photo-reconnaissance aircraft about to embark on a mission. Note the camera mounted on the forward cockpit. (*Library of Congress*)

French troops in reserve positions behind the Somme front. (*Library of Congress*)

up to the Roman road, Flying Section Nr 27 showed through numerous photographs the rapid progression of enemy attack trenches there. However, the same General Headquarters made the assessment, based on the evaluation of photographs, that the works between Rouvroy and the Oise were only for demonstration purposes.[5]

As the Germans had so clearly observed, new French units were also moving to this sector, in spite of the ongoing commitment of the French army in the Verdun sector. Marcel Étévé, a *lieutenant* serving with the French *417e Regiment d'Infanterie* near Maucourt, was one of those who had been moved up to the Somme. He wrote to his mother on 6 June:

We are now to the north, in a horrible flat country, where villages are made of brick and the locals of wood. This is also my country, it seems, for now anyway. We see little of the brick of the houses and even less of the natives; we did five days on the front line in a village which was completely demolished, but this was actually quite nice. The trench there wound its way between avalanches of roofs and walls, it passed through orchards which were once cultivated but from which the produce is no longer harvested. We had to pass through there on all fours, but it was not without a sense of pleasure: the grass in all directions, the strands of barbed wire, and masses of flowers: roses, tulips and carnations that were once ordered and in straight rows, but which now grow in a complete jumble of madness. Not to mention delectable and unexpected strawberries. Our accommodation left something to be desired and our dugouts smelt annoyingly musty, none of which deprived the rats of this sector of their vitality. As for the Germans, they had sent gas over to our predecessors, and, pleased with this practical joke, they left us largely in peace. Apart from a night ambush which they sprung on one of our patrols, and in which they left two of their comrades hanging on the barbed wire, they were decent enough.[6]

In another letter the following day he wrote, again to his mother, of the growing sense of camaraderie between this French unit and their new neighbours the British, in this great endeavour:

> Here we are once more in reserve, 2 kilometers from the line, in a very large village, which was once quite badly bombed, and from which the civilians were long since evacuated. That is to say that we are now the lords and masters, all the houses belong to us, and we select one at our leisure. I live with the officers of the company, in a huge house, a little torn, with a lovely garden and a large shaded courtyard. We have gathered in one place the remaining doors and tiles, and we feel at home. Suspended, above our table, is a swallow's nest; the installation of windows has rather upset these creatures, who now await the moment when the door is open to come flying around us. It is certainly nice. In a nearby house, I found an old Pleyel (made by Pleyel, supplier to the King): a four octave, piano-spinet, completely delightful; I could play Couperin, if I had the music here, and if the instrument were not missing so many keys ... and here, as a distraction, mother, we have an unexpected version of 'Tipperary', which an ingenious type from our company revealed to us this morning; it begins: 'He knows the English, the Pifferari ...' What a charming symbol of the *entente cordiale* between all the allies, is it not?[7]

Among the French troops awaiting the order to advance, there was a mixture of anxiety and anticipation, but this was underlined by confidence that the battle would be a great success. Robert Whitney Imbrie, an American volunteer ambulance driver with the French army on the Somme, remembered the high state of morale among the French soldiers around him:

> We mingled with our neighbors and talked with them, but no matter how the conversation started it was sure to come around to the one, great, all-important subject – the attack. Even for us who were not to be 'sent in' but whose duty it would be merely to carry those who had been, the delay and suspense were trying. How much worse then, it must have been for those men who 'were going over the top,' waiting, waiting, many of them for their chance to greet death. I remember one afternoon talking with a chap who before the war had kept a restaurant in Prince's Street in Edinburgh, a restaurant at which I remember having dined. He was an odd little Frenchman, alert and bright-eyed, and every now and then as he talked he would pat me on the shoulder and exclaim 'Oh, my boy.' He assured me that very soon now we should see the attack. 'Oh, my boy, the world very soon will talk of this place. You will see the name of this village on maps' – a true prophecy, for when the New York papers came to us weeks after the attack had started, I saw a map with Cappy marked upon it. 'Soon greater than Verdun we shall see, great things, and oh, my boy, we are here to see them; we are part of them. *C'est magnifique!* but the waiting, the waiting, why can't they end it? Send us in. *Quant à moi* – I go with the second wave, and if I come out, *après la guerre*, you will come to my place, my place in Prince's Street which you know, and for you I will open

A camouflaged French heavy gun on the Somme front, 1916. (*From the French magazine L'Illustration*)

the finest champagne of *La belle France* and we will raise our glasses and drink to these days, but oh, my boy, the waiting, *c'est terrible*.'

My journal for these days reflects a feeling of suspense. 'Tuesday, June 13th: on repos today for which I was thankful, since the rain still continues, with a low temperature. Spent most of the day in my bag reading as being about the only place I could keep warm. The 20th Zouaves marched into town today, their bugles playing. Their arrival and the presence of the Senegalese can mean but one thing: the attack will soon be launched. Well, if it's coming it can't come too soon. This suspense is trying. If this weather continues I will have trench foot again as my shoes are leaking. Firing has been unusually heavy today, and tonight a terrific bombardment is in progress.'[8]

Another American ambulance driver, William Yorke Stevenson, wrote of the reason for much of the buoyant French confidence on the Somme in June 1916 – the overwhelming superiority of firepower being brought together on this part of the front:

June 8. Big train of great '220' mortars came by on their way to Chuignes this morning, eight of them drawn by huge Renault & Jeffery (American) trucks, whose wheels in front, as well as rear, were tractors – the couplings of these to the carriages carrying the trails and 'camion' were the same as those on railways, and the carriages were made in Troy, Ohio. They shoot a shell five feet high weighing three hundred kilos, and carry about ten kilometers. They are meant only to reduce fortifications ... The big-gun train is camping here temporarily until the emplacements are finished. Everywhere house barracks and log protections are being erected and the country is simply alive with working men. One hundred 'camions' turned up here to-day, of the largest size. They are just the ordinary service wagons for the '8-270s'! Another train of '220s' passed later. The gunners had amused themselves by naming them 'Le Bourdon,' 'Le Gueuleur,' and so on. All their guns and their accessories are in the multi-colored tones of paint, green, ochre, black, and brown, and look like maps. One 'camion' drags the base and turntable, another the gun itself; the rest, gasoline and ammunition.[9]

A heavy shell about to be loaded into a French artillery piece. French superiority in heavy guns contributed greatly to their success in the first phase of the Somme battle. (*From the French magazine L'Illustration*)

A few days later Stevenson also writes of the torrential rain in late June, which threatened to derail the timetable of the battle. In fact, by the final week of June, so wet was the ground after the heavy rain that the date of the offensive was put back two days in order to give the battlefield a chance to dry out. Originally planned for 28 June, the attack would now be launched on 1 July. There was immediate concern that as a result, British artillery ammunition would be insufficient for an additional two days of bombardment, and batteries were ordered to slacken their rate of fire. This had the unfortunate effect of letting the pressure off the Germans at just the vital moment, and there were even reports in some cases of Germans being able to rebuild damaged defences as a result. Stevenson also describes Senegalese shock troops moving forward, a clear indicator of an imminent attack, as these West African colonial troops were frequently used by the French in the vanguard of an assault. Other French preparations were more sombre:

> In addition to the customary bombardment we are in the midst of a violent thunder and hail storm; the crashes of thunder and lightning mingling with the roar of the guns certainly is creating a real pandemonium. This makes one week so far of solid rain and the roads are almost impassable from mud and traffic combined ... The roads are so blocked that the food is slow to reach the Front just now. Today, for instance, we were on half-rations here at Cappy. As we sat at our coffee however, the 'ravitaillement camions' turned up and there was great rejoicing.
>
> June 13 ... Shoals of Senegalese are passing toward the Front, and it certainly looks as if the offensive was coming soon ... I hear we are going to be shifted again; headquarters to be at Proyart and evacuate to the new hospital at Marcel Cave. This will be just before the big attack. At Marcel Cave the French have erected an enormous hospital on the railway. To illustrate what is expected, they have purchased from the town an additional site for a graveyard to accommodate five thousand dead, expected to

French Senegalese troops moving forward in readiness for the attack on the Somme. (*Library of Congress*)

be the casualties from this hospital alone – not from the trenches, but those who cannot survive treatment. This gives more of an inkling as to the preparation in our Sector than anything else I have seen. And our Sector only covers some three or four miles of the Front.[10]

Preparations, however, consisted not just of the physical accumulation of materiel, but also of ensuring the mental and psychological readiness of those who were to take part. In the British army, at a regimental level, morale was heavily based upon esprit de corps. A sense of belonging to a particular unit with unique geographical distinctions was a major factor in ensuring self-worth, pride in one's work, and a common outlook. Good relations between officers and their men was another key aspect in developing morale. Men who feel that they know and can trust their officers – indeed that the officers share the same dangers and hardships as them – invariably make for better soldiers. Many commanders at battalion level did their utmost to foster esprit de corps in their unit, and in many cases the colonel of a battalion was something of a father figure. One of the best of such men was Frank Maxwell VC, commanding the 12th Battalion Middlesex Regiment, who wrote to his wife about his briefing to his men on 2 June:

I told them to break off and get as close round me as possible, sit down and smoke, and listen. I began by saying that I liked this sort of way of seeing and speaking to the regiment when I had something to say that concerned them all. Oftener it has to be through regimental orders, or through officers and NCOs, but when we can be a family, we'll be one and talk to each other as one. Then I said I was new to them, and as most of them didn't know my handsome face, I took off my hat and told them to have a good look at it. This immense jest was enormously appreciated, and after that we were on great terms, and I am ashamed to say I stood there in the middle of that 800–900 men, alternately grave and laughing at what I had to say, for over three-quarters of an hour. I don't suppose you knew I had the gift of this sort of gab; but I must have, and shall, no doubt, appear in Hyde Park the first Sunday I get home. When in full flight about the fighting spirit, which I said meant you wanted to kill a German so much that you felt you could eat him after it, I looked round to see the Padre standing amongst the officers. I begged his pardon, told him he'd have his turn next Sunday (if we weren't digging), and carried on to worse. Afterwards I spoke to him, and was surprised to hear him say he agreed with all I said. One of the lessons of Christianity was to do your task well and thoroughly, and if, as undoubtedly it was, it were the soldier's task to kill, then he must be in earnest about it, and kill and want to kill as thoroughly as I insisted.[11]

The sense of 'family' which Maxwell describes here would of course be so much higher in the New Army 'Pals' formations, where men from the same streets and factories had enlisted together, and where their platoon officer was frequently the son of the factory owner or a local professional man. Thus morale in the BEF was undoubtedly high. It was noted by many officers that as the date of the offensive approached, numbers on sick parades actually declined as no one wanted to miss it. Charles Douie, an officer of the 1st Battalion Dorsetshire Regiment at this time, has written:

'an atmosphere inimical to anxiety'. That happy phrase most adequately expresses the morale of the Dorset Regiment, and indeed of the British Army, in June of 1916[.][12]

Yet in many cases, certainly among the British, the state of mind was more than what could simply be described as a 'good mood'. By 1916 the grim reality of warfare on the Western Front was clearly apparent to all, yet there was still an overwhelming and serious sense of duty and purpose among the young men in khaki and *horizon bleu* who were about to go forth into battle. One young officer, Arthur Ratcliffe, who was to be killed on the first day of the battle, wrote in a letter published posthumously that

We are on the eve of a great battle ... The great moments which are the test of our sacrifices are at hand. We shall go not boasting, but with steadfast hearts and may the day be well crowned.[13]

Another British officer, Stephen H. Hewitt of the Royal Warwickshire Regiment, was also to lose his life on the Somme. He wrote to his parents in late June:

... we have not had an uneventful unlaborious time in the past three months, and at any moment now we are ready to enter into something ten times as bad. Fairly narrow escapes, 'windy' experiences, patrols to the enemy's wire, wiring-parties in the neighbourhood of Boche machine-guns, are of course part of the routine: in addition to this I have already been on the fringe of one exceptionally fierce bombardment. Leave I have had the ill-luck to miss by a few days. But bother leave and past experiences! We are all anxious to be up and at it now, believing that our lot has been cast into a historic enterprise, which will end in success; thanking our stars that if we fall it will be in something big; and feeling that the hazards which are a stimulus in the trenches, are a dead-weight on our thought when we are doing nothing; and that we want only one rest, the rest at Home.[14]

Second Lieutenant Ashley McGain, clearly understanding the strong possibility that he would lose his life, had prepared a letter for his parents in the event of his demise. Part of it reads:

Within the next day or so it is possible – indeed probable – that I shall die while attacking the Germans. If I do, then know that I have died happy, having done my duty. Grieve not for me, Mother mine, but rather rejoice that you were able to give a son for our noble cause. I shall do my duty – never fear … I am glad now that I live in these present times so that I am and have been able to take part in this, the greatest … of all wars.[15]

Second Lieutenant Ashley McGain, 11th Battalion Suffolk Regiment. (*Manx National Heritage*)

This soldier from the Isle of Man, who so clearly identified with his cause, was indeed to be killed on the opening day of the battle, serving with the 11th Battalion Suffolk Regiment. Lest it be thought that McGain's letter was unique or an aberration, a strikingly similar example comes from Lieutenant Billy Goodwin of the 8th Battalion York and Lancaster Regiment, writing home on 27 June:

I'm feeling most excessively cheerful – our guns are simply deafening and only bombarding deliberately at that. It's the first time the ever too late – I don't think – British have been able to show their hand genuinely! The amount of guns and infantry and cavalry – hopes of open fighting at last! – we have behind us and on a 25 mile front is perfectly amazing! We've only got to go a paltry mile or so and I tell you I'm not sorry we're the first lot to go over. I think with all our jolly artillery barraging a few yards in front of us the whole way, Mr Fritz won't dare to look for us until we're on top of him. Everybody is feeling gloriously confident which of course is half the show.[16]

Like Ashley McGain, Goodwin, who was a native of Exeter and a former scholar of Corpus Christi College, Oxford, was to lose his life on the opening day of the battle. However, it was not just the academic elite of Great Britain which would be involved in this forthcoming battle. The American war poet Alan Seeger, serving in June 1916 with the French Foreign Legion, wrote in a similar vein to a friend at home:

We go up to the attack tomorrow. This will probably be the biggest thing yet. We are to have the honor of marching in the first wave. No sacks, but two *musettes*, *toile de tente* slung over shoulder, plenty of cartridges, grenades, and *baïonnette au canon*. I will write you soon if I get through all right. If not, my only earthly care is for my poems. Add the ode I sent you and the three sonnets to my last volume and you will have *opera omnia quo existant*. I am glad to be going in first wave. If you are in this thing at all it is best to be in to the limit. And this is the supreme experience.[17]

Born in New York, Seeger was a Harvard graduate and had spent some years living a Bohemian lifestyle as a poet in Greenwich village. He had been resident in Paris in 1914, and together with a number of Americans volunteered for the French army upon the outbreak of war. Another US citizen, Harry Butters, was serving in the British Royal Field Artillery. He had a strength of feeling similar to that of Seeger towards his adopted army and

Second Lieutenant Billy Goodwin, York and Lancaster Regiment. (*Liddle Collection, University of Leeds*)

its cause, writing to his sister in California of the uncomprehending nature of many of his compatriots as to what the war was really about:

> Leave to return home is out of the question, dearest, these people have been too kind to me as it is, to bother them further and besides, I have no wish to see home again until the war is won. You are the only one who understands at all.
>
> To the others it is some far off dream of exciting news to read about. What does it mean to them! NOTHING AT ALL! They don't realise what England is standing for any more than they understand what made the moon! Tell them that she is standing for THEIR freedom and right to live in the world free from the rule of the Prussian brute, and they'll laugh at you! Ask 'em.[18]

In fact, Butters had already suffered a bout of shell-shock after experiencing heavy fighting at Loos the previous year, and might reasonably have returned home having 'done his bit' for the allied cause. However, he had refused the option of a medical board, and the probability of being discharged, in order to carry on fighting and to take part in the Somme battle. Yet another American, Charles D. Morgan, likewise an officer with the Royal Field Artillery on the Somme, wrote:

> The inspiration of the men under one is enough in itself to make it worth while. They are really splendid – far ahead of their officers, I fear, in relative efficiency. And so far as it is possible in this selfish world, we all feel we are fighting more or less for an ideal. It stirs inarticulately even in the breast of the Tommy, I think… .[19]

The last days before the breaking of the storm were characterised by an increase in activity in the immediate environs of the front line as final preparations were made. Charles Douie's battalion was in the sector between Thiepval and Authuille Wood. They had been there since the spring of 1916, taking their turn in the line under the watchful and ever-vigilant eye of the Germans in this sector, but as spring turned to summer there was a noticeable increase in activity:

> The near approach of the battle redoubled the calls on the infantry for fatigue parties, and in the last days we knew no rest. In the line the incessant shell fire and unrelenting vigilance deprived us of rest by day or night; in support we were constantly called out on working parties. At Blackhorse Bridge we paraded at 8 in the morning for day working parties, returning in the late afternoon. At 8 in the evening we went out again, returning at dawn. Officers and men grew desperately tired, and the prospect of attack which could not but terminate in a period of rest became more than ever alluring.[20]

There was also a noticeable increase in aerial patrols. In the weeks before the attack, efforts had been made to photograph the entire front line faced by the Fourth Army. Some aircraft bombed and harassed German reserves and reinforcements, whilst others attacked enemy observers in kite balloons. In the last days of June the RFC used a new British weapon, the Le Prieur rocket, together with phosphorous bombs, to bring down eight such balloons. Perhaps the most important duty of the allied airmen was counter-battery work, as Captain George F. Campbell, testified, writing:

On the morning of June 28, then, we proceeded out with grim determination to clear the air of the Hun. We also wanted to maintain the prestige which the Flying Corps had secured in its infancy, when it was outnumbered and battered about, in the early days of the war. Our Squadron and each of us as individuals had this prestige to maintain. Having left the drome and rendezvoused high over a very prominent landmark, then known as Bootleg Wood, from its shape, we met two other squadrons of fighting patrol. Altogether we numbered between 50 and 60 machines, this being a very heavy fighting patrol for those days. Our orders were to advance at several different altitudes and sweep everything before us, maintaining this formation throughout the duration of our 'trick' in the air. It looked very easy to me, with this number of machines. Nothing in the air can stand against us, I thought, but I was soon to find out that such was not the case. Crossing the line like so many swarms of

A German observation balloon being launched. Known to the British as a 'sausage', a balloon of this type gave its name to Sausage Valley on the Somme. (*Library of Congress*)

bees, at heights ranging from 8,000 to 18,000 feet, we started our campaign of clearing up. It was between 6 and 7 o'clock in the morning, and at first our flight did not offer any excitement, Fritz not appearing in the sky at that hour. Looking down on crossing the line, I noticed very heavy barrage fire in progress, and spotted several of our contact and reconnaissance planes busily engaged in dealing out destruction to the enemy, through the medium of our batteries, which they were directing.[21]

However, it must also be stated that the bad weather and cloud in the last two days before the attack seriously interfered with the ability of the RFC to undertake this work. Patrols in No Man's Land and small-scale raids into the enemy lines were also carried out by the infantry, in order to try to establish the strength of the enemy barbed wire, the numbers of enemy soldiers in the front line, their state of alertness and so on. An American soldier of British parentage, New Yorker Private Arthur Guy Empey of the 1st Battalion London Regiment, was involved in just such a trench raid on 29 June 1916, near Gommecourt:

The bullets were cracking overhead. I crawled a few feet back to the German barbed wire, and in a stooping position, guiding myself by the wire, I went down the line looking for the lane we had cut through. Before reaching this lane I came to a limp form which seemed like a bag of oats hanging over the wire. In the dim light I could see that its hands were blackened, and knew it was the body of one of my mates. I put my hand on his head, the top of which had been blown off by a bomb. My fingers sank into the hole. I pulled my hand back full of blood and brains, then I went crazy with fear and horror and rushed along the wire until I came to our lane. I had just turned down this lane when something inside of me seemed to say, 'Look around.' I did so; a bullet caught me on the left shoulder. It did not hurt much, just felt as if someone had punched me in the back, and then my left side went numb. My arm was dangling like a rag. I fell forward in a sitting position. But all fear had left me and I was consumed with rage and cursed the German trenches. With my right hand I felt in my tunic for my first-aid or shell dressing. In feeling over my tunic my hand came in contact with one of the bombs which I carried. Gripping it, I pulled the pin out ... and blindly threw it towards the German trench. I must have been out of my head because I was only ten feet from the trench and took a chance of being mangled. If the bomb had failed to go into the trench I would have been blown to bits by the explosion of my own bomb. By the flare of the explosion of the bomb, which luckily landed in their trench, I saw one big Boche throw up his arms and fall backwards, while his rifle flew into the air. Another one wilted and fell forward across the sandbags – then blackness. Realizing what a foolhardy and risky thing I had done, I was again seized with a horrible fear. I dragged myself to my feet and ran madly down the lane through the barbed wire, stumbling over cut wires, tearing my uniform, and lacerating my hands and legs. Just as I was about to reach No Man's Land again, that same voice seemed to say, 'Turn around.' I did so, when, 'crack,' another bullet caught me, this time in the left shoulder about one half inch away from the other wound. Then it was taps for me. The lights went out.

When I came to I was crouching in a hole in No Man's Land. This shell hole was about three feet deep, so that it brought my head a few inches below the level of the ground. How I reached this hole I will never know. German 'type-writers' were traversing back and forth in No Man's Land, the bullets biting the edge of my shell hole and throwing dirt all over me. Overhead, shrapnel was bursting. I could hear the

Men of the Bavarian *Infanterie Regiment Nr 15*, photographed around 20 June 1916 on the Verdun front. Shortly after this photo was taken the men were posted to the Somme sector, in order to strengthen German defences there.

fragments slap the ground. Then I went out once more. When I came to, everything was silence and darkness in No Man's Land. I was soaked with blood and a big flap from the wound in my cheek was hanging over my mouth. The blood running from this flap choked me. Out of the corner of my mouth I would try and blow it back but it would not move. I reached for my shell dressing and tried, with one hand, to bandage my face to prevent the flow. I had an awful horror of bleeding to death and was getting very faint.[22]

Left behind by his comrades, Empey would still be lying wounded in No Man's Land when the battle itself was launched. He was, however, subsequently rescued, but was discharged from the army as a result of his wounds.

What of the men across No Man's Land, in *feldgrau*? How were they coping with the strain of the relentless allied bombardment, and the knowledge that when it came to an end this could herald only one thing – the beginning of a general offensive. Gerhard Siegert was a German artillery NCO on the French front. In his memoir he describes the growing intensity of the French bombardment in the final days of June. In the nearby village of Estrées, the high street lay under almost continuous fire from a French heavy battery firing 9cm projectiles. On 25 June one house in particular was badly damaged, and the occupants fled to the positions of the nearby German battery for protection from the rain of shells. Siegert tells us:

The women were in a dugout of the battery. There, they had taken shelter. The men of the battery were now extremely worried about the two women. Even an old man had taken refuge with them. He had been driven out of his home and did not want to go back. He had nothing with him, only the violin of his son, who, he said, fought on the other side. How the poor people have suffered psychologically in those terrible days, one can only guess! Hopefully they are thinking favourably of the members of the first battery of Breslau Field Artillery Regiment Nr 6! The bombardment did not stop. In the battery position everything was upset. Everyone knew the great offensive was imminent. To be able to move faster and more freely, and especially to be able to unload ammunition more comfortably, the oats were mowed, but left lying on the ground. This was not noticed by the enemy air observers. The four guns of the third battery were now partly shot up, and sometimes became unusable. They were replaced immediately. The other batteries had already suffered heavy losses.

Every night the 'Light columns' brought enormous amounts of ammunition to the front. For the column people it was particularly difficult; they came out of their peaceful, quiet villages far behind the front; they knew only the main roads, and suffered most severely from the enemy fire. Our observers had very exciting, but interesting service. There was always one officer and one sergeant before the trench telescopes. Each change and movement of the enemy was reported. The barrage on our trenches was the most horrible thing they had ever seen; the opponents bombarded them with 'heavies'. Although our batteries were particularly targeted by the enemy guns, they were seldom able to reach us installed meters deep into the ground. Our poor infantry sat idly in their well-developed dugouts and suffered horrible losses due to being buried. Only the flare-posts stood in the terrible hail of fire in the trenches, so as to be able to alert the artillery. This went on day and night. Without ceasing. Without a break.[23]

Evidence of the ferocity of the French bombardment of the Germans on the Somme: empty 75mm shell cases piled up in a village behind the front.

Even Siegert, who had served at Verdun, found the intensity of this French bombardment awe-inspiring. On 28 and 29 June German observers reported the French trenches to be crowded with men, and to the Germans it appeared that the attack they had been expecting for so long must now be imminent. In spite of the battering they had received from the allied artillery, the morale of the German soldiers remained high. Siegert continues:

> The observers cheered with excitement. Communication with the batteries was no longer possible. All telephone lines were shot to pieces. To try to mend the wires would be madness. As a final means of communication there remained the flares, and white signal flags that stood out from the green of the forest. At every moment the observers in the trees were fired upon. Sometimes people had to flee, but only for a minute, then they stormed back up the ladder to the tree. The sense of duty drove them on: 'If the French break through, then the survivors of the battery are finished!' Not everything returns to me in exactly the way that it was. What I tell, is only one person's view. One could write a book just about these days alone. Yet over everyone floated a horrible anxiety: our one thought was this – when will they attack? ... That which they had had to endure for what would soon be a week, day and night, was no longer life. They worked mechanically. The ingeniously built battery position, and a benevolent God, had so far saved us from losses. All other batteries had now lost, in the meantime, so many old comrades. One of the first batteries to be hit, and completely destroyed, was the 9cm 'schoolhouse battery'. She was half right of us in the courtyard of the school. Almost all the guns were smashed into small pieces.[24]

Moving forward into attack positions, it was understandable that even those with the strongest commitment to their country's cause would feel nervous, even nauseous. Would their legs fail them, or would they simply freeze up when the whistles blew? The question many, particularly officers, asked themselves was 'will I let myself down in front of my men?' It was a fear of the effects of the nervous tension, rather than of battle itself, which many men experienced. Edward Liveing, a lieutenant with the 12th Battalion London Regiment (The Rangers), summed this up well. He wrote of moving up to the attack on 30 June:

> As we marched on towards the village (I do not mind saying it) I experienced that unpleasant sensation of wondering whether I should be lying out this time tomorrow – stiff and cold in that land beyond the trees, where the red shrapnel burst and the star-shells flickered. I remember hoping that, if the fates so decreed, I should not leave too great a gap in my family, and, best hope of all, that I should instead be speeding home in an ambulance on the road that stretched along to our left. I do not think that I am far wrong when I say that those thoughts were occurring to every man in the silent platoon behind me. Not that we were downhearted. If you had asked the question, you would have been greeted by a cheery 'No!' We were all full of determination to do our best next day, but one cannot help enduring rather an unusual 'party feeling' before going into an attack.[25]

A British staff officer named Richard Vincent Sutton made an entry in his diary at 11.35pm on the night before the battle. The tone of the entry was cautiously optimistic, an optimism which was based upon the relentless groundwork undertaken by the British, yet there is also an awareness of the dangers that just a few determined Germans could pose towards an undertaking such as this:

> We have now had four months of ceaseless preparation. Every Brigade has six times attacked similar trenches to those we are attacking tomorrow, which have been dug in the training areas in rear. Every officer and every man knows exactly what he has to do, and is determined to do it. For seven days our artillery have been bombarding the enemy's position. Numerous gas and smoke attacks have been launched, and when the enemy has manned his parapet he has been slated with artillery. The various plans of attack that have been decided upon by the Army Commander are to my mind first-rate. They are ... too lengthy and intricate to enter upon in these notes, but one point that I think should be mentioned here is that the whole attack is to be carried out on a time-table until the objectives are reached. The infantry are to occupy each position as the intense artillery fire lifts off it on to the next one. In my opinion everything depends on the infantry following upon the heels of the artillery barrage, which will go in front of them in each task. The weather appears to be favourable, which is an enormously important factor in modern battles. There are, however, two things which may defeat us; or rather, I should say, not two, but a combination of both. These are the magnificent fighting qualities of the enemy and his ever-present machine-guns. No matter how long or how heavy the bombardment, it is impossible to knock out every machine-gun, or kill all the detachments. One machine-gun may hold up a whole Brigade if it is properly handled, and a quantity of machine-guns may hold up our whole attack, and slaughter us in thousands. We have reason to hope that only a small number of machine-guns will be properly handled owing to the great physical strain which the enemy have had to bear during these seven days' bombardment.
>
> Deserters have told us they have been able to get no rations up for three days and very little water. Another man captured in a recent raid was staring mad; another said he was one of the last survivors of his company. It appears that the morale of the enemy is shaken, and that he is not in a position to fight his machine-guns to the end, but if he does, God help us. The suspense is great. The feeling is like that of a man watching his horse go down to the starting post, when he has staked his last penny and the welfare of his family upon it. But in this case it is the British Empire that is the stake, and incidentally probably one's last penny as well. This time to-morrow we shall know for better or for worse. One thing I do know is that all has been done in the way of forethought and preparation that it is possible for human creatures to do, and that it is now in God's hands to do as He pleaseth.[26]

It must be stated that, among the British staff, optimism was not universal. There was a feeling in some quarters that such was the political pressure for this offensive to proceed rigorously according to time-table that any dissenting voices were either ignored or sidelined. Some officers felt that the whole machinery of the preparation for battle had taken on such momentum that by this late stage nothing could be done to halt or delay it. The staff are often derided for their ineffectual performance during the First World War but one particular officer at the headquarters of Lieutenant General Sir Aylmer Hunter-Weston certainly does not fit this stereotype. Second Lieutenant F.P. Roe was diligent both in his efforts to investigate how thorough the preparations had been, and in reporting his findings to higher authority. Despite his misgivings about the lack of damage achieved by the British artillery barrage, one detects that there was perhaps also a sense of resignation that nothing now could be done to halt or delay the rigid time-table according to which the battle was being run:

> I knew General Hunter-Weston [VIII Corps commander] for many months daily, he was not optimistic, he was being pressed right from GHQ that this attack must be persisted with because otherwise … as far as France was concerned the game was up. General Hunter-Weston was a most considerate officer. He was not optimistic – I have read stories where he said even a rat couldn't live [in the German lines and] that it would be a walk through … I believe this to be a total invention. I don't think he was capable of it, he was a very fine soldier … In the main, speaking for VIII Corps, very little of the enemy wire was cut. It was very strong indeed, it had apron defences for sometimes as much as twelve feet thick, and as far as VIII Corps was concerned, it

Lieutenant General Sir Aylmer Hunter-Weston, commanding the British VIII Corps on the Somme. In spite of the extensive preparations for the forthcoming attack, he was not optimistic.

German soldiers constructing barbed wire defences. On some parts of the Somme front these were as much as twelve feet deep. (*Library of Congress*)

was only cut in certain places much further in the south of the corps. It was my job as a Forward Intelligence Officer to a Corps to visit the whole of the three-divisional front line. I was personally aware that as it stood, with the French unable to play their part that they had aimed to take, in view of their losses at Verdun [and] in view of the fact that our flank in VIII Corps was completely open [which] I saw and reported at the time … Just to put it in a nutshell, I am sure there was no great optimism on the part of the Corps Commander, or in fact on the part of the Fourth Army commander, General Rawlinson. There was no optimism of any kind what so ever, absolutely none; in fact there was a feeling of oncoming disaster which we felt very strongly at the time.[27]

Of course, in most cases, such concerns would have been beyond the awareness of the soldiers in the front line, in whose hands everything now lay. Generals had done what they could to bring men and materiel together in sufficient quantities at the right place and the right time, but very soon the conduct of the battle would be largely beyond their influence. Such was the nature of combat in the First World War, and the primitive communication equipment which existed, that soon after soldiers went over the top their senior officers effectively lost control of a battle, and success or failure devolved onto much more junior commanders. One of these men, who would play his part in the coming day's fighting, was Edward Liveing, of the 12th Battalion London Regiment. He remembered with clarity the surreal quality of the early hours of 1 July 1916:

Dawn was breaking. The morning was cool after a chill night – a night of waiting in blown-down trenches with not an inch to move to right or left, of listening to the enemy's shells as they left the guns and came tearing and shrieking towards you, knowing all the time that they were aimed for your particular bit of trench and would land in it or by it, of awaiting that sudden, ominous silence, and then the crash – perhaps death. I, for my part, had spent most of the night sitting on a petrol tin, wedged between the two sides of the trench and two human beings – my sergeant on the left and a corporal on the right. Like others, I had slept for part of the time despite the noise and danger, awakened now and then by the shattering crash of a shell or the hopeless cry for stretcher-bearers. But morning was coming at last, and the bombardment had ceased. The wind blew east, and a few fleecy clouds raced along the blue sky overhead. The sun was infusing more warmth into the air. There was the freshness and splendour of a summer morning over everything. In fact, as one man said, it felt more as if we were going to start off for a picnic than for a battle.[28]

Among the soldiers waiting to go over the top that morning there was a variety of feelings and emotions. Arthur Mack, another British soldier of American birth, who was serving with the London Regiment, probably summed up the feelings of many when he wrote:

All the rookies who had come up with me were on the ragged edge of nervous prostration and the chaps who had been there when we came were nearly as bad. Our morale was bad. We had got some used to being shelled – just enough so we were able to figure out the mathematical chances of being hit by the next one – and that's a bad state to be in. Most of us had never been under rifle fire in the open or under machine guns, and we were so shaken that we dreaded it. And that's the shape we were in when we went over the top on the morning of the first of July.[29]

So much anticipation and preparation had led up to this point, and now the destinies of three great nations (and countless other smaller ones) would lie with the men crouching in trenches or dugouts, awaiting the sound of whistles blowing, and the order to advance, or to rise up and repel. For all too many, sadly these would be the last hours of their lives. So too would these be the last hours of the great Franco-British ambition to break through to Bapaume and drive the Germans back to Berlin. It is a military truism that no plan survives first contact with the enemy, and perhaps never was this borne out more clearly than on the Somme, where the coming weeks would see the objectives of the campaign eroded and transformed by the pressures of combat on a previously unprecedented scale. All three armies would be forced to make changes to their objectives, their tactics, their command structures and their weaponry as the battle forced lessons to be learned at an extraordinary rate. This four-and-a-half month long struggle would also make its mark indelibly both on the landscape and upon the men who lived through it, for almost all those who returned from the battle would be affected by it in some way or another.

Chapter Two

Get Out … Get Out … They're Coming!

I f the weather can ever be taken as an omen for the success or failure of an operation, then the allied generals must have felt that the gods of war were indeed smiling favourably upon them, as the morning of 1 July 1916 dawned bright and cloudless. What was to follow, however, certainly for the British, was a day of disappointment and ultimately recrimination, for in many cases their soldiers went over the top to face uncut barbed wire, and Germans who had not been killed or demoralised, and who manned their guns defiantly. They were – along most of their line – to sustain heavy casualties in exchange for limited gains. Only in a few places would the British seize their objectives in the way that had been planned. By contrast, to the south the French would achieve significantly more progress, and theirs is the real success story of the first day of the Battle of the Somme.

The extreme left flank of the allied frontage on this battlefield faced the fortified village of Gommecourt and its adjacent park, heavily defended by a German garrison. Two British divisions were assigned the task of attacking it that morning. The 46th (North Midland) Division was the most northerly attacking formation, and together with the 56th (London) Division it was tasked with pinching out the German salient here. A sad irony of the fighting at Gommecourt was that, bitter as it was, the objective of the attack was to be no more than a diversion, in order to draw in German troops and thus provide flank protection for the attacks planned further south. Nevertheless, among the troops waiting to advance, the apprehension and tension were real enough. Lieutenant Edward Liveing, serving with the 12th Battalion London Regiment, was awaiting the order to advance:

I have often tried to call to memory the intellectual, mental and nervous activity through which I passed during that hour of hellish bombardment and counter-bombardment, that last hour before we leapt out of our trenches into No Man's Land. I give the vague recollection of that ordeal for what it is worth. I had an excessive desire for the time to come when I could go 'over the top', when I should be free at last from the noise of the bombardment, free from the prison of my trench, free to walk across that patch of No Man's Land and opposing trenches till I got to my objective, or, if I did not go that far, to have my fate decided for better or for worse. I experienced, too, moments of intense fear during close bombardment. I felt that if I was blown up it would be the end of all things so far as I was concerned. The idea of after-life seemed ridiculous in the presence of such frightful destructive force. Again the prayer of that old cavalier kept coming to my mind. At any rate, one could but do one's best, and I hoped that a higher power than all that which was around would not overlook me or any other fellows on that day. At one time, not very long before the moment of attack, I felt to its intensest depth the truth of the proverb, 'Carpe diem.' What was time? I had another twenty minutes in which to live in comparative safety. What was the difference between twenty minutes and twenty years? Really and truly what was the difference? I was living at present, and that was enough. I am afraid that this working of mind will appear unintelligible.

I cannot explain it further. I think that others who have waited to 'go over' will realise its meaning.[1]

Any nerves which Liveing may have had whilst waiting to advance soon left him once he had gone over the top, where the terrible panorama before him played out with the surreal quality of a cinema film. He continues, describing his battalion's advance towards the German line:

One thing I remember very well about this time, and that was that a hare jumped up and rushed towards and past me through the dry, yellowish grass, its eyes bulging with fear. We were dropping into a slight valley. The shell holes were less few, but bodies lay all over the ground, and a terrible groaning arose from all sides. At one time we seemed to be advancing in little groups. I was at the head of one for a moment or two, only to realise shortly afterwards that I was alone. I came up to the German wire. Here one could hear men shouting to one another and the wounded groaning above the explosions of shells and bombs and the rattle of machine-guns. I found myself with J, an officer of 'C' company, afterwards killed while charging a machine-gun in the open. We looked round to see what our fourth line was doing. My company's fourth line had no leader. Captain W_k, wounded twice, had fallen into a shell-hole, while Sergeant S_r had been killed during the preliminary bombardment. Men were kneeling and firing. I started back to see if I could bring them up, but they were too far away. I made a cup of my mouth and shouted, as J was shouting. We could not be heard. I turned round again and advanced to a gap in the German wire. There was a pile of our wounded here on the German parapet. Suddenly I cursed. I had been scalded in the left hip. A shell, I thought, had blown up in a water-logged crump-hole and sprayed me with boiling water. Letting go of my rifle, I dropped forward full length on the ground. My hip began to smart unpleasantly, and I felt a curious warmth stealing down my left leg. I thought it was the boiling water that had scalded me. Certainly my breeches looked as if they were saturated with water. I did not know that they were saturated with blood.[2]

Things initially went well for the London troops, with smoke released on time to mask their forming-up in No Man's Land, and sufficient wire cut in front to enable them to make progress. However, matters quickly began to go awry at Gommecourt. Despite the fact that the leading formations took the first two lines of German trenches with comparative ease, the defenders launched a vigorous counter-attack which effectively pinned down the advanced parties and prevented any reinforcements from reaching them. Corporal Reginald Davis was serving with the 1st/9th Battalion London Regiment (Queen Victoria's Rifles), which was in the first wave of the attack here. In a letter home he wrote:

I was in charge of the Battle Police that day, and we had to accompany the bombers. We started over the top under heavy fire and many were bowled over within a few minutes. Lanky of limb, I was soon through the barbed wire and came to the first trench and jumped in. Some seven of us were there, and as senior NCO I led the way along the trench. One Hun came round the corner, and he would have been dead but for his cry 'Kamerad blesse'. I lowered my rifle, and, making sure he had no weapon, passed him to the rear and led on. We had just connected up with our party on the left when I felt a pressure of tons upon my head. My right eye was sightless, with the other I saw my hand with one finger severed, covered in blood. A great desire came over me to sink to the ground, into peaceful oblivion, but the peril of such weakness came to my mind, and with an effort I pulled myself together. I tore my helmet from my head, for the concussion had rammed it tight down. The man in front bandaged my head and eye. Blood was pouring into my mouth, down my tunic. They made way for me, uttering cheery words, 'Stick it, Corporal, you'll soon be in Blighty!' one said. Another, 'Best of luck, old man.' I made my way slowly, not in pain, I was too numbed for that. My officer gave me a pull at his whisky bottle, and further on our stretcher-bearers bandaged my head and wiped as much blood as they could from my face. I felt I could go no further, but a runner who was going to HQ led me back. I held on to his equipment, halting for cover when a shell came near, and hurrying when able. I eventually got to our First Aid Post. There I fainted away.[3]

Davis underwent an operation at a Casualty Clearing Station, and under an anaesthetic his damaged eye was removed. He was placed on a hospital train the following day, bound for the coast. The next five days he spent at a hospital near Le Treport. His mother was sent for, and a piece of shell was extracted from his head by means of a magnet – it could not be done by knife, as it was too near the brain. His soldiering days were now over, as would be those of Arthur Empey, still lying wounded in a shell hole in No Man's Land. From this position he witnessed the attack on Gommecourt carried out by troops of the London Scottish, part of the same division:

An intense bombardment was on, and on the whole my position was decidedly unpleasant. Then, suddenly, our barrage ceased. The silence almost hurt, but not for long, because Fritz turned loose with shrapnel, machine guns, and rifle fire. Then all along our line came a cheer and our boys came over the top in a charge. The first wave was composed of 'Jocks.' They were a magnificent sight, kilts flapping in the wind, bare knees showing, and their bayonets glistening. In the first wave that passed my shell hole, one of the 'Jocks,' an immense fellow, about six feet two inches in height, jumped right over me. On the right and left of me several soldiers in colored kilts were huddled on the ground, then over came the second wave, also 'Jocks.' One young Scottie, when he came abreast of my shell hole, leaped into the air, his rifle shooting out of his hands, landing about six feet in front of him, bayonet first, and stuck in the ground, the butt trembling. This impressed me greatly.

Right now I can see the butt of that gun trembling. The Scottie made a complete turn in the air, hit the ground, rolling over twice, each time clawing at the earth, and then remained still, about four feet from me, in a sort of sitting position. I called to him, 'Are you hurt badly, Jock?' but no answer. He was dead. A dark, red smudge was coming through his tunic right under the heart. The blood ran down his bare knees, making a horrible sight. On his right side he carried his water bottle. I was crazy for a drink and tried to reach this, but for the life of me I could not negotiate that four feet. Then I became unconscious.[4]

Empey's war was over. He recovered, but the severity of his wounds resulted in his discharge from the British army. He returned to the United States, where his war memoir *Over The Top* became a bestseller. It was later made into a movie, with Empey cast as himself. The role eventually led him into a career as an actor in Hollywood. Arthur Mack, the other American serving at Gommecourt with a London battalion, wrote frankly of his experiences, and indeed of his own personal lack of courage, as he went into battle:

> We had a fair artillery preparation – enough to batter down their wire and that was all. We went over early in the morning. There was no barrage – and we simply climbed out and went forward on the double. There was no smoke screen in front of us and we were open to the sight of the strongly emplaced German machines. Besides that we had very few grenades. The Mills bombs had come in only a short time before and had not yet reached us. We had some of the old-fashioned hairbrush and jam-tin grenades, but they were worse than nothing, as the men didn't trust them. Those old jam-tin bombs were sure suicide tools. They were made, as the name implies, of old jam and marmalade cans. You'd light the fuse and then had a matter of four seconds to throw the thing … So that's the way we went into

Arthur Empey, recovering in hospital after the first day of the Battle of the Somme.

the July first attack, without barrage and without bombs. Nothing but rifles and the bayonets. It was eight hundred yards to the German trenches. We crossed it on the double with two rests of about a minute each to catch our breath. The whole attack as far as our sector was concerned was a washout. The division on our left had a mix-up on orders and didn't go over with the rest of us. The result was that we were enfiladed and raked fore and aft. I was so scared that I was petrified. I remember that all the way across I was praying that I wouldn't have to use the bayonet or to face the bayonet. I have read a good deal of tommy-rot from time to time about the German being afraid of the cold steel. The fact is that any Anglo-Saxon hates it. The Scotch and the Irish like the bayonet. The Englishman hates it as bad as any German. I dreaded it on my first charge, and in all the many months of service after that, and I hate the idea now. I had that dread topside in my mind all the way across.

When we made the German trenches we found no Fritzies there. The Hun was playing it low down and foxy on us. He had raked us all the way across and had quietly abandoned his front line when we arrived. I dropped into a bay and waited there for as much as half an hour. The suspense was just what was needed to give me a let-down and knock out what faked-up courage I had left in me. I stood there alone, shaking all over, and very badly nauseated, until an officer came along and told me to join some of the men two traverses further down. I moved down and joined them. There was little shellfire and we were fairly safe from the typewriters. I was just getting a little courage back when a commotion started around the comer in a communication trench, and a second later around the corner came crowding about twenty Heinies. They had come out of a dugout. They were on top of us in an instant. A big fellow made a thrust at me.

I parried perfectly. He dropped his rifle. I made a thrust at his chest. He caught the rifle with both hands and seemed to pull the bayonet into his throat. And then a strange thing happened. When the steel went into him my head cleared. The lump went out of my throat. My solar plexus stopped squirming. My knees were solid. I let go a glad yell and kicked him off the pin. It broke at the butt, but I didn't care. I clubbed old Sarah Jane and went after the next Fritz, knowing I was just twice as good a man as he.[5]

As Mack's account implies, the difficulties encountered by the London division on this part of the front were exacerbated by the complete lack of progress made to the north by the other attacking division, the 46th (North Midland). Here, the leading waves, comprising battalions of the North and South Staffordshire Regiments, together with those of the Nottinghamshire and Derbyshire Regiment, were met by intact barbed wire, hand grenades and fierce enemy fire. The supporting waves were greeted by shell fire, and those few troops who entered the German lines were soon cut off. In support here was the 1st/5th Battalion Leicestershire Regiment, including Captain Aubrey Moore. Having gone forward early in the morning, Moore was stunned by the concussion of a nearby shell burst, which killed his company sergeant major. Only later in the day did he fully recover his senses, and met two returning Staffords officers – both badly shaken – who told him of the failure of their assault. Later he took an independent (and, with hindsight, brave) decision not to continue the offensive in his own part of the line:

Lieutenant J.W. Tomson, 1st/5th Battalion Leicestershire Regiment. He led 'D' Company on the morning of 1 July 1916.

> Somewhere about midday I had a verbal message that the attack would be resumed at 1500 hours. No confirmation came. We had now got things sorted out and I had my company in my own part of the line. Most other units had also got into some sort of order. When 1500 hours came no confirmation had been sent, no artillery barrage opened. Those of us in command of companies said we would not go, it would have been sheer murder. Half an hour later a written message came to me saying the attack had been cancelled.[6]

Despite the individual bravery shown by many of its men, such was the subsequent disquiet at British General Headquarters over the performance of the 46th Division that it became the subject of a Court of Enquiry into why it had failed to close with the enemy on 1 July.

South of Gommecourt lay the village of Serre. On the morning of 1 July it was heavily attacked by the 'Pals' battalions of the 31st Division. These battalions, raised in the autumn of 1914 in response to Kitchener's call for volunteers, were recruited in the northern industrial regions from men who knew one another in civilian life, worked in the same factories or industries, played in the same cricket or football teams, and in many cases lived on the same streets in the rows of terraced housing in Leeds, Bradford,

The ruins of the village of Serre, on the German front line. Heavily fortified, it was attacked by some of the British 'Pals' battalions on 1 July with disastrous results.

Accrington or Sheffield. The devastation wrought upon these close-knit communities when their battalions suffered heavily in action can only be imagined. The 15th Battalion West Yorkshire Regiment (Leeds Pals) was one of the first units into action that morning, going over the top with a great shout of 'Now, Leeds!', but sustained particularly severe casualties, the men being stopped in No Man's Land by rifle and machine-gun fire. A handful of men from the 11th Battalion East Lancashire Regiment (Accrington Pals) and the 12th Battalion York and Lancaster Regiment (Sheffield City Battalion) managed to reach Serre, but were subsequently lost. In reserve was the 18th Battalion Durham Light Infantry (Durham Pals); among them was Private George Ramshaw, who remembered sixty years later:

> I had to follow the first line ... Or the first few lines with ammunition, and the trench was full of men, and when the whistle went these men went over first, and you never heard anything like it, it was pandemonium – I don't think there were any of them got more than fifty yards away ... I could see it, and the men were dropping into the trenches in terrible conditions, there were some of them that had had their faces blown off – they staggered back [and] our supports were coming on top of them, [the front line] was choked. We never got out of that trench with the ammunition – never got out of it.[7]

It was sheer good fortune for Ramshaw that he was in a later wave, and in the event never went over the top on the first day of the battle. Indeed, this probably saved his life.

Across No Man's Land from Ramshaw was Otto Lais, a German soldier in the front line near Serre, who wrote vividly of his experiences as a machine-gunner here. He and his comrades were still dazed from the week-long preparatory bombardment when the attack began, and for Lais the intensity of the moment was such that he was barely able to carry out his duties as a gunner and indeed had to fight to regain control of himself:

> The idea that there could still be life or any resistance in us (after this week) seems absurd to them! But now men crawl out of half-crushed dugouts, now men squeeze through shot-through tunnels, through buried dugout entrances, through broken, shattered timber frames, now they rise up between the dead and dying and call and cry out: 'Get out! Get out! It's the attack!' … 'They are coming.' The sentries, who had to remain outside throughout the drumfire, rise out of the shell-holes. Dust and dirt lie a centimetre thick on their faces and uniforms. Their cry of warning rings piercingly in the narrow gaps that form the dugout entrance. 'Get out … get out … they're coming!' Now men rush to the surface and throw themselves into shell holes and craters; now they fling themselves in readiness at the crater's rim; now they rush forward under cover from the former second and third lines and place themselves in the first line of defence. Hand-grenades are being hauled by the box from shell-hole to shell-hole.

Private Tom Scawbord, 15th Battalion West Yorkshire Regiment (Leeds Pals), who was killed in action on 1 July 1916 near Serre. (*Courtesy of Mike Wood*)

There's a choking in every throat, a pressure which is released in a wild yell, in the battle-cry 'They're coming, they're coming!' Finally the battle! The nightmare of this week-long drumfire is about to end, finally we can free ourselves of this week-long inner torment, no longer must we crouch in a flattened dugout like a mouse in a trap.

No longer do we feel the dull impact of the shelter-breaker exploding downwards (an impact like a hammer-blow on the helmeted skull). No longer must we calm, hold down, tie down those men who almost lose their minds through this pounding, booming and splintering, through difficulty in breathing and through the jerking and swaying of the dugout walls, and whom with overtly trembling limbs want to get up away from this hole and this mousetrap, up into the open air, into a landscape of raging flames and iron – a landscape of insanity and death. We call for a barrage! Red flares climb high then fade away as they fall to the ground. Destructive fire and barrage fire leave masses of green and red marks in the sky! Dear God! The German barrage fire! Behind us the guns lie destroyed in their emplacements, their wheels upwards, their barrels in the dirt.

An enormous crater left by the impact of the English heavy shells yawns at the site of the gun emplacements. Most of the crews are dead, lying buried in tunnels and bunkers. On the waggon-tracks that led to the gun batteries lie shot-up ammunition waggons, shattered gun-limbers, spilled cartridges and shells, dead drivers, and the carcasses of horses torn apart by direct and near-hits.[8]

German soldiers, with bayonets fixed, await the moment when the barrage will cease and they will leave their dugout.

To Lais the German barrage seemed pitifully weak, and it is true that the German batteries were under a great deal of pressure that morning. After sustaining a week-long hammering, they were now attempting to break up British infantry attacks whilst still under fire themselves. So it was that on 1 July 1916, from the German point of view, almost everything depended on the infantry. Overhead, shots flew, whipped and cracked wildly into the British ranks, above them shells hissed, whizzed and roared like a storm, or perhaps more accurately a hurricane; British shells fell on what little German artillery was left, on the support troops and on the rear areas. Amidst all the roar, the clatter, the rumble and the bursts, the shouting and wild firing of the riflemen, the firm, regular beat of the machine-guns was solid and rhythmical – tack-tack-tack-tack – a terrible sound to the British, but it gave a degree of comfort and inner calm to Lais and his comrades in the German infantry. He goes on:

> The machine-gunners, who in quieter times were much mocked – and envied (they were excused from hauling ammunition) – are popular now! One belt after another is raced through! 250 shots – 1000 shots – 3000 shots. 'Bring up the spare gun-barrels' shouts the gun commander. The gun barrel is changed – carry on shooting! – 5000 shots – the gun-barrel has to be changed again. The barrel is scorching hot, the coolant is boiling – the gunners' hands are nearly scorched, scalded. 'Carry on shooting' urges the gun commander 'or be shot yourself!'
>
> The coolant in the gun jacket boils, vaporised by the furious shooting. In the heat of battle, the steam hose comes away from the opening of the water can into which the steam is meant to re-condense. A tall jet of steam sprays upwards, a fine target for the enemy. It's lucky for us that the sun is shining in their eyes and that it is behind us.

Had the enemy used close-in covering fire in 1916, as became customary for both sides in 1917 and 1918, the situation would have been highly critical for us. The enemy is getting closer; we keep up our continuous fire! The steam dies away, again the barrel needs changing! The coolant is nearly all vaporised. 'Where is there water?' shouts the gunlayer. There is soda water (iron rations from the dugout) down below. 'There's none there, Corporal!' The iron rations were all used up in the week-long bombardment. Still the English attack; even though they already lie shot down in their hundreds in front of our lines, fresh waves continue to pour over from their jumping-off positions. We have to shoot!

A gunner grabs the water can, jumps down into the shell-hole and relieves himself. A second then also pisses into the water can – its quickly filled! The English are already in hand-grenade range; grenades fly to and fro. The barrel has been changed, the gun jacket filled – load! Hand-grenades and rifle-grenades explode violently in front of the gun – it's not just unsettling, the loading gets into a tangle! You recite loudly, slowly and clearly saying to yourself: 'Forward – feed – back!' (knock the cocking handle forward – feed in the belt – throw back the cocking handle) – the same again! Safety catch to the right! – 'Feed through!' … tack-tack-tack-tack … a furious sustained fire once more strikes the 'khakis' in front of us! Tall columns of steam rise from almost all the machine guns. The steam hoses of most guns are torn off or shot away. The skin of the gunners, of the gun commanders, hangs in shreds from their fingers, their hands are scalded! The left thumb is reduced to a swollen, shapeless piece of meat from continually pressing the safety catch. The hands grip the lightweight, thin gun handles as if locked in a seizure. Eighteen thousand shots! The platoon's other machine-gun jams. Gunner Schw. is shot in the head and falls over the belt that he feeds in. The belt is displaced, taking the cartridges at an angle into the feeder where they become stuck! Another gunner takes

German machine-gunners set up their weapon on the top of their shell-battered trench. (*Library of Congress*)

over! The dead man is laid to one side. The gunlayer takes out the feeder, removes the cartridges and reloads.

Shooting, nothing but shooting, barrel changing, hauling ammunition and laying out the dead and wounded in the bottom of the trench, such is the harsh and furious pace of the morning of 1st July 1916.[9]

Franz Seldte was a machine-gun officer in the nearby German *Infanterie Regiment Nr 66*. On the morning of 1 July this unit was positioned north of Serre. Seldte published his memoirs after the war, a now almost forgotten account in which he refers to himself throughout in the third person as 'Helmut Stahl'. Like Otto Lais, he also describes the tension and apprehension of the build-up to the British attack, the barrage, and the nerves as the German soldiers waited for the Tommies to advance on this beautiful summer's day. He even makes reference to Royal Flying Corps aircraft buzzing low over No Man's Land. His powerful account tallies with British descriptions of the Germans in places leaving their lines and setting up their machine guns out in front of the trenches, the better to engage the enemy soldiers advancing ahead of them:

Thereafter, clouds of smoke develop over the English lines. And now the battle that burns over the forest of Gommécourt draws Stahl in. He sees through his field glasses flames, smoke and dust rising. But the view is obscured. It seems to him, however, as if heavy fire from German machine guns plays on the ground in the distance. Beyond the meadow Stahl recognizes movement in the English trenches, drifting to the northeast, and further back in the ruins of the village of Hebuterne, behind the Toutventferme [Touvent Farm], and behind the Signyferme [La Signy Farm] men seem to accumulate. To the right and left of the regimental front the barrage begins again. The view of the battlefield in front of him is getting worse. The fire bursts over him with renewed force. No doubt they will come.

Stahl lets the machine-gun team make ready. Then he roars down into the dugout and flies out with the spare rifle, which he has reserved for his own use. Everything happens fast. He holds on to the machine-gun sled. They jump over the shattered parapet, kneeling on sandbags. He himself kneels behind the MG and draws back the cocking hammer. Stahl opens fire, carried away by the excitement of the moment. As he begins to load in a new ammunition belt, one, two, three, four, and then again one, two, three, four black grey earth fountains erupt before him. A stream of hot gas blows at him. He realizes that he, with his MG, is the target. Just as he is about to call a command to his gunners something hot, fiery and reaching high carries him over the trench wall and lands him with a crash on the rough trench floor.

The breath has been knocked out of him; he is winded. Laboriously he gets to his knees; it feels like he has been shot through the mouth. He straightens his muddy field glasses and spits blood and saliva into his open right hand. Then he notices his left arm. From the half-shredded sleeve two bone stumps stick out like two pointed fingers. The left hand, yes, his left hand, hangs down strangely by ligaments and from the sleeve drips blood …

Stahl wants to say something, but he cannot hear his own voice and in his ears there is a sound, as if the sea was rushing through there. The realisation dawns upon him: your left hand is gone. Near him is his orderly, Grube, pale with terror. He yells at him: 'Cut it off, man.' The man stares at him wordlessly.

Stahl finds a hideous form of courage. He spits. He speaks. He hears his own voice through the damned rushing in the ears as if from a distance. Trembling, he opens with the other hand the buckle of his waist belt. The Parabellum pistol hangs heavy against his thigh. With the right hand he unbuttons the tunic. He finds it very difficult. He next undoes the braces, bites into it and with the help of Grube wraps the gray rubber band around the stump, so that finally the damned bleeding stops.

Then somehow a medic appears there and wraps the thing together better and binds his arm to his body. Stahl leans panting against the dugout wall and yells: 'Give me the medicine tablet man, give me cognac.' Grube crashes down into the dugout and appears once again with white tablets, which Stahl devours, washed down with cognac from an aluminum cup. Stahl plunges down the liquid fire. He leans panting and slightly insane at the trench wall. Is this the end, he thinks. He has further thoughts, but they do not come through. Thinking is terribly difficult.[10]

Franz Seldte, seen in later life in Nazi uniform. On 1 July 1916 he lost his hand as a machine-gun officer serving near Serre.

Seldte continues with a description of his medical treatment as he proceeded to hospital; for him active service was over, though he would return to the front before the end of the war as a newspaper correspondent. His *nom de plume* was not chosen at random: after the war he was a founder of the *Stahlhelm*, the German paramilitary veterans' association. The organisation had right-wing leanings and eventually allied itself with the Nazis, Seldte himself becoming Reich Minister of Labour in Hitler's government.

South of Serre lay the Redan Ridge, named after the major German strongpoint which commanded the slopes up which any British advance must come. This was the sector of the 4th Division, among the units of which was the 10th Field Ambulance RAMC. Private Charles Barton of Wigan was serving with this unit; in the days following the attack he wrote about his experiences on 1 July. The work of the stretcher-bearers was perhaps the most dangerous of any who went forward into the attack. Unarmed, unable to take cover and required to cross and re-cross No Man's Land, the men of the RAMC were often deliberately picked out by German snipers, their red cross brassards offering no protection whatsoever. Barton describes going forward under terrific shell fire, the section sergeant being hit and losing an eye even as they were moving up to the front line. He states that the anticipation of going into the attack had played upon the nerves of many of the men of his section, as they waited at the reserve position known as White City during the night before the battle. They received the order to go over the top fifteen minutes after the main attack, expecting a slight resistance, but by this point the enemy fire had developed into an inferno. Prior to the battle, a captain and sergeant had fixed two marker flags in the British front line, in order to act as guides for the stretcher-bearers returning with wounded, and to prevent them wandering into another division's sector by accident. Barton continues:

> We got the order to go over, and the reception we got I shall never forget. It was terrible, we had not even a sporting chance. However, we got to our poor wounded comrades, and set to work dressing [their wounds] and getting them back to our lines from where they were taken from us by another section. After about eight hours' hard work I got hit. Shells [were] bursting all round us but I managed to take another of my wounded comrades with me. I got two more pieces of shrapnel, but I just managed to creep back to our lines. I was then put on a stretcher and taken to an aid post where I was attended to.[11]

Barton subsequently received the Military Medal in recognition of his bravery, awarded to him at a presentation ceremony in England following his recovery from his wounds.

Beaumont Hamel, the next village on the German front line, was attacked on the first morning of the battle by the 29th Division, a formation which had not long arrived in France, having served with distinction at Gallipoli. Ten minutes before zero hour a mine containing 40,000lb of ammonal had been blown under the nearby Hawthorn Redoubt (a strongpoint in the German front line). The explosion of this mine was actually filmed by Lieutenant Geoffrey Malins, the official cameraman with the British army, who wrote an extraordinarily vivid account of his time in the front line, shooting the footage which would eventually appear in British cinemas later that year as the acclaimed film *The Battle of the Somme*. Malins tells us in great detail how he came to be in position to capture the Hawthorn Redoubt explosion:

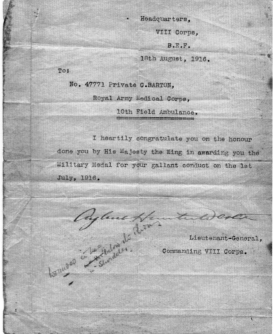

Private Charles Barton RAMC of Wigan, with the letter from Sir Aylmer Hunter-Weston congratulating him on the award of the Military Medal for bravery on 1 July 1916. (*Courtesy of John Davies*)

Our guns were still pounding heavily, and the din and concussion was awful. To hear oneself speak it was absolutely necessary to shout. 'You are in a pretty rocky position,' someone said to me. 'Fritz will be sure to plaster this front pretty well as soon as our men "get over".' 'Can't help it,' I said; 'my machine must have a clear view. I must take the risk. How's the time going?' 'It's "seven-ten" now,' he said. 'I am going to stand by. Cheero; best of luck!' I left him, and stood by my machine. The minutes dragged on. Still the guns crashed out. The German fire had died down a bit during the last half-hour. I glanced down our trenches. The officers were giving final instructions. Every man was in his place. The first to go over would be the engineers, to wire the crater. They were all ready, crouching down, with their implements in their hands. Time: 7.15 am! Heavens! how the minutes dragged. It seemed like a lifetime waiting there. My nerves were strung up to a high pitch; my heart was thumping like a steam-hammer. I gave a quick glance at an officer close by. He was mopping the perspiration from his brow, and clutching his stick, first in one hand then in the other – quite unconsciously, I am sure. He looked at his watch. Another three minutes went by. Would nothing ever happen? Time: 7.19 am. My hand grasped the handle of the camera. I set my teeth. My whole mind was concentrated upon my work. Another thirty seconds passed. I started turning the handle, two revolutions per second, no more, no less. I noticed how regular I was turning. (My object in exposing half a minute beforehand was to get the mine from the moment it broke ground.) I fixed my eyes on the Redoubt. Any second now. Surely it was time. It seemed to me as if I had been turning for hours. Great heavens! Surely it had not misfired. Why doesn't it go up? I looked at my exposure dial. I had used over a thousand feet. The horrible thought flashed through my mind that my film might run out before the mine blew. Would it go up before I had time to reload? The thought brought beads of perspiration to my forehead. The agony was awful; indescribable. My hand began to shake. Another 250 feet exposed. I had to keep on. Then it happened. The ground where I stood gave a mighty convulsion. It rocked and swayed. I gripped hold of my tripod to steady myself. Then, for all the world like a gigantic sponge, the earth rose in the air to the height of hundreds of feet. Higher and higher it rose, and with a horrible, grinding roar the earth fell back upon itself, leaving in its place a mountain of smoke.[12]

That Malins had managed to capture this enormous explosion – one of the largest ever made by man up to this point, was a remarkable achievement, and it is all the more extraordinary when one considers the personal danger in which he placed himself and the cumbersome equipment with which he was working. Not content with capturing the mine explosion, he proceeded to record the advance of Z Company of the 2nd Battalion Royal Fusiliers to seize the crater:

From the moment the mine went up my feelings changed. The crisis was over, and from that second I was cold, cool, and calculating. I looked upon all that followed from the purely pictorial point of view, and even felt annoyed if a shell burst outside the range of my camera. Why couldn't [the] Bosche put that shell a little nearer? It would make a better picture. And so my thoughts ran on. The earth was down. I swung my camera round on to our own parapets. The engineers were swarming over the top, and streaming along the sky-line. Our guns redoubled their fire. The Germans then started H.E. Shrapnel began falling in the midst of our advancing men. I continued to turn the handle of my camera, viewing the whole attack through my view-finder, first swinging one way and then the other. Then another signal rang out, and from the trenches immediately in front of me our wonderful troops went over the top. What a picture it was! They went over as one man. I could see while I was exposing that numbers were shot down before they reached the top of the parapet; others just the other side. They went across the ground in swarms, and marvel upon marvels, still smoking cigarettes. One man actually stopped in the middle of 'No Man's Land' to light up again. The Germans had by now realised that the great attack had come. Shrapnel poured into our trenches with the object of keeping our supports from coming up. They had even got their 'crumps' and high-explosive shrapnel into the middle of our boys before they were half-way across 'No Man's Land.' But still they kept on. At that moment my spool ran out. I hurriedly loaded up again, and, putting the first priceless spool in my case, I gave it to my man in a dug-out to take care of, impressing upon him that he must not leave it under any circumstances. If anything unforeseen happened, he was to take it back to Headquarters.[13]

Musketier Johann Reger, Bavarian *Infanterie Regiment Nr 8*, who was killed in action on 1 July 1916 near Beaumont Hamel.

Another witness to the events taking place here was using a different example of the latest in twentieth-century technology: an aeroplane. Lieutenant Edward Packe of 15 Squadron RFC was flying as an observer in a two-seater BE2c, with his cockpit in front of that of the pilot. He was on reconnaissance on the morning of the attack, and found the Germans in a hostile mood, writing in his diary for 1 July:

We were delayed taking off as the mechanic had over-filled with oil, but we were off by 7.20am and over the lines by Zero Hour 7.30am. It was an awful sight to see our men lying out in lines opposite Beaumont Hamel, either dead or wounded. Only in two places did I see any of our troops reach the German trenches, and only a handful at each. I got a bullet into my buttock whilst we were at 2000ft. over Beaumont Hamel, the bullet having gone through our petrol tank first; there was no future in staying out, so we returned. I went to the Squadron Office and gave a verbal report to Brock, who disbelieved me at the time. (Events subsequently proved me right.) I walked up to my hut in the woods and the R.A.M.C. orderly came and patched me up, having pulled bits of horse hair and petrol tank out of the hole. After about a couple of hours the ambulance arrived and took me to Gizaucourt. Tucker, the other Contact Patrol Observer, was also wounded by a bullet that went through the fleshy part of both legs, thus acquiring four holes from one bullet. The hospital very quickly filled up to overflowing and I spent an unpleasant night on a stretcher on the floor.[14]

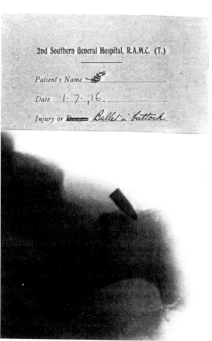

2nd Southern General Hospital, R.A.M.C. (T.)

Patient's Name

Date 1·7·,16.

Injury or ~~Disease~~ *Bullet in buttock.*

Lieutenant Edward Packe of 15 Squadron RFC, together with an X-ray photograph of his buttock, showing a German bullet still embedded. He was hit by fire from the ground on 1 July 1916. (*Courtesy of Jo Edkins*)

It is hardly surprising that Packe, with an uncomfortable though not serious wound, was a low priority for treatment. From early morning on 1 July hospitals and casualty clearing stations behind the lines had held themselves in readiness to receive the thousands of expected casualties, and it was not long before they began to arrive. Indeed, by 10am some of the hospitals had been totally overwhelmed. Olive Dent, a VAD (auxiliary nurse) at one such hospital, recounts the scene that morning:

We knew what to expect. For days and nights past we had heard the guns ceaselessly cannonading. So when the batman woke us at six one morning with the message that every one was to go on duty as quickly as possible, we were not surprised. We washed, dressed, and breakfasted hurriedly. It was a glorious morning with great glowing shafts of streaming sunlight warmly irradiating the camp. The tent walls had as usual been rolled back, thus making of the wards a roof and a floor. We could see therein a great stir and bustle, but what was it caused a sick pain at the heart and hastened our hurrying footsteps? In every walk there were wounded soldiers, a bus-load of the more slightly wounded cases at one marquee, motor-ambulances with stretcher after stretcher of more seriously injured burdens bringing up the rear, men being carried pick-a-back by orderlies, others being brought on the 'four-handed seat', others trudging along with the aid of a walking-stick. Tunics had been torn to free wounded arms, breeches had been ripped for access to injured legs, boots had been discarded in favour of huge carpet slippers or bandages, heads were swathed, jaws tied up, bandages stained with dirt and blood. Almost every boy was clay-caked, the hair full of yellow clayey dust, the face thinly crusted with it, the moustache partly embedded in it. One Jock I subsequently found with puttees caked to the legs which were covered with set clay as evenly as a plaster-of-Paris limb. 'Good morning, boys,' we called as soon as we were within speaking distance. And a very volley, a regular cheer came to our white-clad, white-capped party. 'Good morning, sisters.' 'We'll soon have you fixed up.' 'That's all right. We've shifted them, so it's worth it.' The first batch of patients we treated stands out in any memory. They were fed, bathed, put into clean pyjamas, had their wounds dressed, were each given Blighty tickets and cigarettes, and lay with faces expressive of the personification of blissful contentment.[15]

Dent must have been putting a brave face on what can only have been a truly horrendous situation as the casualty evacuation chain was strained to its limits that morning. Difficult decisions had to be made by doctors as to who was too far gone, and who they had a chance of saving. The situation was not totally dissimilar behind the German lines, as one British officer was about to discover.

South of Beaumont Hamel, across the marshes of the River Ancre, lay the mass of Thiepval Wood, where soldiers of the 36th (Ulster) Division had assembled prior to their attack on the German stronghold of Thiepval. Among these men was Second Lieutenant J.W. Shannon, serving with the 10th Battalion Royal Inniskilling Fusiliers. Shannon moved off with his unit from the safety of the wood at zero hour and managed to advance a considerable distance into the German lines, the Ulstermen dropping Stokes trench mortar bombs down the protruding chimneys of occupied German dugouts as they went. Some units of this division, through bypassing German strongpoints, managed to reach the German third line, but the failure of the divisions on either side of them to advance meant that they were both subject to enfilade fire from the flanks and liable to be cut off by a counter-attack. Shannon wrote in a subsequent report:

On reaching the 3rd line system of German trenches during the attack carried out by my battalion … [I was] engaged digging an advanced position on the road Thiepval–Grandcourt, at a point south of the River Ancre. The battalion suffered severe and heavy casualties under an intense bombardment. I was severely wounded in both legs, just immediately before the few survivors of the battalion were compelled to fall back on the 2nd line trench. I could not move, owing to the shattered condition of my right leg, and the pain caused by bullet wounds in the left leg.

I was taken absolutely by surprise when a large body of German soldiers came along the 3rd line trench to the counter-attack. I was the only survivor in that portion of the trench. The German party did not attempt to kill or injure me; indeed on observing my helpless condition, they were rather sympathetic. Several soldiers offered me field dressings &c and one man remained with me for some considerable time, and set my leg in temporary splints and bandaged the wounds.[16]

Shannon's journey into captivity would continue the following day. Although not deliberately mistreated, he was frequently overlooked or ignored and had to make repeated requests for assistance from German medical staff; at one dressing station he noted they were dealing with over a thousand cases, so the Germans to some extent had the excuse that they were overstretched. Another officer with the 36th (Ulster) Division was Major F.P. Crozier, commanding the 9th Royal Irish Rifles. He wrote:

That half-hour is the worst on record for thoughts and forebodings; so we sing, but it is difficult to keep in tune or rhythm on account of the noise. At last our minute, our own minute, arrives. I get up from the ground and whistle. The others rise.

We move off with steady pace. As we pass Gordon Castle we pick up coils of wire and iron posts. I feel sure in my innermost thoughts these things will never be carried all the way to the final objective; however, even if they get halfway it will be a help. Then I glance to the right through a gap in the trees. I see the 10th Rifles plodding on and then my eyes are riveted on a sight I shall never see again. It is the 32nd Division at its best. I see rows upon rows of British soldiers lying dead, dying or wounded in No Man's Land. Here and there I see an officer urging on his followers. Occasionally I can see the hands thrown up and then a body flops to the ground.

The bursting shells and smoke make visibility poor, but I see enough to convince me Thiepval village is still held, for it is now 8am, and by 7.45am it should have fallen to allow of our passage forward on its flank ... My upper lip is stiff, my jaws are set. We proceed. Again I look southward from a different angle and perceive heaped-up masses of British corpses suspended on the German wire in front of the Thiepval stronghold, while live men rush forward in orderly procession to swell the weight of numbers in the spider's web.[17]

Crozier reached the edge of Thiepval village, and waited for those of his men following him – no doubt all heavily laden with extra ammunition, picks, shovels and barbed wire – to catch up with him. A machine gun opened fire on him from the direction of the village, but the range was wrong and the bullets flew high:

I survey the situation still; more machine-gun fire; they have lowered their sights: pit pit, the bullets hit the dry earth all round. The shelling on to the wood edge has ceased. The men emerge. A miracle has happened. 'Now's the chance,' I think to myself, 'they must quicken the pace and get diagonally across the sunken road, disengaging from each other quickly, company by company.[18]

Having escaped from the wood more or less unscathed during a break in the German shelling, most of Crozier's men none the less walked into a barrage of German fire in No Man's Land. Thiepval, as he put it, was masked by a wall of corpses. The nerves of those men who remained alive were shot by this time and in the afternoon Crozier saw one party attempt to retire without orders:

A ... party cuts across to the south. They mean business. They are damned if they

Major F.P. Crozier, who led the 9th Royal Irish Rifles into action near Thiepval.

are going to stay, it's all up. A young sprinting subaltern heads them off. They push by him. He draws his revolver and threatens them. They take no notice. He fires. Down drops a British soldier at his feet. The effect is instantaneous. They turn back to the assistance of their comrades in distress.[19]

The 36th Division had been recruited en masse from the Ulster Volunteer Force, the protestant paramilitary force raised by Sir Edward Carson in 1912 to oppose Home Rule in Ireland – by force if necessary. Many of the men of this division were Orangemen, and a good number went over the top on 1 July wearing their Orange Order sashes – for them the date marked the anniversary of the Battle of the Boyne some 224 years previously. An Ulsterman named James Hannay was a padre at a convalescent camp behind the British lines in 1916. Many of the lightly wounded of 1 July were diverted to his facility, and he wrote of the 36th Division casualties from Thiepval whom he saw and met in the hours following the attack:

> The very first day of the rush of the lightly wounded into our camp brought us men of the Ulster Division. I heard from the mouths of the boys I talked to the Ulster speech, dear to me from all the associations and memories of my childhood. I do not suppose that those men fought better than any other men, or bore pain more patiently, but there was in them a kind of fierce resentment. They had not achieved the conquest they hoped. They had been driven back, had been desperately cut up. They had emerged from their great battle a mere skeleton of their division.
>
> But I never saw men who looked less like beaten men. Those Belfast citizens, who sign Covenants and form volunteer armies at home, have in them the fixed belief that no one in the world is equal to them or can subdue them. It seems an absurd and arrogant faith. But there is this to be said. They remained just as convinced of their own strength after their appalling experience north of the Somme as they were when they shouted for Sir Edward Carson in the streets of Belfast. Men who believe in their invincibility the day after they have been driven back, with their wounds fresh and their bones aching with weariness, are men whom it will be very difficult to conquer.[20]

Today the memory of the Battle of the Somme still burns fiercely within the Ulster protestant community. For many years there was a widely held belief among them that the 36th Division had been given the most difficult objective on 1 July in order to destroy the UVF and thus nullify post-war opposition to Home Rule in Ulster. Though this is an intriguing idea, it seems to be entirely unsupported by historical evidence, and in any case considerations of the post-war political structure in Ireland must have been of limited concern to the British high command in the planning of a major offensive designed to break nearly two years of deadlock in France.

On either side of the Albert–Bapaume road lay Ovillers and La Boisselle, and among the British soldiers in this sector was Captain James Jack of the 2nd Battalion the Cameronians (Scottish Rifles). Jack was a regular officer who had seen service in the Boer War, as well as on the Western Front from 1914 onwards. He and his men were under orders to follow on, after the leading waves from other battalions had gone over the top, and to consolidate newly won objectives. Jack for his part had a grandstand view as the men of two full battalions, who had crawled out into No Man's Land, rose to their feet at the moment of zero hour and began to advance through the swaying knee-high grass and weeds at a quick march. They came under a hail of rifle and machine-gun fire, much of it from Germans who had escaped the barrage falling on their own lines by sheltering in craters in No Man's Land, and almost to a man the attacking waves were cut down.

Waiting in a communication trench, Jack and his men were showered with dirt and debris from a German howitzer barrage which was falling around them. This, however, was the least of Jack's problems, for he now had a serious dilemma. His orders were to take his two companies over the top in support of the troops which had gone over first, but he had plainly seen that hardly any of these men had reached the German front line. Those few who had got there had either been killed or driven back into No Man's Land. Should he exercise discretion, or obey his orders? The latter might be pure madness, but the former might lead to accusations that the Cameronians had abandoned their comrades on the battlefield. A stark scene lay before him:

> The sun had now dispersed the morning haze and the day promised to be warm. On the upward slope behind us lay many bodies of the West Yorkshire [regiment] ... No Man's Land was strewn with prone forms; up against the hostile wire they showed thickly, the regimental helmet badge being easily recognised on some. Not all of these were casualties, however; among them were men driven out of the German trenches and taking what cover they could in shell holes amid the long grass decked with sunlit scarlet poppies on our side of the enemy's wire entanglements. These men remained still as the dead to avoid drawing fire till darkness should screen their escape; others not so close to danger would make a dash singly or crawl patiently towards our trenches, sniped at on the way.[21]

Jack's conundrum was resolved when orders reached him countermanding his instructions to go forward. Later that afternoon he was told to prepare to attack following a brief bombardment of the enemy trenches, but to his relief these orders were also subsequently cancelled for fear of hitting any British troops who may have been in the German lines. In Jack's view, if an attack which had taken months to prepare and which made use of fresh troops had utterly failed, then an assault on the same positions made with tired and shaken troops after a scratch bombardment stood even less chance of success. Although other battalions from their division had taken heavy casualties, the Cameronians escaped relatively unscathed, probably because Jack had kept his men under cover wherever possible. GHQ instructions stated that any advance from the rear areas to the front line and beyond must be done above ground, thus exposing the men to enemy fire for a considerable distance. New Army officers would have felt less able than an old hand such as James Jack to disregard such a regulation; Jack for his part took his men up as far as possible using communication trenches, despite their congested state.

South of La Boisselle was the Fricourt salient. Lieutenant B. Gordon was serving here with the 9th Battalion King's Own Yorkshire Light Infantry and wrote a highly detailed account of the first day of the battle while the events were still fresh in his mind. His testimony reveals that the British bombardment in his sector at least had succeeded in disrupting the German defences to a considerable degree, and both structures and defenders were in a disorganised state. Gordon set off at 7.30am through thick smoke caused by British shelling, as well as enemy machine-gun fire and shrapnel. Despite being slightly wounded in the chin by a fragment, which caused bruising and bleeding, he pressed on:

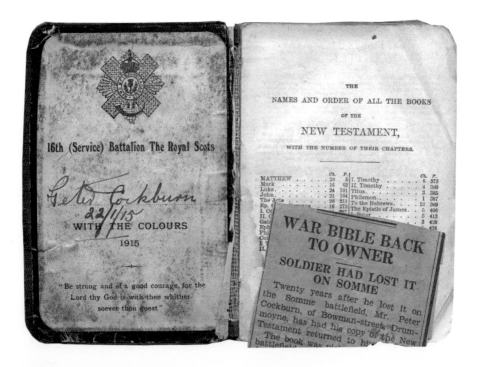

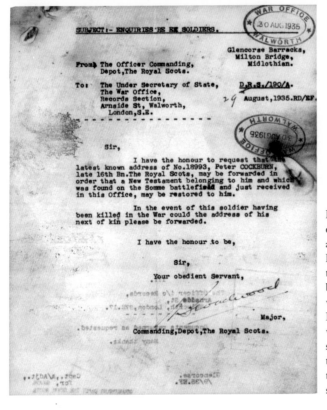

Peter Cockburn, a 25-year-old grocer from Edinburgh and a member of the 16th Battalion Royal Scots, lost this New Testament on the battlefield when he was wounded on 1 July 1916 near La Boisselle. Amazingly it was later found by another soldier, who in 1935 managed to return it to him, despite the fact that Cockburn had since emigrated to Australia.

In places one came to a bit of 'pukka' trench almost untouched. This was comparatively rare. The German machine-guns and infantry must have been preserved owing to the deep dugouts. These were numerous and elaborate, most of them with two or three entrances. The enemy wire entanglements had everywhere been completely destroyed by our artillery.[22]

Gordon had drifted to the right and was now in the vicinity of Fricourt. He decided to try to recover his direction and whilst doing so he encountered a party of Germans:

While we were moving to our left we suddenly came upon a dozen Germans about ten or twelve yards off. They fired at us with rifles. I whipped out my revolver and fired several rounds, and some of my men also fired. One of the Germans dropped, and suddenly [one of my men] rushed forward shouting, 'Come on boys, the buggers are on the run!' The enemy would not face the bayonet. We captured the wounded man and one other, who threw down his rifle and held up his hands; the rest fled.[23]

After clearing a German dugout, Gordon continued to advance, reaching the sunken road between Fricourt and Contalmaison. Here he instructed his men to dig in and hold on. They were fortified by soda water and gold-tipped cigarettes found in an enormous German dugout which had been a battalion headquarters, the water in particular being invaluable as it was by now midday and the sun had become almost unbearably hot. Early in the afternoon Gordon received orders to advance a little way to Crucifix Trench and occupy this position. This was his battalion objective and Gordon and his men held it until they were relieved that night by two reserve battalions, making this at least one success for the British that day. Gordon recalled that it was a particularly trying afternoon, however:

The men were hot and exhausted but the job of consolidating the trench had to commence at once as our position was very exposed. Shelter Wood, Birch Tree Wood and Fricourt farm were full of Germans with machine-guns. My flanks being somewhat in the air, I sent bombing squads and machine-guns to cover them … It was a most unpleasant afternoon, and difficult to carry on owing to the extreme shortage of officers … I feared a counter-attack but we were being well supported by our own heavy artillery and shrapnel and I have no doubt the enemy were at that time disorganised if not demoralised.[24]

Only near Mametz and Montauban were the British notably successful on 1 July 1916. By the end of the day the 7th Division had captured Mametz, after heavy fighting in and around Danzig Alley. One of the most famous actions on this part of the front was the advance by the 9th Battalion Devonshire Regiment on Mansell Copse. They were met with heavy enfilade fire which caused many casualties. The 8th Battalion Devonshire Regiment was sent forward in support but it too sustained severe losses. One soldier of the 9th Battalion, Lance Corporal Oliver Elmer, wrote to his platoon commander (who had missed the attack):

I expect you have seen the good news in the papers lately, well the 9th Devons have been in the thick of it again, and I'm proud to say have come out with great honours. We had a very difficult task, and we did it although it cost a lot … We are now back having a spell of reorganising and shall soon be ready for them again if needed.[25]

Between Mametz and Montauban lay the British 18th Division. After initially being held up by German machine-gun fire, this division was also successful in taking almost all of its objectives. It was on this part of the front that Captain Billy Neville of the 8th Battalion East Surrey Regiment famously supplied footballs for his men to dribble forward across No Man's Land. Lieutenant T.R. Price was another officer in this division, serving with the 6th Battalion Northamptonshire Regiment. Price in later years had nothing but praise for one particular general's performance on this day, stating:

We in the 18th Division thought that the day had been a tremendous success, of course we took our final objective and we had practically no casualties whatsoever … The whole reason why we did, ourselves, and the whole division did so well that day was because of our divisional commander … Sir Ivor Maxse was the only one to my mind who'd really prepared for the battle. For three months before the battle – we dug the whole of the position we were to attack in a back area – and attacked it every day for about three months. We got very fed up with it but the consequence was on the morning in question every single man in the whole division knew exactly where he was expected to go and got there.[26]

The village of Montauban was protected by a brickworks under which the enemy had burrowed so as to make an underground fort, for which the ruins of the works made excellent head-cover. The fort was strengthened with concrete, reinforced with iron

A platoon of the 20th (Service) Battalion Manchester Regiment (Manchester Pals) just before the Battle of the Somme. Of the twenty-seven men in this photo, five would be killed on 1 July 1916 and a sixth died of his wounds the following day.

girders. It contained living rooms for many men, and emplacements for machine guns. As it lay on a plateau-top, well back from a contour line, it had a good field of fire in all directions. All that could be seen from outside it was a heap of bricks.

Two other outlying forts covered the Montauban–Mametz Road; although these were wired, it was thought that they were not likely to be so dangerous as the brickworks. British preliminary fire upon the brickworks and Montauban was exceedingly heavy, constant and accurate. It could be precisely observed and corrected from observation posts in the trees behind the British lines, and the enemy at this part of the line had not, at that stage of the battle, any great concentration of men and guns. It happened that the British attack upon the brickworks, Montauban village and the road down to Mametz, all on the extreme right wing of the British advance, was swiftly successful, and without great losses. The brickworks had been so deluged with shells that the fort gave little trouble, and the British were established there and in Montauban village before noon. This was

Second Lieutenant F. Gordon Ross, 20th Battalion Manchester Regiment. A Stalybridge mill director before the war, he was killed in action on 1 July 1916.

British soldiers returning with German prisoners, 1 July 1916. (*From the French magazine L'Illustration*)

the sector of the 30th Division, comprised in the main of battalions of the Liverpool and Manchester Pals. Thomas Crebbin, before the war, was a shipping clerk employed at the Garston Bobbin Works in Liverpool. Typical of the brighter class of recruits who were attracted to the Pals battalions upon their formation, he joined the 18th Battalion King's Liverpool Regiment (2nd Liverpool Pals). This battalion was in the first wave on the morning of 1 July and made rapid progress, advancing along Train Alley to Glatz Redoubt, which they reached by 8.35am. Crebbin wrote afterwards:

> We went over about 7.30 on Saturday morning, July 1st. I don't think I ever felt so excited in my life before. Our lads were in the best of spirits, laughing and joking; but we soon came to the real work. The Germans fought hard until they saw they were getting beaten. Then they would throw up their hands and cry 'Mercy Komerade.' We took a lot of prisoners, but at the same time we lost a lot of men. I got hit when I reached the Germans' fourth line of trenches. While trying to make my way back a shell burst nearby, and a piece of shrapnel grazed one thigh and went in the other, and another bit went through my leg just above the ankle.[27]

On the left of this successful attack, where men had to storm the steep little hill on which Mametz stands, the approach was slower, but by the late afternoon Mametz, or what was left of it, was in British hands, and the cellars and piles of rubble covering machine guns had been bombed into silence. One German soldier in this area that day was Emil

French soldiers moving swiftly forward into action, 1 July 1916. The French used infiltration tactics, with small teams using cover to cross No Man's Land, rather than advancing in rigid rows – the tactic favoured by the British. (*From the French magazine L'Illustration*)

Goebelbecker of the *Reserve Infanterie Regiment Nr 109*. He recalled approximately sixty years later that on the morning of the attack he was in the command dugout in the rear:

> From this position, the front lines were clearly visible to me. The first line was empty, the troops were in the second & third lines. The bombardment of the front line & No Mans Land suddenly stopped at I believe 9am or 10am & the British troops left their trenches & attacked en masse. Our front lines gave in immediately. There were very few defenders left & with no NCOs or commissioned officers to take command, everyone dropped back on their own. I was left with two riflemen in a hole & when we crawled back one was killed … What puzzled me most all day was the lack of further forward movement by the British troops after the initial attack. The whole German line had collapsed & it would have been a simple matter for them [the British] to make a much larger advance than they did.[28]

Unlike the British, whose fortunes on 1 July were mixed to say the least, the French attacking to the south of the allied front had almost unalloyed success on that first day, and penetrated deeply into the German lines along most of their frontage. The French sector of the Somme was bisected by the river itself, and included its associated marshland, which spreads for a mile or more on the southern side as the watercourse breaks up into a hundred streams and channels, which meander between islands green with little bushes and thick reeds. North of the Somme it was necessary to move eastward so as to clear the enemy from strong positions on the cliffs cut by the river in its meanders, positions which were sometimes very difficult to attack because they were protected on one side by the valley marshes at the base.

A stiff engagement took place at the scarp known as the Gendarme's Hat, near Curlu, which runs along the north bank of the Somme, on the opening day of the offensive. This cliff face was formed by one side of an abandoned quarry, and prior to the attack French artillery had stripped the top of the little vegetation it possessed and at the same time smashed the German defences at the top. This position was attacked by the French 39th Division, the so-called 'Iron Division', one of the elite formations of the French army. Whilst some men scaled the steep hillside, others swarmed around the less precipitous flanks and joined their comrades on the crest, cheering and waving their handkerchiefs to indicate to aerial observers that the position had been captured. Three lines of German trenches were taken here. H. Warner-Allen, a journalist who was present, gave a description of the French advance towards the village of Curlu, which was the southernmost point of the attack on 1 July on this bank of the Somme:

> By 3pm they had reached Curlu, but in the village itself on the higher ground, round the church and cemetery, they met with a desperate resistance. The French artillery had demolished all the complicated defence works in the village itself, which was no more than a pile of ruins, but a portion of the very powerful underground fortress constructed by the enemy in the cemetery and in the vaults of the church had escaped destruction, and one or two Maxims remained uninjured. In accordance with their orders the French infantry halted and sent back word to the artillery behind. At 6 o'clock the fire of every gun available was concentrated on the church and cemetery of Curlu. In half an hour all was over. Church, cemetery and all the German defences had been utterly shattered. The French infantry swept forward relentlessly, and by 9 o'clock the whole village was in their hands.[29]

In fact, as the triumphant French troops were investigating the area in front of the church, German machine guns concealed in barns had opened fire, causing heavy casualties and an immediate withdrawal. A heavy bombardment by French howitzers and 75s firing gas shells between 6 and 6.30pm flattened the village, and the French occupied the eastern edge and several small quarries nearby. The next advance would be towards Hem and Monacu Farm.

South of the Somme, in a bend of the river, lies Frise. The village itself was not assaulted on 1 July but the 31st Brigade of the 16th Colonial Division encircled it on the heights to the south and east, and it fell on the following day. However, the lock (*eclusier*) at Frise was taken by the troops of the 16th Colonial Division on 1 July. While some men attacked along the canal that runs along the south bank of the Somme, others moved along the heights above the river. Georges Lafond, a sergeant major in the machine-gun section of a French colonial infantry battalion, was in action here on 1 July, and provides a graphic account of the fighting in this part of the battlefield south of the river. The Germans were rather more surprised by the French attacks here, though this is not to say, however, that they did not mount a stout defence of their positions:

A hundred yards in front of us the company reaches its objective, the hill and the Boche blockhouse. Two sections have rushed in and are already in action. Two more sections throw themselves into a crater more to the left opposite a clump of trees which is still held by the enemy. Suddenly there is a terrific explosion, and the most violent clap of thunder that can be imagined sends us head over heels. The ground trembles, the earth cracks, and through the crevices oozes a black smoke which envelops us. Everything is black. Are we entombed? A mine has been exploded near us in the entrance. They shout; they cry. Belts of cartridges burst in the furnace. A swarm of bees seems to fly over our heads. The blockhouse has just blown up with our two sections. It was mined.

When the smoke lifts from the overturned ground, all we can see are corpses scattered about. Our comrades … our dead! The enemy wanted to prevent our companies capturing and organizing it. We try to see something from the shell hole where we remain. It is certain death even to try to raise the head. The bullets glance off the ground. Morin wants to join the lieutenant and finish his errand in spite of everything, but where is he? Was he in the blockhouse? We can't see anyone in front of us. Our waves of infantry have turned to the right, invested Herbecourt, and taken it. They are now fighting in the village. We judge from the columns of smoke that there are fires. The noise of the explosion of grenades reaches us.

But in front of us there is no one. It is a breach. The breach our company ought to have held firmly closed with its machine guns during the attack on the village. The enemy knows this without a doubt. He has calculated his blow well. He has succeeded. He is going to launch out from the clump of trees and take our companies in the rear. Indeed that is the case. Groups of gray worms crawl out of the thicket. They reach the ridge. They are a hundred yards from us. There is no one to stop them. But where are our two sections? Are they wiped out too?

'My old Morin, we're done for.'

Our hands clasp in a fraternal farewell. In three minutes the Boches will be on us. They will kill us pitilessly. We hold our revolvers ready, fingers on the trigger. At least we won't go alone. They stand up now and shout. They are going to make a dash. '*Vorwaertsf Gottfordamisch!*'

The harsh sound of the command and the oath comes to us clearly. They dash forward to take the crater. But almost at the end, at scarcely fifty yards, the four guns of our two sections, hidden in the shell holes, receive them with a withering fire. The Boche line cracks, breaks; groups of men fall in heaps, like puppets. Our guns fire constantly. The Boche line wavers, hesitates, the ranks thin out. We can hear the dead sound of the falling bodies. We laugh and laugh; we applaud, crying like fools: 'There are our two sections. Bravo!'

But behind the files that fall are others in greater numbers which advance in close ranks, one after another. Our fire is slower. Our munitions are exhausted – the gun crew is firing all the cartridges of their carbines. The assailants realize this. Some of the groups have already reached our emplacements. An incredibly tall and strong officer hurls himself on a gun. It is Marseille's gun. It has been silent just a moment, but it hasn't finished its task for all that. Marseille tears the barrel from the tripod, and using it as a gigantic mace beats the officer to death. A terrible hand to hand fight follows. The lieutenant, wounded, dripping with blood, on his knees on the parapet, stops the demoralized enemy with shots from his revolver. But this heroic defense of the breach can't last long. Most of our men have fallen and most of the rest are wounded. The enemy is still advancing, in close ranks now. He is going to get by … Then, from the support trench, which the first Territorials hold, a company dashes out like a whirlwind, with an irresistible dash. It throws the mass of the enemy into disorder, and it is soon just a mob, which turns its back and flees frantically, as fast as it can go, falling under our rifle fire, and strewing the ground with corpses and innumerable wounded who drag themselves along on the ground begging for mercy.[30]

Soldat Mathieu Jouy (*centre*), from a French colonial regiment, receives the *Legion d'Honneur* for his bravery on 1 July 1916. Armed with a light machine gun, he single-handedly captured the strongpoint of Beauséjour. (*From the French magazine L'Illustration*)

Further south still, the German artillery NCO Gerhard Siegert provides us with a graphic account of the perspective of the German gunners facing the French onslaught, desperately aware that they must fire as rapidly as possible to protect their infantry in the front line, but equally certain that if they run out of ammunition then in the rear areas they too are done for. Siegert also captures the sense of claustrophobia induced by the gas mask, an essential but unpleasant piece of equipment:

It was around 5 o'clock in the morning. The sun shone again, as on previous days. There was an eerie calm. The days were so terribly long: it was not until 10 clock in the evening that the sun set. There would be again 15 to 17 hours of battle – 'Who will endure and get through?' The Frenchman's artillery was like a drumroll, but the impacts seemed dull. Many of the burning fuses popped in front of us. The clouds from them hung like white balls, motionless in the air. The stench from the smouldering flares drifted on the pure morning air over to us. 'Gas! So today begins the attack?' The hours of trepidation had passed; we tied our gas masks over our faces. Suddenly Sergeant Lindner called down a barrage with a terse sign from the flare post! We now knew that the storm would begin! The observer from the 'French watch' had given the first signal! The next moment they were showered by our guns. Every gun had 1000 rounds at its disposal. With an average rate of fire of 20 rounds per minute, we laid down a barrage. Vizwachtmeister Grande was in charge of the fire. Contact with our observation point was interrupted. Mending the telephone line was impossible. Dust and dirt swirled up high. The gas smokescreen standing before us acts as a backdrop to the chaos around and behind our trenches and becomes thicker. Our barrage helped to fight off the attack for which the French artillery was preparing.

After just a quarter of an hour cease-fire was called: the luminous flares no longer appeared. We had to show consideration for our guns and our ammunition: one-third of the stock had already been fired in these minutes, and the day was still long! Again, bright red tumbling flares called for help. Again the battery raced to action. We operated purely mechanically, no orders were called between us, because the gas masks hung like muzzles in front of our faces. I could hardly set the 'bubble', the tiny spirit level on the top part of the gun, on which accurate shooting depends, because my gas mask was so steamed up, but I was not permitted to remove it. The other gunners dragged ammunition from protected niches: our ammunition reserves had to be depleted! How long before we had no more? We heard nothing but the impacts. No one paid attention. Barrage firing in anticipation of an enemy attack required the greatest exertion of nerve.

The hellish work was almost unbearable; we were wearing a gas mask, moreover, in extreme heat. The masks no longer drew in fresh air. The filter was hot. The sweat ran down in rivulets from the face and body. In the lower part of the gas mask, small pools were formed by sweat. How long should this go on? To have to work and fight in this polluted, toxic air threatened to rob us of the tiny remnant of our power. The greatest concern was the ammunition. On this, everything depended. We wanted to fire slower, but could not. We knew that in the attack, everything depended on our barrage. The infantry clung to it, were protected by it. Yes, what of our infantry? Were they still in front? For a week we had seen nothing of them. We knew that the enemy trenches were filled with assaulting columns. They had to overrun our first lines. If we used up our ammunition all at once, would they overrun the artillery positions? The sergeant had told us that behind were no more reserves. The sergeant knew the lie of the land!

This knowledge ate into us, and stuck in our throats, so we shot slower.

Drumfire continued to fall on the front line, thus the infantry positions were not yet ready to fall, even though it had been bombarded by fire from hundreds of guns and mortars for seven days and seven nights.

The heavy artillery fired now mainly on the bridges across the Somme and on the roads. 'Perhaps our reserves are on the march?' – 'They are wanted indeed, but we will continue to do our duty, as long as we live, and if we know help is approaching, everyone will again pull together and hold out till the last man!' Again cease-fire was ordered. The gunners threw the empty shell cases away. They were in our way, hindered us, and only increased the heat in the gun emplacement. We took off our coats, worked in our shirt sleeves or drill order. One threw everything off oneself, wanted to be free. If we could, we would have fought naked. I sat exhausted on my directional seat, leaned disorientated on the gun and struggled at the same time desperately for air. I knew that I would in the next moment tear-down the gas mask; I had the feeling I would suffocate if I could not breathe better soon.[31]

Some German artillerymen believed that the intensity of the gas laid down by the French on their batteries at this time exceeded anything experienced at Verdun. German field batteries suffered particularly badly on the French front on 1 July. Contact with the observers and infantry in the front line was quickly lost, because smoke and gas obscured the flares used for communication, and indeed many front-line positions were overrun. Some batteries worked in isolation, unsure what was going on ahead of them. Others received the shocking message that there was no longer any of their own infantry in front of them. In some areas German artillery officers took forward some of their own men, equipped with grenades, to try to hold the trenches; an artillery *leutnänt* with ten gunners manned 500 metres of a trench; artillery NCOs and officers carried up wire rolls to try to close gaps in the defences, and in one case a single gunner collected scattered infantry and led them forward again. In these critical hours sometimes one self-disciplined individual with initiative proved vital to holding a section of the front.

The batteries remained in action until the last moment. Some guns were still firing despite having worn-out barrels or having sustained damage. One such gun at Estrées carried on alone, the two other guns having long since been hit and put out of action, until a shot set the ammunition on fire and the whole gun emplacement was completely burned out. In another battery an attempt to put a wheel on gun 2 from gun 4 failed, and so the battery commander ordered his men to blow up the barrels, then withdraw the limbers to save them.

In this sector the French 1st Colonial Corps advanced across the open and totally flat terrain of the Santerre plateau, with little cover of any description, towards the twin villages of Dompierre-Becquincourt. Their advance would continue almost without halt until they reached the Somme opposite Peronne at Biaches a week or so later. The largest allied advance since the onset of trench warfare on the Western Front, it was a great morale raiser for the French, and was due largely to the weaker German defences on this part of the Somme front – the Germans had quite reasonably assumed that any breakthrough here would ultimately be contained by the loop of the River Somme west of Peronne, and so it eventually proved.

Recounting his experiences of 1 July later that summer, the adjutant of a Silesian regiment recalled the French practice of infiltration – small groups moving forward from

A smashed German 77mm field gun, in the remains of an emplacement on the Somme battlefield.

shell hole to shell hole to reach the enemy front line. This was in marked contrast to the British tactics employed on the first day of the battle, which involved rigid lines moving forward across No Man's Land together, and was another reason for the greater degree of allied success in the southern portion of the battlefield:

Then came the first big storm – the beginning of July. The French followed a new tactic. Even during the barrage they broke into our lines. But what does one call the line? I was once forward during these days. There I met – crawling – a man who was sitting in a shell hole. 'Where is your front line?' I asked him. – 'I'm in it' – he replied. So they came creeping in thick blue masses, even before the barrage was over, at about 10 o'clock in the morning. Well, and then it started.

How this is – as it was – no one can tell. There are only loose details. No one at the front learns what happens on the left and right, and no one behind as the front changes from minute to minute ... The men are sitting on tenterhooks, waiting. Only later, gradually, the picture emerges, but it is not easy, because the living here with us do not like to tell of it ... At noon on 1 July our main front was still holding – to Soyecourt no Frenchman had exceeded our front shell holes. Only our right wing had to fall back. We were originally up to Fay. Now the French were in Estrées and our neighbouring division in Belloy. From a straight line our front had become a right angle. At that time we had a dismayed look in our eyes. Only afterwards we saw what we had held – and that our angular position had become the cornerstone of our entire Somme front. After a few hours we surveyed the situation. The enemy had also swept right over Frise, Dompierre and Fay ...[32]

French soldiers returning from the front line at the end of the day on 1 July 1916. (*From the French magazine L'Illustration*)

Nevertheless, in spite of making considerable inroads into the German positions, the French did not have things all their own way. One of the few features of any height in this area is the rise upon which lies the village of Fay, at the head of a small valley. The French attacked and overran Fay to a position on the far side of the village in front of Assevillers, which was the scene of the only major French setback on 1 July. The village was occupied by a battalion of Senegalese tirailleurs in the early evening, which had advanced further and faster than planned. A fierce German counter-attack caught them unawares and they were ejected in some panic. The French then formed a front just to the west of Assevillers until the Germans themselves withdrew. The Silesian adjutant continues:

> It was natural that we should want to retake the lost terrain on the wing. At 4 o'clock in the afternoon our Silesians drew up, reinforced by some reserves, before the right wing. They attacked angrily – even the reserves. My God, they were all weary regiments, while the French, who were facing us, came from weeks of rest. We entered Estrées again, captured the village and were by the evening of that day holding ground north of the old Roman road... .[33]

This German officer was in the extreme southern portion of the French sector, and by the close of the day the line here rested upon Soyecourt, the French troops having been pushed back perhaps a kilometre west of Estrées by the German counter-attack described above.

Back in the extreme north of the allied line, Lieutenant John Morris of the 1st/5th Leicesters, who had been in a reserve position during the 46th Division's unsuccessful attack, wrote afterwards of the aftermath of this day's fighting. His description is highly evocative of the aftermath of a major battle:

> When dusk fell [my second in command] and I, still without any orders, decided to go forward. An acrid pall of smoke had settled low over the land. Many of the trenches had

collapsed in the bombardment and those that still remained were choked with corpses. Small parties of men were to be seen wandering about trying to find their own units. Nobody talked; the men moved in a sort of trance, like sleep-walkers. All noise had ceased; a stunned hush had fallen over the blasted moon-like landscape. We wondered if the attack would be continued.

The next day was very hot, and already the dead had begun to stink. A number of badly wounded men could be seen trying to crawl back towards our trenches. It was still very peaceful; only an occasional rifle-shot disturbed the quiet. As soon as night fell we took our small party out into no-man's-land to see what we could do. We made no attempt to conceal our movements, and although it would have been easy to shoot us down, nothing happened. We worked on through the night, carrying our burdens back as far as our old front line, where emergency dressing stations had by this time been set up. When dawn broke and we felt we could do no more, we carried our last casualty right back to an emergency hospital. I needed some food, also I was tired and dirty. The man we were carrying seemed to be terribly mutilated, but he only moaned quietly. We carried him to the post, and the doctor, in a weary voice, told us to lay him on the rough deal table, which was all he had for his operations.

There was a sickening smell of gangrene and ether. It fascinated me, and I sat down on a bench, exhausted and unable to drag myself away. I was almost at the end of my tether and could hardly keep my eyes open. The doctor's voice came to me out of a haze. 'You'd better get out of this,' he said; 'it's not going to be pleasant.' I stumbled outside and an orderly gave me a mug of tea.[34]

As journalists are so fond of reminding us, purely in terms of casualties 1 July 1916 was the worst single day in the history of the British army, with close to 60,000 men killed, wounded or missing. Yet we must bear in mind the fact that this figure alone does not tell the whole story of the first day of the battle, for the Germans also suffered heavily; there were some British successes, and the French did well. Ultimately of course the engagement was to last four and a half months, and we must remind ourselves that it is upon the battle as a whole, and not on individual days, that we should base any assessment of success or failure. The doctor's parting words to Morris could almost be taken as a prophetic indictment of the weeks and months which now lay ahead, for the events of 1 July were merely the curtain-raiser for the series of violent and ever more devastating battles that would follow, through the heat, dust and flies of August and on into the mud and slush of November. As the battle drew ever more men, British, French and German, into its jaws, so too it would devour trees, houses, churches, indeed whole villages, leaving a shell-scarred moonscape in its wake.

Chapter Three

The Menace of Outraged Nature

In the days following 1 July both the British and French would consolidate the gains made in their respective sectors on that date. The French continued to attack towards Belloy en Santerre, and the British sought to exploit the foothold they had established in the German lines in the southern part of their sector, with the next major assault being that planned for the Bazentin Ridge on 14 July. The British high command still cherished hopes of a breakthrough on the Somme, and indeed perhaps it was in the fighting on 14 July that they came closest to achieving this. However, the mixed fortunes of the first day would continue to have repercussions inasmuch as it was no longer possible for the two allied armies to advance shoulder to shoulder in an eastward direction as had previously been envisaged. Instead, the direction of the British advance was now slewed northwards, and the focus of their attention for much of the month would be the horseshoe of dark and brooding Picardy woods – Mametz, Trones, Bazentin and High Wood – that now barred their path. The French in contrast would turn their attention southward, as they also sought to exploit their advances.

On 2 July the 3rd Battalion of the French Foreign Legion was given the task of taking Belloy en Santerre on this southern part of the battlefield. The advancing troops moved forward at the double until German machine guns hidden along the Belloy–Estrées road opened fire, cutting down officers and NCOs and leaving the men to continue the assault on their own initiative. Alan Seeger, the American war poet, would lose his life in this assault. His friend Rif Baer, an Egyptian, described the action:

During the night of June 30–July 1 we left Bayonvillers to move nearer the firing line. We went to Proyart as reserves. At 8 o'clock on the morning of July 1st there was roll call for the day's orders and we were told that the general offensive would begin at 9 without us, as we were in reserve, and that we should be notified of the day and hour that we were to go into action. When this report was finished we were ordered to shell fatigue, unloading 8-inch shells from automobile trucks which brought them up to our position.

All was hustle and bustle. The Colonial regiments had carried the first German lines and thousands and thousands of prisoners kept arriving and leaving. Ambulances filed along the roads continuously. As news began to arrive we left our work to seek more details; everything we could learn seemed to augur well.

About 4pm we left Proyart for Fontaine-les-Cappy and in the first line. Alan was beaming with joy and full of impatience for the order to join the action. Everywhere delirious joy reigned at having driven the enemy back without loss for us. We believed that no further resistance would be met and that our shock attack would finish the Germans. After passing the night at Fontaine-les-Cappy we moved in the morning toward what had been the German first lines. I passed almost all the day with Alan. He was perfectly happy.

'My dream is coming true,' he said to me, 'and perhaps tomorrow we shall attack. I am more than satisfied, but it's too bad about our July 4th leave. I cannot hope to see Paris again now before the 6th or 7th, but if this leave is not granted me, "Maktoob, maktoob,"' he finished with a smile.

The field of battle was relatively calm, a few shells fell, fired by the enemy in retreat, and our troops were advancing on all sides. The Colonials had taken As.sevillers and the next day we were to take their place in the first line. On July 3 about noon we moved toward Assevillers to relieve the Colonials at nightfall. Alan and I visited Assevillers the next morning, picking up souvenirs, postcards, letters, soldiers' notebooks, and chatting all the time, when suddenly a voice called out: 'The company will fall in to go to the first line.'

About 4 o'clock the order came to get ready for the attack. None could help thinking of what the next few hours would bring. One minute's anguish and then, once in the ranks, faces became calm and serene, a kind of gravity falling upon them, while on each could be read the determination and expectation of victory. Two battalions were to attack Belloy-en-Santerre, our company being the reserve of our battalion. The companies forming the first wave were deployed on the plain. Bayonets glittered in the air above the corn, already quite tall.

The first section (Alan's section) formed the right and vanguard of the company and mine formed the left wing. After the first bound forward, we lay flat on the ground, and I saw the first section advancing beyond us and making toward the extreme right of the village of Belloy-en-Santerre. I caught sight of Seeger and called to him, making a sign with my hand.

He answered with a smile. How pale he was! His tall silhouette stood out on the green of the cornfield. He was the tallest man in his section. His head erect, and pride in his eye, I saw him running forward, with bayonet fixed. Soon he disappeared and that was the last time I saw my friend....[1]

Belloy was taken that day. For an American soldier as patriotic as was Seeger, to be killed on 4 July was particularly poignant. The French Foreign Legion covered itself in glory on this day, receiving a commendation from the commander of the French Sixth Army, who praised the unit for having taken a village from the enemy at bayonet point, advancing with remarkable vigour and energy, and capturing around 750 prisoners in the process. Some evidence of the battering which the Germans had taken here comes from the captives themselves. A few weeks later another American encountered some German prisoners digging graves at a hospital behind the lines, and engaged them in conversation:

Most of them were taken at Herbecourt and Belloy-en-Santerre, at the beginning of the

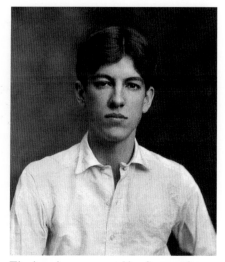

The American war poet Alan Seeger, who died whilst serving with the French Foreign Legion.

Legionnaires await the order to go forward, 4 July 1916.

offensive. Speaking of the attack, they said it was terrible, especially the bombardment preceding the assault. One man said that of his battalion, one thousand strong, only one officer and eighty-two men escaped alive. 'We all gave it up when we saw what troops were in front of us,' another man told me. To my question as to what regiment had attacked, he answered, 'The Foreign Legion.'[2]

Despite the setback the British had suffered on 1 July, they too were quickly back on the offensive. Between 2 July and 4 July heavy attacks were made towards Fricourt, which soon fell, and on 3 July Bernafay Wood was captured after a lightning bombardment. La Boisselle was also taken the following day – as Harry Trounce, an American serving as an officer with the Royal Engineers, would discover, it was a scene of utter destruction and carnage. Trounce was part of a tunnelling company, seconded to repair and consolidate trenches and dugouts in the newly won ground. Moving up the La Boisselle valley at night in the wake of the offensive, he remembered:

The surface of the ground everywhere around was so pitted with shell-holes that it was impossible to find a piece of ground five feet square which did not have one or more shell-holes in it. The bodies of German and British soldiers were lying around us in thousands. The fitful glare from the star-lights and flashes from the guns showed these bodies and portions of bodies lying in every conceivable pitiful and grotesque position. Most of them were lying face down in the shell-holes and almost filled trenches, while others stretched on their backs stared up to the skies with glassy, unseeing eyes. Rifles, bombs, and all manner of small weapons and equipment, German and British, were scattered around on all hands. We had all seen plenty of the horrors of war before and were just fresh from the Vimy Ridge trenches, where bodies also were numerous, but here it was a veritable shambles. These men had all been killed within the last two or three days. Freeman, the reliable guide with me, warned us about stepping on the bodies in the dark. To my disgust, I stepped on a body right away, and, in climbing over an earth mound, placed my hand on another. I thought I was pretty well inured to these horrible sights, but my revulsion was so strong that I vomited on the spot.[3]

Trounce and his men wanted to bury some of the British soldiers whose bodies they found there, but this was impossible. They did, however, bury a few bodies the next night, after taking their identity tags and effects from their pockets. The grim task of clearing the battlefield and identifying the dead wherever possible would take on new significance during the Somme battle, as the scale of losses on the British side was hitherto unprecedented in the war. Yet despite the fact that the heavy casualties on 1 July were common knowledge, there was surprisingly little adverse effect on British morale in the days which followed. Lionel Crouch, an officer in the Buckinghamshire Battalion of the Oxford and Buckinghamshire Light Infantry, was well aware that part of his division had been badly mauled on that day, mentioning the fact in a letter to his father on 6 July, and yet he went on to state:

… by the time you get this letter we shall be back in trenches leading the normal life, but I sincerely hope that it will be only temporary. When we came out of trenches (for the last time, we hoped) we were all as cheery as crickets, in spite of the fact that we were probably going into a boost [attack]. I would rather boost twice over than go back to the monotony of trench life.[4]

The following day, despite describing convoys of wounded returning from the front, with the worst cases swathed in bandages within motor ambulances, he was still able to write:

Our Brigade with others actually had orders to attack, and marched some way, and then the orders were cancelled. The men were furious. We were all very disappointed. I would rather go through anything in an attack than go back to this infernal trench monotony, but perhaps it will be only temporary.[5]

British commanders sought to exploit their success in the southern portion of their front by attacking now in a northerly direction, rather than easterly as had originally been envisaged. The first major objective was Mametz Wood, standing squarely in the path of any advance in that direction. What would become a bitter and protracted struggle on this part of the battlefield was now beginning. The ferocity of the continuing British artillery bombardment is borne out by the testimony of a German

Two comrades of the 9th Battalion Northumberland Fusiliers, who both died on the Somme. Private Frederick Watson (*right*) was killed in action on 5 July 1916; Private Adolphus Truttman was killed two days later in an unsuccessful attack on Quadrangle Trench, south of Contalmaison.

soldier here; Adolf Keller was an artillery signaller with the *5. Garde Feldartillerie Regiment*, operating a field telephone in a forward observation post in Mametz Wood. Adjacent to him were infantrymen, some of whom were from his home town in western Germany:

> If I recall correctly, the ditch was occupied by men of the 6th company of the Lehr Infantry Regiment. These comrades were presumably mostly Silesian compatriots. I became especially close companions, however, with those men from Elberfeld. The company had sent in the evening of 6th July possibly sixteen to eighteen men to fetch rations from the sugar factory near Longueval. The ration party did not return. Who knows what became of them? The next day the sergeant comrade from Elberfeld produced a mess tin in which were the remains of a sordid lard substitute. He warmed up the contents with the help of a candle stub, and thus we three held a banquet with tiny servings.
>
> On our section of ditch there fell a heavy hostile fire. All of the infantrymen temporarily moved forward about fifty meters from the ditch. I stayed behind in the slit trench, and was buried shortly after. Immediately behind followed a second hit, which pressed me still more deeply and more firmly into the earth, and took away my every hope for rescue. In the meantime, the infantrymen had taken their earlier places in my vicinity once again, and were expecting a hostile infantry attack. My comrades from Elberfeld missed me straight away. Here, on the position in which I had dug myself in the day before, they saw the pouting masses of earth and supposed me to be properly under it all. With untiring diligence they started to dig me out. One of the Elberfeld men especially tried over and over again to dig through to me, in spite of the heavy hostile artillery fire and the machine guns of the airmen, which he was under. His trouble, his courage and his willingness to sacrifice all were greeted at the last minute by success. When I again saw the daylight, I gave him my photograph as a token of my thanks.[5]

The following day the 38th Welsh Division launched its attack against the wood, beginning at 8.30am. This was a locally raised division, sometimes nicknamed 'Lloyd George's Welsh Army' in acknowledgement of the role the Welsh politician had played in its formation. Like many of the New Army units it had a unique character: its men were largely drawn from sections of chapel-going Welsh society who had previously viewed the army with deep suspicion – a suspicion which it had taken some time (and a goodly number of senior positions allotted to prominent local dignitaries) in order to overcome. At Mametz the division attacked at first with two brigades, meeting murderous German machine-gun fire, and over the next five days the Welshmen would make repeated attempts to take the wood. Private D.G. Gregory of the 13th Battalion Royal Welsh Fusiliers, writing in his diary for 10 July, noted:

> Entered wood and were greeted with machine-gun fire. Dense undergrowth made movement difficult – walls of young saplings not thinned for two years … Our work was to drive and clear [a] wood 220 acres in extent.[6]

Captain R.H. Hutchings of the 16th Battalion Welsh Regiment reported in a letter to his parents:

> Imagine, if you can, crumps at the rate of 2 per minute bursting within 200 yards of you the whole time and the horrible sickly smell of dead men, high explosive and tear shells & the ceaseless din and racket of thousands of guns of all calibres.[7]

Another ferocious day of fighting in Mametz Wood followed on 11 July. One of the best descriptions of this action comes from Captain Llewellyn Wynn-Jones of the 15th Battalion Royal Welsh Fusiliers. By the end of this day of disappointment, he had come to appreciate the tactical conundrum which the British faced in this kind of warfare, in that as soon as the infantry began to advance, communication was quickly lost, and so the artillery was blinded and no longer able to perform its function of protecting them. In this action Wynn-Jones was attached to the headquarters of the 115th Brigade, and was soon a helpless observer as things quickly began to unravel:

At eight o'clock the artillery began its bombardment of the edge of Mametz Wood. A thousand yards away from where I stood, our two battalions were waiting. I read the orders again. The attack was to be carried out in three stages, beginning at half-past eight, reaching in succession three points inside the wood, under the protection of an artillery barrage. Smoke screens were to be formed here and there. Everything sounded so perfectly simple and easy. A few minutes after eight all our telephone wires to the battalions were cut by the enemy's reply to our fire. There was no smoke screen, for some reason never explained – perhaps someone forgot about it. This was the first departure from the simplicity of the printed word. Messages came through, a steady trickle of runners bringing evil news; our fire had not masked the German machine-guns in Mametz Wood, nor the wood near Bazentin. The elaborate timetable suddenly became a thing of no meaning, as unrelated to our condition as one of Napoleon's orders; our artillery barrage was advancing in mockery of our failure, for we were two hundred yards away from the wood.[8]

Private Griffith Thomas, 14th Battalion Welsh Regiment (Swansea Pals). A labourer in a steel tube works before the war, he survived the battle at Mametz Wood.

Wynn-Jones and his brigade commander, Brigadier-General H.J. Evans, subsequently received a new set of instructions to the effect that the artillery barrage would be renewed in twenty minutes and the troops were to try again. The two men set off on foot, and found the remnants of the brigade sheltering in some dead ground, unable to move forwards or retire in the face of the deadly machine-gun fire. Fortunately, a working telephone line was found and Evans was able to advise his divisional headquarters of the extent of the casualties sustained so far, and the impossibility of going forward.

The French advance in the south meanwhile continued unabated. Captain Augustin Cochin was an officer with the *10e Regiment d'Infanterie*. He wrote to his mother on 7 July describing conditions in the captured German lines, and also his own feelings of contempt for the enemy before him:

An obsolete Russian field gun, captured and put into use by the Germans, lies abandoned amid the wreckage of Mametz Wood, July 1916.

Captured German trenches between Mametz and Hardecourt.

What an odious war, days and days in holes in the ground, each with his own niche in the wall of a trench. No breaks: the Germans shoot stubbornly three hundred yards away, and the 'zzz boom' is continual! There is no way to wash of course, just untie one's boots. ... To our right we have broken through, but not the left (where the English are), and then we expect 1200 meters from the point of departure, the attack is delivered every day. There is a terrible racket all night on the side of the English, uninterrupted rolling cannon fire. Is it a Boche attack? A British victory? Nobody knows. We may be mouldering here for a long time.

I'm in the middle of the spoils of the Boche and could send you a variety of things, but it would be necessary to delve into shelters full of corpses, and I do not have the courage. I collect only postcards, which all talk about the great German youth, it is the only subject outside of politeness, which also makes up a huge part. 'How are you? Very well, I hope' etc etc. There is nothing so flat as these letters, there is not one that is funny or specific, like those of the least of my men. Awful, awful race, the more closely we see them, the more we abhor them. Bands of prisoners are despicable to see, down, anxious to get well ahead, delighted to be taken. More were taken yesterday, with their short jackets, and carrying a small bundle of supplies for the trip. It's annoying to get killed from behind the parapets by such animals. They have a special smell, very strong, which we can not get rid of, when you live like us in their lines, [one finds they have] special lice too – these famous great lice have iron crosses ... I am deep in my hole, and was half asleep in the middle of a terrible racket! Physically I am well, and morale is good also, but the intellectual side of life does not exist.[9]

Cochin was to lose his life in the following day's advance, a brother officer recording that:

The order to attack was given for 8 July, 9 o'clock in the morning. Despite the fatigue, exhaustion, deprivation, and rain, the troops advanced beautifully. Having captured several German trenches which were smashed by artillery, and taken Hardecourt they arrive at a wayside calvary. Captain Cochin, in the first wave, directs one of his men, who fires a machine-gun lying on the stone base of the calvary. A Fritz takes aim from a trench behind a barricade of sandbags, with a periscope rifle, mounted on a stand. It is 10.10am.

Gravières, the medical orderly, a youth with the face of a choirboy, rushes forward: a bullet has entered near the mouth, and has come out through the neck, the blood flows freely. 'He has not missed me,' said his captain. 'Take my equipment from me, take me away.' But he is still absorbed by the concerns of command: 'Forward!' He indicates, with his hand, for the advance to continue. 'My poor ninth company! Always forward, always on towards the glorious victory.' He thinks of Captain Carpentier: 'I want to see Captain C ... here behind me. Alas, it is true that we can not be everywhere at once. Tell this to Captain C ... say that my men were admirable, and followed me everywhere.'

We attempt to dress the wounds, but the captain, who feels smothered, twice pulls away the dressings. 'Embrace for me my poor father, my poor mother, my brother, the whole family.' Then he said aloud the act of contrition, but soon he can talk no more, and Gravières must finish with him.[10]

Cochin was a writer and historian before the war, and was well known in France at the time. His loss was deeply felt nationally, as well as among his family and immediate comrades.

At dawn on 8 July the 5th and 6th Battalions of the *38e RIC (Regiment d'Infanterie Coloniale)* were also in position for their attack, one in front of the trench at Bigorres, the other to the west side of Barleux. For this action the regiment had intermixed its black and European companies, a common practice in the French army. The French military authorities believed that, whilst the Senegalese possessed the necessary courage and elan for the attack, they lacked the organisational skills to consolidate captured ground which European troops had. At the moment of the attack the forward troops came under violent German fire. Many were driven back, but the 6th Company was at least in a position to open fire on Porpoise Trench. The neighbouring formation, a Moroccan division, had failed in its attack, and the Germans remained stubbornly in possession of the cemetery to the south of Barleux. Despite the desperate heroism of Senegalese assaults here, the attack was a failure. That night, reinforcements

Capitaine Augustin Cochin, the French historian and writer, who was killed in action at Maricourt on 8 July 1916.

arrived; at dawn a patrol, guided by a sergeant named Imbert, was sent to investigate the defences of the trench at Bigorres. He found it was not strongly manned, and indicated as much by means of an agreed sign; French sections duly occupied it and, commanded by a second lieutenant named Amtigue, held it firmly, in spite of the counter-attacks of the enemy. At one instant they were gripped by anxiety as ammunition began to run low, and they feared that the enemy would return, because the trench continued up to the village where the Germans were still present in strength. Hastily, with bodies, they made a barricade and armed themselves with German grenades left by the previous occupants. A Senegalese sergeant named Dougoutigni-Da-Kita explained the handling of these to his men and, standing alone behind this dam of the dead, he prepared to defend it. Despite the bullets that were continually fired at him, he came out of this epic conflict unharmed, the *Medaille Militaire* and the braids of a warrant officer being his justly deserved rewards.

Both black and white soldiers suffered greatly from thirst in this action: having advanced ahead of their supplies, they were frequently short of drinking water. The Germans often suffered similarly but on one occasion it was something more than water which was coveted. Old soldiers often cherished above all others the memory of humorous events which occurred in the midst of bitter fighting, but the account of Hans Korfmacher, of *Infanterie Regiment Nr 174*, who was serving on this front, is something more than merely a humorous anecdote. It clearly illustrates the German tactic of repeatedly counter-attacking and contesting every yard of lost ground, which was the policy of the German commander, General von Falkenhayn. It was a tactic which was to cost them dearly in terms of manpower, but on this particular occasion Korfmacher remembered a much more amusing aspect of the situation. He tells us:

The battle at Estrées on the Somme had been going on with unabated fierceness for some time. However, it may have been on the 8th or 9th July 1916 when our ration carriers succeeded in catering handsomely for us. Among other things, we received a barrel of cranberries, which to distribute amongst us all at once, however, was totally impossible. Thus we agreed to take what we wanted from the barrel when we could. As a result of the frequent attacks of the French, which always came from the flank, we were often forced to evacuate our trench, go over the lane and settle in the adjacent roadside ditch; at the same time, naturally, on each occasion, we had to say goodbye, even if only temporarily, to our cranberries which we had put in a rabbit hole [German term for a shelter under the fire step of a trench], underneath a piece of tent for a cover.

After a break of twenty minutes we went over to the counter-attack, under the lead of our sergeant Emil Liebert, of *Reserve Infanterie Regiment 207*, 3rd kompanie. So it was that we promptly threw the French out of our trench again. All at once, however, our sergeant found out that the French had gone to our cranberries. Our feelings were now expressed in strong words. It seemed, however, as if the French did not take exception to this, because after a short time there beat once more a wagonload of grenades upon us, and we withdrew again offended into our roadside ditch. When I got there, I noticed that the sergeant was missing. I was about to jump back over the edge to search for him, when he appeared with the words: 'The only cranberries we eat, are those that we get!' and I thought, God's Truth, for on his back was the barrel with the cranberries in! The hilarious part came when the barrel hit the ground. When Sergeant Liebert had run to and fro perhaps three or four times with the tub, and was half way back to our ditch after a counter-attack, he stumbled over the legs of a comrade, bounced with a swish into a shell hole and emerged with one side of his face and up to his breast covered in the red berries … I can tell you this, it was a sight to gladden the heart of every old crock, laughter would be too mild a word, no, we screamed … Sergeant Liebert, who later was killed, was a dear companion, and I think back with pleasure to him.[11]

Still on the French front, on 9 July the French *37e R.I.C.* was ordered to encircle and capture the hamlet of La Maisonette and Blaise Wood, by attacking both from the south and the east. Two groups were formed to accomplish this task; the northern group was given the task of attacking La Maisonette directly, while the southern group had to seize Porpoise Trench, then come up the eastern crest of the plateau between Hill 623 and the captured trench, and neutralise the resistance facing the northern group. The southern group was composed only of Europeans, but in the northern group the first line was composed entirely of black troops from Senegal, supported by the second line, comprising European troops, who were responsible for organising the position as soon as it was in French hands.

At 2pm on 9 July the attack began, with the northern group seizing its first objective. The second group, including the Senegalese, fulfilled its role with equal mastery. The first wave, a Senegalese company, reached Thalweg Bottom without a halt, but suddenly cleverly concealed enemy machine guns took them in enfilade, and their losses became significant as they continued to climb the slope leading to Porpoise Trench. Soon just forty men were left. Too weak to continue, they stopped on an oblique slope at the leading edge, while trying to dig in to avoid the fire from the defenders of Porpoise Trench. The second wave, launched in turn, suffered roughly equal losses, and the few survivors swelled the small isolated group. Meanwhile the members of the northern group strove to bring the fire of their machine guns to bear to support their comrades; keeping this up with heroic obstinacy, they forced the enemy to stay holed up in their shelters. Between 6 and 7pm a bitter struggle with grenades took place, ending with the capture by the French of two guns and twenty-seven prisoners. For their part, the Senegalese were able to take advantage of this diversion. They crept silently forward again, finally approaching Porpoise Trench, but they could not yet take it. Suddenly, at around 8pm, a young officer named Lieutenant Meyer noticed a slackening in the fire of the enemy; at once he sprang forward, and behind him came a heroic handful of survivors. This time the trench was taken, along with seven officers and 123 men, with five machine-guns. However, the cost had been high for the French, with all the officers involved in this action being killed or wounded. A citation written afterwards stated:

> Meyer (Auguste-Marie-Maurice): an energetic officer with remarkable composure. On 9 July 1916 he successfully led his company to assault the enemy positions. All officers of the neighbouring companies having been knocked out, he wisely took steps first to resist enemy attacks.
> Lamine Kamara, sergeant;
> Demba Ba, corporal;
> Moussa Cissoko, soldier: have demonstrated, on July 9, 1916, the most brilliant valour in the assault, walking on a path of 700 meters, under a murderous fire of machine guns and artillery. Unable to engage the strongly defended German trench, they clung to the ground for five hours, a few meters from the enemy. At dusk, benefiting from the progress of a neighbouring troop, they set off with a group of riflemen to the trench, where 130 prisoners were taken, including 7 officers and 5 guns.[12]

Everyone involved in this costly affair showed great courage. The officers led their men with a disregard of danger that was reflected in their casualty figures. With three exceptions, all the companies in the first line lost all their officers. The soldiers of the *37e R.I.C.* showed they were worthy of their leaders and of their previous exploits. The history of the regiment states:

> The Senegalese and their leaders, who for the most part were coming under fire for the first time, have amply justified their reputation through the bravery and sacrifice which they have shown in this harsh business. At the time of departure for the assault, the Senegalese were smiling and full of vibrant enthusiasm. They left singing, with a calm and beautiful composure. As soon as their

The grave of Matinda Yande, a Muslim soldier of the French 61st Senegalese Battalion from Upper Volta, who died of wounds received on the Somme on 15 July 1916.

ranks came under murderous machine-gun fire, not a failure was noticed among them. It was the same in the second wave, despite having a clear view of the losses sustained by the first. They moved forward to the cheers of the Europeans, infantry or artillery, who remained in the departure trench, and who they enthused with their attitude. When they had got to within a few meters of the enemy trench, the survivors had only one desire: to try to reach their adversary![13]

Even when not directly facing the enemy, the strain of battle conditions on the Somme took their toll on the composure and the capacity of officers and men to continue with their duties. Second Lieutenant Mark Plowman (who wrote under the pseudonym Max Plowman) was serving with the 10th Battalion West Yorkshire Regiment, part of the 17th Division, which was in support in the middle part of July. After a testing spell in the second line, during which he was engaged in digging communication trenches under shellfire, he wrote:

It is marvellous to be out of the trenches: it is like being born again. The cloud of uncertainty that hung above us every moment while we were under fire, putting its minatory query before the least anticipation, is lifted, and we are free to say, 'In an hour's time' without challenging Fate with the phrase. When freedom to anticipate is being persistently challenged, one understands as never before how much man lives by hope. To be deprived of reasonable expectation – even of the next moment – is the real strain. I had not thought of that. Certainty, even of violent death, would often come as a relief. It is the perpetual uncertainty that makes life in the trenches endurance all the time. 'Stick it' has become a password: intelligibly the right one. We have to forget 'I shall.' It is this constriction of hope that depresses men in the trenches. 'If' stands before every prospect, and it is no small 'if' in this war.[14]

Plowman was an unusual character, not typical of British officers in the line. Initially a pacifist, after much soul-searching he had joined the ranks of the RAMC before being commissioned as an infantry officer. After suffering shell-shock later in the war, he resigned his commission and reverted to his pre-war stance, declaring himself a conscientious objector. Nevertheless his views on the difficulty of maintaining composure under steady harassing fire are supported by those of Lieutenant William Strang of the 4th Battalion Worcestershire Regiment. Strang's diary from around this time provides moving testimony of the way in which prolonged exposure to danger in the front line could wear down even the strongest resolve. Strang seems to have been an introverted soul, perhaps over-inclined towards self-doubt (as he himself seems readily to admit), though his account suggests that he was not alone in his unit in succumbing to mental exhaustion under the relentless bombardment:

I was ill-tempered, worried, querulous and absolutely lacking in energy or interest in my work. I managed to show a good face to the men but could not before my pals ... Our tenure [in this place] seemed interminable: day after day and no sign of relief ... The men broke down slowly, most of them. Some of my men stood firm – Smart and Cross, Helly and York, Dare and Hunt ... Sgt W. stuck to the end but only just ... It needed a great effort and much self conquest to [enable] him to perform his duties ... I am not brave and I think about things too much. Much shell fire would drive me mad. I am disappointed with myself and am terribly afraid of giving way.[15]

With the capture of Mametz Wood finally achieved, by mid-July the British were in a position to launch a major new offensive. Now the objective would be to drive the Germans off the Bazentin Ridge, a significant spur of high ground running roughly northwest to southeast between Pozières and Longueval, and hopes were again entertained of a breakthrough if all went well. Despite the insistence of the French that it could not be done and would result in disaster, the British planned to launch the first phase of the assault under cover of darkness on 14 July. In order to secure the right flank, at 2.30am soldiers of the 18th Division were ordered to make a last-ditch attempt to take Trones Wood, which had thus far held out against a number of British attacks. A key figure in this action was Lieutenant Colonel Frank Maxwell, who wrote home to his wife:

To talk of a 'wood' is to talk rot. It was the most dreadful tangle of dense trees and undergrowth imaginable, with deep yawning broken trenches criss-crossing about it; every tree broken off at top or bottom and branches cut away, so that the floor of the wood was

Corporal Joseph Richard Dobson, 7th Battalion Royal West Kent Regiment, killed in action in Trones Wood on 13 July 1916. He was, before enlisting, a shipwright at HM Dockyard, Chatham.

almost an impenetrable tangle of timber, trenches, undergrowth, etc., blown to pieces by British and German heavy guns for a week. Never was anything so perfectly dreadful to look at – at least, I couldn't dream of anything worse – particularly with its dreadful addition of corpses and wounded men – many lying there for days and days.[16]

Maxwell's 12th Battalion Middlesex Regiment and the 6th Battalion Northamptonshire Regiment (also placed under his command) were given the task of clearing the wood. He continued his letter with a description of the tactics which he employed:

I organised a line or drive, formed up scattered bodies of Northants and a nucleus of about one and a half companies of my own, under a job lot of about five very young officers, all the rest being hors de combat. After infinite difficulty, I got it shaped in the right direction, and then began the advance, very, very, slowly. Men nearly all much shaken by the clamour and din of shell-fire, and nervy and jumpy about advancing in such a tangle of debris and trenches, etc. I had meant only to organise and start the line, and then get back to my loathsome ditch, back near the edge of the wood where we had entered, so as to be in communication by runners with the Brigade and the world outside. It is a fundamental principle that commanders of any sort should not play about, but keep in touch with the Higher Authorities behind. But though old enough soldier to realise this, and the wrath of my seniors for disregarding it, I immediately found that without my being there the thing would collapse in a few minutes. Sounds vain, perhaps, but there is nothing of vanity about it really. So off I went with the line, leading it, pulling it on, keeping its direction, keeping it from its hopeless (and humanly natural) desire to get into a single file behind me, instead of a long line either side. Soon I made them advance with fixed bayonets, and ordered them, by way of encouraging themselves, to fire ahead of them into the tangle all the way. This was a good move, and gave them confidence, and so we went on with constant halts to adjust the line. After slow progress in this way, my left came on a hornet's nest, and I halted the line and went for it with the left portion. A curtain may be drawn over this, and all that need be said was that many Germans ceased to live, and we took a machine-gun. Then on again, and then again, what I had hoped for. The Germans couldn't face a long line offering no scattered groups to be killed, and they began to bolt, first back, then, as the wood became narrow, they bolted out to the sides, and with rifle and automatic guns we slew them.[17]

Maxwell's almost single-handed organisation of the capture of the wood, due mostly to his personal strength of character, was remarkable and his account illustrates better than most the difficulties presented by the dark and brooding Picardy copses. A good memoir exists from a German officer of *Infanterie Regiment Nr 178*, whose men faced those of Maxwell in Trones Wood at the time. This regiment had recently arrived on the Somme as reinforcements; as they moved up to the front line through the villages in the rear and through the fields of ripening wheat, they did so in formation as if still in a war of movement. Quickly, however, they grasped the reality of the situation as they crossed the shell-tumbled ground to relieve a shattered German battalion, holding a line which in places was little more than foxholes and joined-up shell craters. *Infanterie Regiment Nr 178* now held a considerable portion of the front, from the southeast corner of Trones Wood, where they faced the British, to near the northeast end of Hardecourt opposite the French. So haphazard had been their relief and so few officers remained in the outgoing regiment that there was little clarity regarding the dispositions of the enemy – nor did they have a definite idea of where the neighbouring companies actually were – a situation made good to some extent by courageous officers and men undertaking patrols to establish their location. This German officer tells us:

The artillery fire had gradually increased, more and more over recent days. On the 14th [July] it began again early, and by 4 o'clock in the morning, especially on the right wing, it had swelled into a barrage. We had made completely ready to receive the attack; but oddly enough this was done only in Trones Wood, although enemy soldiers faced us man to man in the opposite trench. Had the enemy airmen who circled with incredible boldness hardly 200 meters above our trench perceived how densely our line was held, and reported it by their horns in warning signals to the other side? Although at 6 o'clock an attempt was made opposite my company to launch a gas attack, it twisted ineffectively in the air and some enemy who wanted then to get out of their trench were quickly driven back by our fire. As we continued to stand on guard, we succeeded in shooting down one of the enemy aircraft, so that he came down right behind the enemy line. The enemy's fire, which had subsided temporarily, began at noon once again to be particularly strong and lasted almost without interruption even during the night.

Not only did it inflict upon us at this time very serious and painful losses, it also threatened to wear down the nerves. The requirements of the previous day had already drawn heavily upon the vigour of our people. Throughout the night they had done either guard duty or digging, and then, when the day came, there remained for those who were not required again for sentry duty no choice but to sleep wrapped up in coat and tarpaulin in the ditch, or gradually to carve out poorly made hollows in the trench walls. And how short were the quiet hours, because as soon as the sun rose higher, the enemy artillery also began their activities which increased more and more until the evening. Added to this were the difficulties of supply. Since the trench was at the same level as that of the enemy it was, before a knee-deep communication trench was dug, in the first days impossible to leave the same without exposing oneself to the most immediate mortal danger; so it was that in the short nights and with the long distances that had to be covered up to the field kitchens, only once during the dark could food and drink be carried. As for heating the former in the trench, of course there was no opportunity and we were particularly tormented by thirst in the blazing heat in the narrow trench; during the long day only bread and canned meat was available, but our men requested that as much coffee, boiled in the cauldron of the field kitchen, or water in canteens, as it was possible to carry be brought to the front. Further it was attended to by the staffs to ensure that seltzer water and other refreshing tonics came up to the front line. Of course, not everything came in a deluge. In the strong artillery fire with which the enemy artillery plastered, especially at night, the adjacent terrain and particularly the roads, the ration party had sometimes to run …[18]

Further north, the leading formation in the British attack on the villages of Bazentin le Grand and Bazentin Le Petit was to be the 21st Division, in particular the 110th (Leicestershire) Brigade, comprising the four New Army battalions of the Leicestershire Regiment. Lying in the debris of shattered trees and branches on the edge of Mametz Wood, whilst awaiting the signal to advance in the early hours of 14 July, were Dick Read

A German photograph of the village of Bazentin le Petit; paradoxically, it was the larger of the two Bazentins.

and his comrade Jackie Johnson of the 8th Leicesters. They had spent the previous night in the vicinity of Fricourt and in Read's words the whole story of the recent days of fighting lay before them like an open book, the dead men on the wire frozen stiff in the act of trying to get through it. Behind the wire was the old German front-line trench, with its shattered dugouts and the bloated and swollen corpses of enemy machine-gunners lying with the wreckage of their gun. For Read, there was none of the camaraderie supposedly felt between front-line soldiers on opposing sides, as was frequently imagined by later writers:

> Here was war as we had not seen it – or smelt it – hitherto. We knew now what to expect when our turn came. Looking around at it, we braced ourselves instinctively in anticipation of our coming ordeal; found ourselves hating those dead machine-gunners as we looked again upon our poor fellows on the rusty wire, and arguing, with a fierce satisfaction, that they had got their deserts.[19]

Captain William Wetenhall, 6th Battalion Leicestershire Regiment. He was killed in action leading his men at Bazentin.

The hours before dawn on 14 July found Read and his pal anxiously awaiting the signal to move forward. As the final shells of the British preparatory bombardment crashed home, and as German retaliatory fire began to burst around them, they were surprised to see their commanding officer moving among the men:

> Just then we saw Colonel Mignon clambering over the fallen trees in our direction, ash plant in hand, with which he thrust aside the undergrowth, bending low here and there and shouting encouragement to the men as he passed. He came to us. 'Not long to go now lads – stick it!' Then, seeing the rangefinder, he exclaimed, 'What the devil are you two doing with that thing here?' I stood to attention and shouted to him above the din and he shouted back, telling me, not unkindly, to dump it at Battalion HQ (for which he gave me a direction) and bring back some S.A.A. – we should want it soon – and look sharp![20]

The kindly words of the colonel – again a father figure to his soldiers, rather like Frank Maxwell – did much to hearten the men, but Mignon was to lose his life in the coming battle. In the same brigade was a sister battalion, the 9th Leicesters. One of its officers, Alexander de Lisle, penned an account of the capture of Bazentin by the Leicesters in the weeks following the battle. It makes for gripping reading, and this young officer's pride in his unit is evident:

> Behind the German first line ... ran the great wood, Bazentin-le-Petit, which itself was spanned at intervals by three successive lines of trenches, each with its separate wire protection. Between these lines were short lengths of trench, so it was a veritable

maze. These fell into our hands, one after the other. It was impossible to march on the intervening ground at the double, so choked with fallen timber, so full of huge shell holes that it was all climbing, jumping, scrambling and sprawling. Whatever the method of going, they got there – Trust the Leicesters for that![21]

In the course of the battle de Lisle was ordered to take a party forward to try to clear the Germans from the northern edge of the wood. He continues his account with a vivid description of the confusion among the trees, and in the process demonstrates that another First World War cliché – that of soldiers continually fighting in muddy trenches – is far from accurate, for here again it was the dense summer vegetation of a forest in full leaf which provided cover for the enemy:

> So as one man we are up and off, not knowing how far the enemy is ahead, but knowing that he is somewhere within the next hundred yards of wood right in front of us. We could only double about ten yards, for the wood was blocked by shell-split fallen trees; and other undergrowth is so thick that soon even walking is impossible. Then the whole line halts, and replies to the murderous hail of bullets still coming from unseen rifles … There is a cry: 'A German sentry on the edge of the wood!' 'Do not worry! Knock the ****** out!' A shot is fired and down he goes.
>
> Then we yell out: 'For God's sake stop this useless firing and go forward with the bayonet and bombs.' But no! [our men] say, and I heard them: 'That is the Germans telling us to stop, and we won't for those b*****s!' I get up to urge the men to stop firing, but almost as soon as I do I receive a bullet in my neck at close range. It penetrated deep, and the blood gushed out. I fell downwards into a shellhole. One of the men quickly applied my first field-dressings as tightly as possible to try to stop the bleeding, for it was bleeding fast. In fact, I thought my number was up, as it bled so hard.[22]

De Lisle was quickly evacuated from the line and returned to England to recuperate. Later in the war he joined the Royal Flying Corps, and lost his life in combat in the air rather than on the ground. For the men of the Leicestershire Brigade, the experience of their first major action had been a mixed one. They had captured all of their objectives, but the cost in casualties had been cruelly high. At the end of a day of bitter fighting, Dick Read and Jackie Johnson had time to reflect on the events of the day; both were dejected and demoralised:

> We watched a fatigue party bringing up our rations, dumping piles of bulging sandbags on the ground near us, and this set us running through the names of our mates we knew already to be killed, wounded or missing. Both of us had lost all our best pals, and we sat there with leaden hearts, lost in our thoughts.

Ludwig Eider, a 26-year-old serving with the Bavarian *Infanterie Regiment Nr 16*. He was killed at Bazentin on 14 July 1916.

Eventually Jackie broke the silence. 'Plenty of rations tonight, Dick!', nodding towards the pile. 'Enough for the whole battalion, eh? About six times too many,' he added bitterly. 'Christ, there'll be hell to pay in Leicester and Loughborough ... and Coalville and Melton ... and Uppingham ... when they know about this. The Leicester Brigade, eh? Bloody well wiped out!' and he trailed off into silence again, immersed in his thoughts.[23]

As far as the Germans were concerned, the first signs now were starting to emerge that their military machine might be beginning – only beginning, mind – to buckle under the relentless pressure that was being brought to bear upon it. Although on the whole it is rare to find German testimony from the Somme which varies from the usual somewhat jingoistic, patriotic tone, by

The bloodstained identity disc of Private Horace Chesham, 8th Battalion Leicestershire Regiment. Chesham was killed at Bazentin, and this disc was sent back to his next of kin with his other personal effects.

this stage clearly not all Germans felt this way. One artillery officer, who was obviously appalled by what was going on around him, wrote on 14 July:

The battle is still raging violently on all fronts; the enemy is still trying to gain a decisive advantage and emblazon victory on his colours. The heroic endurance of our troops deprives him of this hope and defies even the horrible weapons of present day warfare. And in a few days, perhaps weeks, the war will sink back into the old indefinite state of waiting while both sides prepare for further efforts and more gigantic losses, and devise yet more ghastly means of destruction for another struggle, which will again prove useless and will result only in a further loss of hundreds of thousands of young lives. And so it will go on, until – yes, until? And one is right in the middle of it all, no longer marvelling at finding oneself just a small wheel, without volition, driven by those who, fully realizing their responsibility, yet deem it their duty, for the honour and glory of the Fatherland, to send thousands of men to their death – dictating to thousands the way in which their loyalty and courage shall express itself ... Have the German commanders made up their minds to gain some particular point, which they will not give up, and for the sake of which they think it worth while to sacrifice the wishes and well-being of the whole nation, and on which the enemy will not yield, having still too much faith in his own strength?[24]

The author of this letter, Leutnant Eduard Offenbächer, a 21-year-old student from Mannheim, was to lose his life on the Somme just over a week later. It must be stressed, however, that at this stage of the battle such dissent from the righteousness of the national cause was as rare on the German side as it was on the British.

On the same day about half a mile away an officer of the 100th Company Machine Gun Corps, Captain Graham Seton Hutchison, was bringing his Vickers machine guns up in order to support an attempt to clear the western side of High Wood. Here, the Germans had constructed a Switch Line which ran out of the wood and behind Bazentin le Petit.

Its function was to contain any breakthrough, and this is exactly what it would do in the coming weeks. For a brief time, however, the Germans had feared being outflanked, such was the pace of the initial advance on 14 July, and they had abandoned High Wood. If the wood had been secured at this point in the battle, it would have presented the allies with a tremendous prize. As it was, the copse, standing dark and malevolent on the skyline, was subsequently reoccupied by the Germans and would continue to be a thorn in the British side for nearly two months to come. As well as illustrating the surge of adrenaline which many men report having experienced whilst in combat, Hutchison was an eyewitness to one of the most extraordinary incidents during the Battle of the Somme:

> The attack of the Rifles and Highlanders had failed; and of my own Company but a few remained ... A new horror was added to the scene of carnage. From the valley between Pozières and Martinpuich a German field battery had been brought into action, enfilading the position. I could see the gunners distinctly. At almost point blank range they commenced to direct shell-fire among the wounded. The shells bit through the turf, scattering the white chalk, and throwing aloft limbs, clothing, and fragments of flesh. Anger, and the intensity of the fire, consumed my spirit, and, not caring for the consequences, I rose and turned my machine-gun upon the battery, laughing loudly as I saw the loaders fall ... The dismal action was continued throughout the morning, German fire being directed upon any movement on the hillside. Towards noon, as my eyes searched the valley for reinforcements or for some other sign of action by those directing the battle, I decried a squadron of Indian Cavalry, dark faces under glistening helmets, galloping across the valley towards the slope. No troops could have presented a more inspiring sight than these natives of India with lance and sword, tearing in mad cavalcade on to the skyline. A few disappeared over it: they never came back. The remainder became the target of every gun and rifle. Turning their horses' heads, with shrill cries these masters of horsemanship galloped through a hell of fire, lifting their mounts lightly over yawning shell-holes; turning and twisting through the barrage of great shells; the ranks thinned, not a man escaped.[25]

The Indian troops were from the 20th Deccan Horse, who had been sent forward with the British 7th Hussars to exploit a potential breakthrough. Hutchinson's statement that the cavalry was massacred in this incident is a common misconception, though it is true that the cavalry contingent was held too far back in the rear and when open country fleetingly beckoned, not enough was done to speedily bring it forward, one source stating that it took the horses four hours to cover six or seven miles, such was the state of the country over which they had to pass. Even the roads, or what stood for roads, were choked with debris which had to be negotiated. Eventually, too late in the day to make much difference, some of the cavalrymen did get into action. It is fashionable in some quarters to mock the use of cavalry by the British army on the Western Front, as though its horse-obsessed generals were still wedded to some form of medieval warfare. In fact, one British historian has stated recently that the horse remained the most effective form of all-terrain transport until the invention of the Jeep. Even in the static warfare of the Western Front horses could still play a role if conditions were right. The main advantage of the horse in an offensive role was that it was fast, and indeed a troop of cavalry, if they put their mind to it, could be on top of a crew of machine-gunners whilst they were still trying to adjust their sights and reload. In support of this argument a little-known account actually exists from one of the British officers of the Deccan Horse, describing the incident in question:

At 6.30 we started our famous ride into the enemy country, every now and then coming under heavy shell fire – shrapnel and high explosive. No one can believe, without seeing, what a state the ground is in; there is not room for a table cloth on any part of the ground there without some part of it touching a shell hole, so you can imagine the regiment galloping over it at full gallop, barbed wire – well cut by shell fire – old trenches, dead bodies, and every sort of debris lying in every direction. Words fail me to describe it. That was for about three miles; then full tilt down a steep bank like the Haggard field, but steeper, into a very famous valley, where the shrapnel got worse, as we were spotted by one of their sausage balloons. This was soon driven down by the fire of our batteries, which just smothered it with shrapnel. Here we went through our infantry, who cheered us madly as we galloped by, all wishing us luck. On we went past the remains of guns and everything – tons of ammunition and abandoned material and dead Huns everywhere; and we passed here an enormous gun they had left behind, so really I suppose it was we that took it. We were under cover here for half a mile, but suddenly, coming out of the valley, we had to turn sharp to the right up another little valley, and here we came under terrific, but rather inaccurate, machine-gun fire from two directions. I cannot tell you anything about casualties, but it was here my chestnut mare was killed. We went about a mile up this valley, and then got some cover under a bank – by 'we' all this time I mean the regiment and our British regiment. Here we stopped for ten minutes, and then we got orders for our squadron to go on as advance guard in a certain direction. It was now about 7.30 in the evening, and there were twenty-four aeroplanes hovering over us, and one monoplane came down to about 200 feet and fired his machine guns on the Huns just over us – going round and round – the finest sight I have ever seen. Well, we moved out under a heavy fire, and got on about half a mile. During this advance we rounded up eight prisoners, while between us and the British regiment, I suppose, we stuck with sword and lance about forty of them – a glorious sight! Our men were splendid, and didn't want to take any prisoners, but these eight had chucked away their arms, so we couldn't very well do them in. They were simply terrified, and one clung on to my leg and kept calling 'Pity! Pity', his eyes starting out of his head. Poor devil, I pitied him, and we sent him back to the regiment. You see, our job was to push on as far as we could and hold the line to give 'the feet' time to get up. So we did our job all right. We then rode back – 'but not the six hundred'.[26]

Other sources identify the aircraft which dived in support of the cavalry as coming from 3 Squadron RFC, and the pilot of a Morane monoplane from the same squadron, Lieutenant T.L.W. Stallibrass, recorded in his log book the fact that a large force of Germans in the sunken road running south–southeast from High Wood had been poised to inflict serious damage upon the cavalry until his comrade intervened to disperse them. It is interesting to observe cavalry and aircraft working together in this fashion, in a similar way to that in which aircraft and armour would eventually come to work together when the latter had taken over from the horse.

The value of aircraft for photographic reconnaissance work has already been stated, but sometimes there was no substitute for boots on the ground and the Mark I eyeball. Late on the night of 14 July British officer Lieutenant B.U.S. Cripps of the 2nd Battalion

Welsh Regiment was sent by his battalion commander to reconnoitre towards Bazentin for a forthcoming attack. The memory of this strange expedition remained vivid some sixty years later, as he recalled:

> I set off during the night in darkness, and we went for the most eerie walk right up through Mametz Wood, and through a terrible scene of destruction and carnage. Mametz Wood had had a terrific bombarding and trees and things were lying at all angles, and the wood was literally full of dead and dying men, and one had to pick one's way through an enormous number of wounded men, men who were still alive, who implored you to help them. You just couldn't do anything about it, you just had to go on. The number of stretcher bearers was so meagre in those days, these casualties had been there for some of them two or three days and nobody had been near them. They implored you for water – 'help me, give me water,' but you couldn't, there was nothing you could do, and so I stumbled on in the dark with my fifteen

Lieutenant B.U.S. Cripps, 2nd Battalion Welsh Regiment, whose night-time reconnaissance took him on an eerie journey through Mametz Wood. (*Courtesy of Mrs Mavis Cripps*)

The appalling sight of a battlefield strewn with dead.

men, we went through this wood, I can remember some of the corpses and wounded men, I can see them to this day. I remember one Lieutenant-Colonel lying there, shot through the throat. Somebody had tried to put a bandage on his throat, I can remember him to this day just lying on the path through the wood. But anyhow it was just getting light and I got through this wood. There was no hostile activity of any sort. When we got through the wood there was a largeish gap, I suppose about 1500 yards between Bazentin Wood and Mametz Wood and the ground was covered with corpses and quite a lot of dead horses and even some dead cows lying on the ground all with their bellies blown up. Anyhow, I went into Bazentin-le-Petit Wood, not knowing if I was in enemy land or friendly land really, I went into the wood and the first thing I came upon was an enormous concrete pillbox, and so I gingerly opened the door and looked inside and there were I should think about forty wounded Germans in it, and again they implored for help or 'water', but again, one couldn't do anything about it. You just had to ignore such things.[27]

Cripps' remarkable account illustrates the bitter and confused nature of the fighting in the woods, and the difficulties which timely recovery of casualties presented, evidenced by the fact that the wounded from the 38th Division's attack had still not been evacuated several days later. Many of those who died on the Somme did so from wounds that were not in themselves fatal; they died because it was simply not possible to get medical attention to them in a prompt fashion, resulting in shock or exsanguination.

Further south on 14 July the 9th Scottish Division had been allotted the task of taking the village of Longueval and by the end of the day this had largely been achieved. However, the associated German defences in Delville Wood remained a serious problem, positioned as they were on the right flank of the newly won British salient. The following day the wood was ordered to be cleared by the 9th Division's South African Brigade, comprising four battalions raised in the Union of South Africa from those of British or Afrikaans descent. It was to become one of the most gruelling struggles in a battle of bloody encounters. For six days the South African Brigade hung on grimly in the shattered remains of Delville Wood, isolated amid the thick summer undergrowth and fallen branches, pounded by artillery, fighting off local German counter-attacks and harassed by snipers. One of these, who was shot and killed by a member of the 3rd South African Infantry, was described as being dressed in a dirty, torn pair of trousers and a brown sweater to which he had attached leaves, and his face and hands had leaves painted on them. The South Africans were also short of rations and drinking water. A member of the 4th Battalion vividly remembered the foul taste of the latter, which when it arrived at all came up to the line in petrol cans.

Private Nicholas Vlok of Bloemfontain was a South African soldier of particularly distinguished years, aged as he was 49 at the time of the Delville

Private Nicholas Vlok of Bloemfontain, 2nd Battalion South African Infantry. He was wounded in Delville Wood.

Wood battle; he was serving with B Company of the 2nd Battalion South African Infantry, and had previously served as a Boer officer during the 1899–1902 conflict. Vlok was an early casualty of the Delville Wood fighting, being hit on the morning of Saturday, 15 July. He wrote afterwards of the brutal actions of an enemy soldier he encountered in the wood:

At 11 o'clock I was wounded in the right knee, but felt I must still fight on. A little later I received the wound in my back, and for some time no assistance was able to come near us. I lost a fearful amount of blood, and I learnt afterwards it was a marvel that I did not bleed to death. While I was sitting up against a tree in an almost unconscious state, a huge black-bearded Hun came up to me and said in Dutch, 'Come here, you swine-hound.' By some means or other they knew the South Africans were fighting them. I was too ill to move, and without saying another word he drew his revolver and fired point-blank at my head. Although my helmet was blown off he fortunately did not hit me, but I shammed dead in case he should have another try. However, he left me, evidently in search of other helpless men that he could shoot, but before he had gone far one of our fellows rushed at him, sending his bayonet right through him. Before he went down I heard the miserable fellow shout: 'Mercy, Kamerad!'[28]

Another good account of the South African battle in Delville Wood comes from Private G.A. Lawson. He recounts how his unit, D Company of the 3rd Battalion South African Infantry, entered the wood in good spirits and glorious sunshine on 15 July. Two days of continuous shelling and counter-attacks depleted their numbers dramatically, and even reinforcement by the 4th Battalion (South African Scottish) did not for long replenish their strength. Lawson writes:

About 7am I walked along the line, and counted but twenty-two to defend about 150 yards of this front line trench. A number of these belonged to various companies of the 3rd battalion, some to the South African Scottish, but there were very few of the old 'D' Company men left. Sitting in their cramped trenches, facing the enemy, with clips of cartridges neatly laid ready in heaps on waterproof sheets beside them, and lightly holding their rifles in unconscious fingers, the brave lads were all fast asleep … I felt the danger, but who would be so cruel as to awaken them? I certainly could not. Breytenbach and myself resumed the weary watch …

It was as if night for ever refused to give way to day. A drizzling rain was falling in an atmosphere unstirred by a breath of wind. Smoke and gases clung to and polluted the air, making a canopy impervious to light. What a contrast was this Tuesday morning to the morning of the previous Saturday when we first entered what was then a beautiful sylvan scene, but now everywhere a dreary waste. Our little party had to wait in their cramped condition of tortured suspense till nearly 3pm for the only relief we now looked for, the relief afforded by the excitement of the desperate fighting against great odds. The enemy now launched an attack in overwhelming numbers … Once more they found us ready – this small party of utterly worn-out men, shaking off their slumbers to stand up in their shallow trench and face the terrible odds.

As the Germans came on they were mown down. Every shot must have told. Our rifles smoked and became unbearably hot, but though the end seemed near it was not yet. When the enemy wavered and broke they were reinforced and came on again. We again prevailed and drove them back. Only one German crossed our trench, to fall shot in the heart a few yards behind it. Once more they had failed. The lip of our trench told more plainly than words can how near they were to not failing ... Exhaustion now did what shell fire and counter-attacks had failed to do, and we collapsed in our trench, spent in body and at last worn out in spirit. The task we had been set was too great for us.[29]

The stand made here by the South Africans has passed into the national consciousness of that nation, such was the tenacity and heroism with which they hung on against repeated German attacks, amid the shattered stumps of the wood. One of the young South Africans who was captured here also made a deep impression upon a German journalist who interviewed him directly afterwards. A clerk in a shipping company from Johannesburg, the man spoke excellent German, a matter which may well have saved his life. Tall and fair haired, he chatted to the reporter, upon whom the significance of the battle was not lost. The latter wrote that:

Two South African prisoners in German hands. Seated is Private Fred Estill of the 3rd South African Infantry, captured in Delville Wood.

... he told me how he was caught. They had taken Longueval yesterday and had advanced up into the woods of Delville. But as so often before, the guide had let them down. They were suddenly without direction, torn apart into individual small groups who did not know where they were. The Clerk was with a few others in a shell hole in the forest. The stream of fire from the German machine guns whistled over their heads, suddenly from all the craters in front and behind them crawled Germans. It was as if they used an underground tunnel. They emerged literally as if out of the earth. They flung their hand grenades with wonderful precision. Two of his comrades were killed by a single hand grenade – close to him. Then he called to the Germans in their language. For a moment, they hesitated. Then he was disarmed and taken away ... This battle will decide the outcome of the war ... [and] all my thoughts turned to our grey men who defend against tremendous odds each clod of this soil, which is both foreign and yet holy, because it is soaked in blood ...[30]

Around the time that the Delville Wood battle was at its height, Sergeant Hope Bagenal was assisting the Medical Officer of the 27th Field Ambulance, part of the 9th (Scottish) Division, in reserve positions in Bernafay Wood. This wood had also taken a tremendous battering, and Bagenal has left an evocative description of the scene within, where a German dugout, as so many did, became a place of sanctuary for wounded men:

The trees of [the] wood had long ago surrendered their midsummer leaves, and in the dusk held up their stark branches as though asking mercy of the smouldering sky. Looking upwards you could see a lonely leaf flapping. Stars and rags seemed caught in the boughs. To the commoner wilderness of death this place was as a step forward into hell; where forms of fear had their haunts and evil spirits, all but visible, moved in their own paths. The menace of outraged Nature breathed in the startling odour of sap from thousands of bruised tree trunks. Corpses of trees and men mingled corruption, and their limbs lay equally broken. The MO, wearing his cape, walked ahead. We had entered the wood from the corner near the cross roads, and were now wending our way after him. The place was quiet that evening: only an occasional shell fell and echoed. Sticks snapped under our feet. We came at last to a clearing, and descended to a trench that ran left and right. It was one of the two trenches, running the length of the wood, which were held by our battalion. This trench must have been eight or nine feet deep, and was so narrow that a stretcher fully open could not pass along it. But we had not far to go before we turned sharp, descended a little passage and found ourselves in a good dugout roofed with three layers of tree-trunks, very solidly set. This was our new aid-post. The enemy knew every corner of the wood: they had the range of the trench and the position of the dug-out accurately, but the excellence of their own workmanship protected us. The only mistake, from our point of view, was that the door now faced front, so that a shell by ill luck might have fallen in the entrance.[31]

Bagenal describes vividly the scene in this dugout as the Medical Officer worked tirelessly to dress the wounded as a barrage roared overhead. The men in the trench above, less fortunate than him, were visibly shaken by the experience of being under prolonged shellfire:

Down in the dug-out the MO worked cheerfully, though he looked on the verge of collapse from fatigue. Albert, one of our bearers, who was an excellent dresser, quite unperturbed under such conditions, remained to help. Albert had plenty of work, but I fancy he chiefly remembers searching continuously for the iodine bottle, which in the crowd and the semi-darkness was always getting lost. Immersed in our work, we came to feel that time had stopped, and that we were engaged in a void of blood and mud and noise. The creepers hanging down over the entrance moved in the draught from shell after shell. The crash of falling boughs sounded continually, and faces wild with terror appeared and disappeared at the entrance to the dug-out. Although the iodine bottle continued to elude him, the MO never swore. On one occasion, after a crash that sounded immediately over us, he remarked quietly, 'The Saviour loves us.' Certainly Death with a monstrous axe seemed to be striding in the wood above us. The wounded huddled themselves into corners as far as possible from the door. I went out, on one occasion, into the trench and saw that the troops were on the verge of panic. The strain of enduring for hours together the peculiar nameless horror of this place without any allaying occupation was too much for flesh and blood.[32]

For Bagenal, religious faith provided the necessary armour against fear in circumstances of almost certain death or serious wounding. However, it was a conversation with an injured man whose faith was even stronger than his own which really helped to crystallise Bagenal's conviction that here on the Somme he was in the hands of the Almighty:

As we passed the cross roads the shells were falling fairly thick, and we pulled our helmets well down over the nape of the neck. Meanwhile the conversation had taken a religious turn, and I heard him say that he believed in Christ very firmly, and so was not troubled with personal fear. As he spoke a large shell, known as a coal-box, fell about twenty feet on our right. Clods of earth pelted us, and the smoke rose like genii from a bottle. The thought occurred to both of us that the thing was an apparition of evil taking its place captiously beside his declaration of faith. He raised his collar as though at a thunder shower. With his arm in mine I did not even feel surprised at the absence in myself of the common sensations of fear. We did not alter our pace, and in about ten minutes had crossed the barrage area. When we came near the advanced dressing-station I directed him and said good-bye. I had never met as brave a man … Then I continued my return journey to Bernafay Wood, following the same route, familiar by now. First came the shallow communication trench, then the open fields, then the cross roads with its drunken sign-board and shell-pitted pavement. But it was no longer for me a place of terror. As before, the genii arose captiously on every side, the air was full of uncouth sounds; but it was here that that wounded man on my arm had spoken his astonishing words and delivered me from the tyranny of fear. I, too, had believed as he had believed; but it seemed marvellous and as though I had read it in a tale, that I should have been bound with one at such a moment whose faith was greater than my own.[33]

Not every man was as stoical in the chaos and din of battle. The following day at nearby High Wood Lieutenant H.J. Brooks of the 21st Battalion Manchester Regiment was involved in an incident in which – in the bewildering noise and confusion of the fight – a party of his men broke and ran. The resulting scenes of disarray, however, were quickly brought under control. Brooks writes:

> Our three companies were gradually thrown in at High Wood to reinforce the Staffords, and finally we moved our headquarters to join the South Stafford HQs in the bottom corner of High Wood. Here things were not at all satisfactory, nobody knowing where anyone was and especially not knowing where the Bosch was – The morale of our troops was by this time rather shaky and we had a rather bad panic from the wood. We rushed out down the slope in rear. The Colonel and I worked hard and succeeded in rallying a very large proportion and moved forward with them again into the wood. The Colonels of the two battalions conferred and agreed that the position was untenable but this time with approval from Brigade HQ a co-ordinated evacuation of the position was conducted.[34]

This was the first of several fresh efforts which would be made in the coming weeks by the British to clear High Wood. The 1st Battalion South Staffordshire Regiment had penetrated a considerable distance inside the wood, thickly strewn as it was with timber and undergrowth, before they were stopped by fire from the German Switch Line which ran through the northeastern corner of the wood. They were heavily shelled into the bargain, and after further British attacks met with no success, all attacking troops were withdrawn from the wood under cover of darkness.

The battle in the air continued to rage as July passed by. Co-operation between ground troops and aircraft was in its infancy during the Battle of the Somme, but none the less there were flashes of the potential which existed if the two arms could be made to work in unison. Cecil Lewis, a pilot with 56 Squadron RFC, recorded in his log book for 16 July:

> Our fellows almost entirely occupy High Wood. Called for flares with Klaxon. Splendid co-operation! We came lower, and Hun gave away his position by opening machine-gun fire on us. Located parties of bombers from Pozières to High Wood. Hun put up Very lights and turned machine-guns on us again. We cleared up the whole position. Job earned congratulations of General, Colonel and Major.[35]

Captain Robert Saundby meanwhile was serving with Major Lanoe Hawker's famous 24 Squadron RFC, which so dominated the Somme battlefield that summer. Saundby was based at Bertangles, behind the Somme front, and remembered that life at an airfield was for the most part peaceful:

> It was a good aerodrome: just across the railway, which runs in a cutting behind the sheds, there lived a cheery squadron of F.E. 2b's. No. 11. Here ... there [was] nothing to suggest war, except a distant muttering and grumbling of guns ... [When] the last to come home of the patrol, a little delayed by one of the hundred and one causes that might delay him, turns up at last, however [an] almost unconscious relief is felt at the sight of the overdue pilot dropping into the aerodrome ... The quiet village, quiet except when the squadron billeted there was celebrating some occasion in the evening, [stood] in the background.[36]

The main enemy aircraft they encountered was the Fokker *Eindekker* monoplane, which had done a great deal to revolutionise aerial combat (being one of the first aircraft with an interrupter gear to enable its forward gun to fire through the propeller arc). For a time the *Eindekker* had given the Germans a distinct advantage over their British enemies. Saundby remembered a particular characteristic of this aircraft:

> Side-slipping was a favourite trick of the Fokker when caught, and they could lose height very quickly by this method. The Fokker was not very strong, however, and occasionally they broke up when trying to 'stunt' to get away from attack ... Apropos the liability of the Fokker to break up, I know an interesting case in point which occurred in the squadron in which I was serving at the time. Captain —— was leading a patrol of two D.H. 2's and had been asked to keep an eye on a B.E. 2c that was out on photography. He found he had climbed rather too high to be able to watch the B.E. sufficiently closely, and decided to lose a couple of thousand feet. He did so and flattened out a few hundred up over the B.E. 2C, which was then about 8,000 feet. He thought no more about the matter until, on arriving home, the B.E. 2C squadron telephoned and warmly thanked him for saving the Photographic B.E. 2C from a Fokker, which, they said, he had brought down and crashed near. On investigation it appeared that the Fokker had been climbing up under the B.E. 2C to attack it, had seen the Scout patrol diving on him, and spun down and away so violently as to break up in the air and finally crash.[37]

Saundby comments on the fact that during this period of the war, before the Albatros began to appear in German squadrons in significant numbers later that autumn, most enemy fighter pilots were reluctant to cross the front and fight over allied territory. The only such pilot willing to do so regularly was Oswald Boelcke, of whom Saundby says:

> [He], however, was one of the few Huns in those days who did come over our lines. He was a brave man, and commanded more admiration in the Flying Corps in his day, than, I venture to think, any other German Pilot since the war began.[38]

Boelcke for his part wrote of a number of encounters with the pilots of the RFC in July 1916, from which his tally of 'kills' might have been higher were it not for the unreliability of his armament:

> I made good use of my chance to again attack the English at D. I liked it so well, I kept postponing my return to S. One evening I flew a Halberstadt biplane; this was the first appearance of these machines at the front. As it is somewhat similar to an

The German pilot Oswald Boelcke, who flew over the Somme battlefield and commanded more respect than any other German pilot among the British. (*Library of Congress*)

English B.-E., I succeeded in completely fooling an Englishman. I got to within fifty meters of him and fired a number of shots at him. But as I was flying quite rapidly, and was not as familiar with the new machine as with the Fokker, I did not succeed in hitting

Boelcke climbs from his Fokker Eindecker after returning from a sortie on the Somme front, 1916.

him right away. I passed beneath him, and he turned and started to descend. I followed him, but my cartridge belt jammed and I could not fire. I turned away, and before I had repaired the damage he was gone. The next day I had two more opportunities to attack Englishmen. The first time, it was a squadron of six Vickers' machines. I started as they were over L., and the other Fokkers from D. went with me. As I had the fastest machine, I was first to reach the enemy. I picked out one and shot at him, with good results; his motor (behind the pilot) puffed out a great quantity of yellow smoke. I thought he would fall any moment, but he escaped by gliding behind his own line. According to the report of our infantry, he was seen to land two kilometers behind the front. I could not finish him entirely, because my left gun had run out of ammunition, and the right one had jammed. In the meantime, the other Fokkers had reached the English. I saw one 160-horsepower machine (Mulzer, pilot) attack an Englishman in fine style, but as the Englishman soon received aid, I had to come to Mulzer's rescue. So I drove the one away from Mulzer; my enemy did not know I was unable to fire at him. Mulzer saw and recognized me, and again attacked briskly. To my regret, he had only the same success I had had a while before, and as Mulzer turned to go home, I did likewise. In the afternoon, I again had a chance at an Englishman, but he escaped in the clouds.[39]

The Battle of the Somme has a special place in the history of the German air force. It became the high school of aviation tactics and skills, it had a crucial influence on both its organisational and its technical developments, and it shaped the training provided to flight crews until the war ended. Furthermore, these developments came to the fore at the same time as many as virulent attacks were being made in Germany by alleged experts concerning the supposed failures of German flyers before and at the beginning of the battle. These criticisms even reached the proceedings of the Reichstag in Berlin; astoundingly, German pilots who were sorely needed in this period at the front had to leave their units to give evidence there. They underwent their thankless task with good will, and were able to refute the validity of the criticisms, largely because the evidence was obtained from records studied from the safety of a chair at a desk, and from which the weight of personal experience gained in the pilot or observer's seat was absent.

Among Boelcke's students in 1916 was the young Manfred von Richthofen, later to become famous in his own right (indeed, even more famous than his mentor). He wrote of his experiences in aerial combat that summer:

During my whole life I have not found a happier hunting ground than in the course of the Somme Battle. In the morning, as soon as I had got up, the first Englishmen arrived, and the last did not disappear until long after sunset. Boelcke once said that this was the El Dorado of the flying men. There was a time when, within two months, Boelcke's bag of machines increased from twenty to forty. We beginners had not at that time the experience of our master and we were quite satisfied when we did not get a hiding. It was an exciting period. Every time we went up we had a fight. Frequently we fought really big battles in the air. There were sometimes from forty to sixty English machines, but unfortunately the Germans were often in the minority. With them quality was more important than quantity.

Still the Englishman is a smart fellow. That we must allow. Sometimes the English came down to a very low altitude and visited Boelcke in his quarters, upon which they threw their bombs. They absolutely challenged us to battle and never refused fighting.

We had a delightful time with our chasing squadron. The spirit of our leader animated all his pupils. We trusted him blindly. There was no possibility that one of us would be left behind. Such a thought was incomprehensible to us. Animated by that spirit we gaily diminished the number of our enemies.[40]

If the German fighter pilots were reluctant to cross the lines, for the two-seater reconnaissance aircraft and their crews it was part and parcel of their daily duties. The demand for accurate information about the movements of the enemy grew ever greater, and both sides continued to pay the price for an 'eye in the sky'. Whilst the single-seater pilots such as Boelcke and von Richthofen attracted most of the fame and glory, steady, monotonous but just as dangerous work was done by the crews of two-seater Pfalz aircraft on photo-reconnaissance work. The commander of Bavarian Artillery *Flieger Abteilung 102*, Hauptmann Schwink, recounts an incident which occurred over the French lines on 29 July:

Two of us were to record the enemy positions south of the Somme in photographs. Cherdron, for whom the machine gun was closer to the heart than was the camera, wanted to provide cover for his friends. It was a beautiful morning as the three headed out. The enemy, who likes to sleep late, appeared not to be present, and Cherdron's cover vouched for complete safety. The peace, however, was deceptive. When the machines flew over the enemy, up they came. Cherdron took on the first and was pushed by the air battle far from the others. Even as he disappeared from the view of the neighbouring planes, three other single seaters attacked. In a frantic dive the leader of the force tried to escape. Cherdron had received a bullet to the heart, and Sergeant Mielcareck was shot twice in the chest and in the leg. The plane crashed. The others could not see Cherdron's fight. They had to carry out their orders and fulfilled their mission despite several battles.

As I stood at the aerodrome, and saw only two come back, my heart skipped a beat. At first we were not afraid. For when our Cherdron was hunting, it often got late. An hour passed; then another; concern was growing and we began to make inquiries in the hope that Cherdron had made an emergency landing somewhere. But no one knew anything about him. It was not until late in the evening that we received notice from an artillery commander, who said that Cherdron's aeroplane had been hit in combat, Cherdron was dead, [and] the aircraft's pilot Mielcareck, who was severely wounded, had destroyed the machine.

That evening it was quiet in our quarters. Volunteer teams led by Cherdron's friends brought the dead comrades in from the artillery fire; the brave, wounded pilot was taken to a field hospital, where he died after twelve hours. We carried the comrades to the church of Ham and buried them in the cemetery. It was the worst path we had so far taken. The Grim Reaper had announced his presence, and so the fittest and most notable were now torn from our midst; on the way home, we promised all of us that at least the enemy should not notice the gap that had arisen in our little group. I knew my flyers. Their young hearts, which had become so soft at the grave, regained their strength within the hour. Their courage was unbroken, they had already flown a great deal, and now they flew even more so as to avenge the dead. In the shortest time our whole front was re-photographed. So began the detailed work of directing artillery fire on to observed targets and the constant monitoring of the front.

French infantry in a front-line trench.

> … Despite the considerable effort and dangers to which without exception all were
> subjected, towards the end of the battle my little group was still faithfully together. We
> were reinforced and the new ones which came had to pass a variety of tests, both in and
> out of service, until they were deemed to be the equivalent of the 'ancients'. The Battle
> of the Somme had demanded the extreme use of force. It had made my young airmen
> into veterans.[41]

As an insight into the fierce comradeship which grew up among a squadron of pilots, this
account is particularly powerful. The pilot mentioned in the above incident, Unteroffizier
Max Stanislaus Mielcareck, died of wounds at Pargny on 30 July, whilst the observer,
Leutnant Phillip Cherdron, was killed in the action as stated. He was a holder of the Iron
Cross First and Second Class and the Bavarian MVO, and now lies buried in the cemetery
at Ludwigshafen in central Germany; it appears that his family was able to arrange for the
repatriation of his body.

Back on the ground, beyond the army boundary to the south, the French were also
on the offensive. Among those troops moving forward now to renew the attack here was
Lieutenant Marcel Étévé, of the *471e Regiment d'Infanterie*, who went into the line next to
Estrées. He wrote to his mother on 15 July:

> We found the trench in a terribly dirty state: it was the only place where bodily
> functions could be satisfied. We are improving it, and we are digging special hygiene

bays. It is terribly hard work to move about in the trench, where everyone is elbow to elbow; it is necessary for the men to go on on all fours and pass by on top, or else they flatten themselves into their niches. To the right of my section, I am in contact with a village which we have almost completely taken. It is very quaint. We hold a barricade of sandbags (half of French bags, the other half Boche) which blocks the street in front of a house that the Germans still occupy. From there, one has a beautiful view of the village street and the crumbled houses. There is a filthy mess, of corpses, horses and cows burst open, wrecked Boche trucks, boxes of ammunition, etc., etc.

We fire shots into a lime kiln where the Germans are; they respond by firing on a reserve position where they assume us to be. Hun jackets, helmets, shells, and grenades lie all along the trench. Not far away lies a Boche 105mm gun, with two of its gunners. Our area is pretty quiet so far. We had three slightly injured, the sergeant of my second half-section, who has been replaced by a supernumerary sergeant. However, we certainly hear a beautiful racket, particularly that of French manufacture. Good food also leaves much to be desired: everything arrives very cold and full of earth; and there is talk of giving us three days' food in advance, to avoid traffic towards the rear. The most annoying thing is that, at the same time, it will mean a break in correspondence, so do not worry. I think it's going to rain: this would not be nice. I'll keep myself busy making a dry corner.[42]

In another letter to a friend a few days later, Étévé writes from a reserve position in a former German trench about the wastage which his unit has suffered just in holding the line:

We had pretty heavy losses for a regiment which has not attacked yet: almost a quarter of the strength; fortunately minor injuries, mostly. Morale is good anyway, and we're ready for the moment when we charge headlong forward, which will not be long in coming. But I have seen a few sights that I hope will give me the right later to be resolutely pacifist, if I survive. Regarding the demolition of villages: I passed through one which was completely destroyed by our artillery in a way that I never imagined: it was impossible to detect the locations of the houses. And the mine craters, staggering. Also, the demolition of men; but it is better not to dwell on this. For now, our artillery pounds away, and prepares the way ... At this everything in me rejoices.[43]

Just as with the British, many in the French army drew upon religious conviction to sustain them through these difficult times. Etienne Derville, a student at a Catholic seminary before the conflict, had been destined for a life in the priesthood until war intervened. He became a sergeant in an infantry regiment and was badly wounded in the opening battles of 1914, so he was under no illusions about the reality of war. However, for him the conflict

French officer Etienne Derville, for whom the Battle of the Somme was a struggle for the soul of France.

was all about sacrifice for the greater cause, which to his mind was the purification of the soul of France. Through imitating the sacrifice of Christ, he hoped to participate in the re-Christianisation of what he saw as an increasingly secular and irreligious nation. The greater the personal sacrifice, so Derville believed, the closer he came to God. During the Battle of the Somme he requested a transfer away from General Headquarters, where he had been involved in intelligence, and back to the front-line infantry. He wrote in July:

> It is preferable this way. I would have become too 'General Staff' and would not have suffered sufficiently … what else could we ask for at this moment, [except] always to suffer as much as possible, as much as we can stand.[44]

Derville was not the only man of the cloth fighting in the French army. Paul Grall, who was killed in action on the Somme on 24 July 1916, was an ordained priest before the war. It was not uncommon for French clergy to serve in the ranks as ordinary soldiers.

Yet Derville's perceived spiritual dimension to the war would lead to his own increasing disillusion. By the end of the Battle of the Somme he was dispirited that so much suffering had produced so little gain. Not only was France not reconverting to Christianity, but if anything she was becoming more secular and more irreligious. Later commissioned as an officer, Derville was eventually to meet his fate on the battlefield, when he was killed in action in June 1918.

'A great proportion of the trees have been shot down and blown up, while every leaf has been blown off those that remain standing.'

For both attacking and defending troops the strain of living cheek by jowl with death was now becoming almost unbearable, and was testing men of the strongest courage to their limits. South African Brigade Medical Officer C.M. Murray recorded in his diary for 19 July:

Another of our officers came in after having been buried by shell explosions no less than five times. He was a man of iron nerve, but is a total wreck for the present. What with want of sleep and food and the constant narrow shaves, I marvel that more men do not succumb entirely to nerve prostration.[45]

Even the landscape itself now bore stark and chilling testimony to the savagery and ferocity to which it had been witness in the preceding days. Murray again acknowledges that despite the best efforts of his stretcher-bearers, many wounded who might have survived had perished:

To look at the woods it is marvellous to think that anything could remain alive in them. A great proportion of the trees have been shot down and blown up, while every leaf has been blown off those that remain standing. Our bearers have worked nobly and penetrated through Longueval and Delville Woods in bringing away wounded. As the Germans are driven back, the positions that have been blasted by our fire are then further blasted by theirs when we occupy them. The fighting has been so furious that many of the wounded have simply had to be left to die there where they fell, while of course no attempt has been made to bury the dead and the numerous horses and mules that have been killed. No more barbarous warfare can possibly have taken place, in the history of the world, than is going on daily here … Today our bearers are to be relieved which is a mercy. They have now been twenty-one days in the midst of awful surroundings. Incessant din, and working unendingly in momentary risk of their lives, that some have broken down from mental strain and overwork is only natural, the wonder being that more have not succumbed in the same way.[46]

For the next ten days the British would hurl brigade after brigade into the onslaught against High Wood. Standing on the high ground between Bazentin and Longueval, the copse effectively blocked any further advance northwards from these positions. Early on 20 July the 20th Royal Fusiliers launched an attack here; among them was a 17-year-old soldier named Donald Price. He later recalled his experiences of the debacle which followed:

Private Thomas Arthur Prosser, 10th Battalion Royal Welsh Fusiliers, who was killed in action on 20 July in an unsuccessful attack on Delville Wood. His battalion lost direction and walked into the path of British machine-gun fire.

How can one describe that advance? Moving out towards the wood over open land was terrifying. The constant din of our own barrage going over us, and the German barrage falling amongst us was indescribable. Each man was carrying extra ammunition and bombs – and most of us had been issued with a spade. It was a slow walk, impossible to run and if one fell it was an effort to get up again. If we halted at all, I covered my head with the spade – although no use at all for protection it gave me comfort I suppose. Above the drumfire screams for stretcher bearers were continual. How could anyone survive this onslaught? But some of us did, and forced our way into the wood. Streams of machine-gun bullets met us, causing more casualties.

Private Frank Richards DCM, who watched the attack on High Wood from his signalling station on 20 July 1916. (*Courtesy of Margaret Holmes*)

How I became separated from our small group I never knew, but I found myself alone with no sign of any of our men. Our own barrage was now shelling the wood mistakenly, and seeing a dugout handy I decided to take shelter until the shelling died down. Cries of pain were coming up so I cautiously went down and found three very badly wounded Germans who had managed to crawl in. All were crying for 'wasser' which I took to be water, and as I had very little left in my waterbottle, I decided to creep out to find some. A dead German was lying handy and fortunately his bottle contained some.

Dawn came and I was becoming exhausted, not having had any sleep for two nights. I sat down next to one of the Germans hoping to be able to get out at any moment. As it was I fell asleep, and did not wake until dusk. All the Germans had died – I had been leaning against one of the dead. I had no feelings as far as I remember – just an urge for survival.[47]

In the same 33rd Division was Private Frank Richards, another eyewitness to the ferocious fighting for High Wood. Richards had enlisted in the British army in 1902; although he spent the whole of his almost twenty years of service in the ranks, he was an eloquent writer with a sharp memory for detail. His memoir *Old Soldiers Never Die* is rightly regarded as a classic. In it, he gives one of his usual vivid accounts, covering the attack by the 2nd Battalion Royal Welsh Fusiliers against High Wood later on 20 July. Richards himself was a signaller and, although he took no direct part in the fighting that day, from his vantage point in a signal station he had a grandstand view of everything that was happening. He started off using heliograph mirrors to flash morse code messages, but soon resorted to semaphore as conditions worsened:

The position that we had to take up was by a large mill about 600 yards this side of High Wood. The mill was built on some rising ground which made it a very prominent landmark. We had a good view of everything from here, but we also found that when we were exchanging messages with the wood, the enemy would have an equally good view of us, especially when we were flag-wagging … at 8am we were in communication

A memorial card for Herbert Littlewood, 2nd Battalion Yorkshire Regiment, who was killed in action on 23 July 1916. Attacking from Trones Wood, his battalion lost direction in a smoke barrage.

with Brigade. Shortly after this the enemy began shelling us and by 10am they had put up one of the worst barrages that I was ever under. Twelve-inch, eight-inch, five-point-nines and whizzbang shells were bursting around us continually and this lasted during the whole of the day. North, south, east and west it was raining shells, and we seemed to be the dead centre of it all. The barrage of the previous day was a flea-bite to this one. The ground shook and rocked and we were continually having to reset the heliograph. When receiving a message the smoke of the bursting shells and the earth and dust that was being thrown up constantly obscured our vision, and we could only receive a word now and then.[48]

During the afternoon Richards received a signal from High Wood to the effect that it had been captured in its entirety, though this would prove to be premature. About an hour later the signallers in the wood began 'flag-wagging' again, but their messages would soon cease. The difficulties in communication during a major battle are clearly apparent here;

Second Lieutenant Jack Fish, 10th Battalion Worcestershire Regiment. Killed in action near Bazentin le Petit on 23 July 1916, he now lies in the AIF Burial Ground Cemetery, Flers.

the three main methods at this time were telephone (the wires of which were apt to be cut by shellfire), visual signals or runners. All three were haphazard:

We only received about another six words when the signaller in the wood who was sending the message, and the other man with him who was calling it out, both fell; that message was never completed. The message as far as we got it stated that the enemy were counter-attacking. It was the last visual message that arrived from the wood: every message after this came by runner.[49]

Attacks were also now launched pushing out eastwards from Longueval towards Guillemont, but the focus of the battle in the British sector had shifted away temporarily to the Pozières ridge. This village, sitting astride the Albert–Bapaume road, occupied a spur of ground which was to be the objective of the next series of offensives in the northern part of the battlefield. The British 48th (South Midland) Division would make the first of a number of attacks on Pozières, which naturally had been heavily fortified by the Germans. Dominic Devas was a Roman Catholic chaplain attached to the 1st/6th Battalion Gloucestershire Regiment during this phase of the battle. His account gives a vivid impression of the work of a padre behind the front line, ministering to the wounded, as his battalion went into the attack north of Pozières on 23 July. Devas was stationed at an Advanced Dressing Station at Crucifix Corner, between Aveluy and the 'Quarries' to the east of the village:

> The evening opened with a terrific bombardment, which went echoing and re-echoing over the desolate valleys and hills. All through the night I remained in the Dressing Station, helping as far as I could. The place was a regular shambles, full of wounded, with stretcher cases lying in the open outside, and all through the night the stream of stricken humanity flowed unceasing under the gaunt outstretched arms of the great crucifix which marked the cross-roads where we worked. Dawn broke at length, a beautiful summer morning, fresh and cool; but there was no respite till well on in the day, when the rush of wounded slowly subsided and the hard-worked doctors and orderlies were able to take some rest ... Whilst I was at Crucifix Corner I said Mass once or twice in the church at Aveluy. It was badly knocked about, though still serviceable in dry weather. Among my tiny congregation were some cyclists, detached from the 36th Division, who lived by the ADS and acted as escort for the prisoners of war.[50]

Many of those who were wounded on the Somme would experience profound change in their lives as a result. Ian Fraser arrived in France in the spring of 1916 as an 18-year-old subaltern, one of half a dozen fresh from Sandhurst, and destined to join the 1st/4th Battalion Gloucestershire Regiment, also part of the 48th Division. Fraser wrote with remarkable honesty of his fears and anxieties, and the responsibility which lay with him of leading men at such a young age:

> I ... served in the war as a junior officer without distinction. I had not been very brave or very dashing or very otherwise – I had just behaved as all the rest of us did and had done my best. I was a boy of eighteen when I first took my platoon into action, and I was still under nineteen when I was retired on account of my wounds. I [recall] my first experience under artillery bombardment. I had been frightened – frightened on two accounts: first of all for my own life and limb: and secondly, frightened lest I should let the show down; but I got over this as we all did, and though I continued to be frightened from time to time I got used to shellfire, and to crawling about and being sniped at, and to all the other hazards of that war, and even though later on shell splinters and bullets may have come very near to me, I was never so frightened again as I had been at first.[51]

On 23 July 1916 Fraser's battalion was engaged in a bombing attack north of Pozières when he was wounded. A German bullet knocked him over as it entered his temple, and completely destroyed both his eyes as it passed through his head. Again his account is fresh and vivid:

> I didn't think much about blindness when I was hit. I suppose I slept a good deal, and perhaps I was unconscious for a time, though I actually remember being tied up immediately after I was wounded, and I talked to my Company Commander as I walked down the line to a dressing station. I remember being wheeled along on a stretcher – one of those flat things on a pair of wheels, rather like the barrows from which hawkers sell fruit. We seemed to go on for miles down the Pozières–Bapaume road – a shell-swept road. I remember an injection of anti-tetanus serum, and the doctor marking a cross upon my forehead with an indelible pencil. He told me about this; it was a sign that I had been inoculated, so that the next doctor wouldn't do it again. I remember thinking that this was rather funny.[52]

For Fraser, this was but the start of a long journey, both physical and metaphorical: a journey back to civilian life and a journey he would need to make as a person in order to overcome what many today might regard as the end of life – the beginning of many years of permanent blindness.

On the same day that Fraser was wounded, the 1st Australian Division also went into action at Pozières. This unit had arrived in France from Gallipoli, and this was its first taste of battle on the Western Front. The Australian attacks here centred upon the OG lines (OG1 and OG2), two heavily defended trenches east of the village itself. A formidable blockhouse also defended the village; standing at the site of Pozières windmill, it was known to the Australians as 'Gibraltar'. To begin with, in the early hours of 23 July the 1st and 2nd Battalions of the Australian Imperial Force (AIF), part of the 1st Australian Brigade, captured Pozières Trench, which protected the southern side of the village. One of the soldiers present here was Private John Robertson Hawke, a signaller with the 1st Battalion, who describes the advance and also the significance of this battle for Australia:

> Well, the day of the attack we had one of our sigs killed and one wounded. Part of us were told off to act as reserve and two companies of our battalion and two of another slipped quietly over the parapet and made towards the German front line. Hundreds of guns had previously blown the German barbed wire to pieces and at a pre-arranged time the fire was lifted on to his second line. Hardly had the fire lifted [than] all our boys were in amongst the Germans and had completely taken charge of his trench. We took over 40 prisoners in this line including an officer who had enough medals on him to suit a general. Well, the next two companies of our battalion were now on their way over and they went right past the first line and on to the second. This was taken and the third wave now came over and went on into the village and dug in. Fritz had only two lines of trenches here so the third and fourth waves had to make new trenches when they passed over the second line … God knows that every one of our boys played the game and quitted themselves like men. Most of them had not seen any service in Gallipoli but nobly did they keep up the reputation won at Anzac & Lone Pine … Fritz now has as much respect for us as he has for the 'jocks', as they call the highland regiments … Pozières will always be a name of proud memories for the people of Australia although

The wreckage of railway wagons at Pozières station, July 1916.

to a good many it will also mean a name full of regrets for the good men who nobly laid down their lives.[53]

The battle for this village was among the most intense of the entire Somme campaign – indeed, the memorial which now stands on the site of 'Gibraltar' declares that Australian dead lay thicker on this ridge than on any other battlefield on earth. The heavy Australian casualties here were attributed by the British official historian both to what he perceived as the national characteristic of recklessness, but also – and more controversially – to the inexperience of Australian commanders and staff officers. There is, it must be said, some evidence to support this view. Late in the evening of 23 July the 8th Battalion AIF was ordered into the battle at Pozières. There was muddle and confusion as, without maps, the company commanders were given no firm objectives but were ordered simply to 'go as far

ROY VICTOR DRANSFIELD

(An Anzac.)

"A" COMPANY.

2ND BATTALION, A I. F..

23 YEARS OF AGE.

KILLED IN ACTION IN FRANCE.

JULY 25TH. 1916.

A memorial card for Australian Private Roy Dransfield, killed in action near Pozières.

as they could'. Passing through the shattered village, the 8th established a line through the orchard to the north of the ruins. Such was the confusion at 1st Australian Division headquarters over the exact dispositions of its men that a protective barrage was postponed for fear of hitting them, which allowed the Germans an opportunity to bring down their own artillery and launch a counter-attack. Private Reg Johansen of the 8th, writing to his parents, stated:

We lay in shell holes all night and as soon as dawn came they started to shell, and all hell broke loose. They shelled us all day without a break and men were getting skittled everywhere. I shall never forget the cries of the wounded for Stretcher Bearers. We never had a moment's spell from then till the time we were relieved. I could hear the cries for Stretcher Bearers in my sleep for weeks after. We were four days in that hell.[54]

Another Australian soldier here, E.W. Moorehead of the 5th Battalion, recorded later that his unit had also become lost on the way up to the front line. Furthermore, he notes at times disorder and a lack of discipline, as well as officers differing and arguing amongst themselves, presumably in front of their men, which cannot have been good for morale. Yet in contrast with all of this, it seems that sheer Australian bravery was enough to win through. At 3.30am on 25 July the 8th Battalion, behind a supporting barrage, pushed out beyond the cemetery, and in spite of a brief friendly fire incident in which they exchanged shots with the 11th Battalion AIF they had soon secured their objectives. During this time the headquarters of the 7th and 8th Australian battalions was in the captured Gibraltar blockhouse. Australian Private John Bourke was among the first to enter the concrete strongpoint. He wrote home to his mother, describing how he found,

… a heap of cake boxes [made] of cardboard and sewn in with calico, just as the parcels come to us from Australia. The addresses were in a child's writing as were also one or two letters. In another corner was a coat rolled up. I opened it out, and found it stained with blood, and there, right between the shoulders, was a burnt shrapnel hole – shrapnel is very hot … The owner of the coat was a German, and some might say, not entitled to much sympathy. Perhaps not, but I couldn't help thinking sadly of the little girl or boy who sent the cakes.[55]

Even when not actually attacking, soldiers faced extreme danger. Lieutenant Alec Raws of the 23rd Battalion AIF was sent up through Pozières at night on 31 July with a working party to dig a 'jumping off' trench in No Man's Land to be used in the next assault. Under heavy German bombardment it was utterly terrifying work, and required a supreme effort by Raws not just to control his men but to remain in control of himself, as he describes in this frank and searingly honest letter home:

We were being shot at all the time. It was awful, but we had to drive the men by every possible means and dig ourselves. The wounded and killed had to be thrown on one side – I refused to let any sound man help a wounded man; the sound men had to dig. I took it on myself to insist on the men staying, saying that any man who stopped digging would be shot. We dug on and finished amid a tornado of bursting shells. All the time, mind, the enemy flares were making the area almost as light as day. We got away as best we could. I was buried twice, and thrown down several times – buried with dead and dying. The ground was covered with bodies in all stages of decay and mutilation, and I would, after struggling free from the earth, pick up a body by me to try and lift him out with me, and find a decayed corpse. I pulled a head off – was covered with blood. The horror was indescribable. In the dim misty light of dawn I collected about 50 men and sent them off, mad with terror, on the right track for home. Then two brave fellows stayed behind and helped me with the only unburied wounded man we could find. The journey down with him was awful. He was delirious – I tied one of his legs to his pack with one of my puttees ... The sights I saw and the smell can, I know, never be exceeded by anything else the war may show me ... I have had much luck and kept my nerve so far. The awful difficulty is to keep it. The bravest of all often lose it – courage does not count here. It is all nerve – once that goes one becomes a gibbering maniac.[56]

Raws, a journalist with the Melbourne *Argus* in civilian life, was to be killed by a shell on 23 August 1916, and was buried where he fell on the battlefield. His grave was lost in later fighting.

Thus, although the hoped-for breakthrough had not been achieved by the allies, in the first month of heavy fighting on the Somme they had undoubtedly inflicted severe losses upon the Germans: some six German divisions and a number of heavy guns had been withdrawn from the Verdun front in order to reinforce their troops on the Somme. Furthermore, in their first major offensive on the Western Front the British, with their Commonwealth allies, had shown both their ability and their determination to fight. They had captured Fricourt and La Boisselle, Mametz Wood,

Sergeant Phillip James Molloy, 6th Battalion AIF. He suffered a gunshot wound to the arm on 23 July 1916, and was subsequently awarded the Military Medal for his part in the fighting at Pozières.

Bazentin Wood and Delville Wood, although High Wood remained a stubborn centre of resistance. The Germans, who had some of their best men on this front, had been driven from many of their strongest positions, and there is no doubt that they were shaken by what they had been through. The French, despite their commitment on the Verdun front, had also achieved considerable gains alongside the British. The following month would see the Allies further increase their pressure upon the Germans west of Bapaume and Peronne.

Chapter Four

The Choosers of the Slain

The month of August 1916 on the Somme was largely characterised by a long-drawn-out and bitter slogging match between the two sides. By the end of July the British commander Sir Douglas Haig in particular was moving away from the idea of breaking through the German lines, following the failure of the 14 July assault to achieve this aim. For Haig, now, the objective had become the wearing down and destruction of the German army. With more than ten weeks of good weather still in prospect before the onset of winter, Haig was confident that much could still be achieved on the Somme front, particularly as more was now expected from the French with the close of the German offensive at Verdun. However, the Germans, despite having been driven from many of their well prepared positions in July, had constructed new defences, some of which were equally strong and still defied Haig and his men. High Wood, in particular, would remain a stubborn obstacle to progress. The growing strength and confidence of the French meanwhile would be underlined by their successful attack on 12 September.

On 30 July the French pushed eastward on their entire frontage on the Somme. The troops comprising their left flank, part of the French XX Corps, obtained a footing on the ridge outside Maurepas. The day before, on 29 July, in a shelter near the village, a German soldier named Georg Sieber committed his thoughts and experiences to paper in a letter to his family:

> I squat now in an insignificant small hole, in order to gain some protection against the lethal shell splinters; it must not be thought that this is a proper dug out. One's back becomes quite stiff over time and useless, and little by little one becomes quite rigid. One writes some lines huddled in a sitting position, then one feels pains in the back and neck, thus more writing is impossible, then one lies down a short time on the back, later on the belly, then sometimes again to the right and then to the left, until the letter is ready. As a base, use is made of the thighs and knees which also hurt now and again, then one soon gets cramp in the legs.
>
> You really cannot imagine this minor misery. Now and again 'heavies' arrive suddenly nearby, so that one must creep away to the outermost corner in order not to be caught by it, then one crawls again on all fours to the entrance to the hole in order to have light for writing. Tonight I received a letter from Hedwig; she told me much, mostly about the holiday, whilst I poor fellow must crouch here. Hopefully I will get through this and then I can come on leave. Then the joy will be great and the reunion will be so beautiful.[1]

Such improvised positions, which the Germans were now often forced to use, were a far cry from the well constructed dugouts in the original German front line. For Sieber the longed-for reunion was never to come – he was killed in action the following day as French troops swept forward.

Smoke from the explosion of minenwerfer shells masks a German counter-attack on the Somme.

Further north, the British were still attempting to push out beyond Delville Wood and Longueval, but High Wood continued to cause them difficulties. The first week of August was one of the hottest of the summer, with temperatures every day reaching the high seventies or eighties Fahrenheit, adding to the unpleasant nature of a battlefield strewn with unburied bodies, as well as to the difficulties of the soldiers in combat. On 4 August a young American known as Patrick Terrence McCoy took part in an attack on Intermediate Trench (so named because it lay between the British front line and the German Switch Line) north of Bazentin-le-Petit. McCoy's real name was van Putten, and he had enlisted under an alias into the 16th Battalion Royal Scots. When it became caught up in the German lines without support, the battalion was ordered to withdraw. In his account of the action, van Putten offers a frank description of the sheer terror he felt whilst trapped in No Man's Land, and his emotional reaction after the immediate danger had passed. He takes up the story at the point at which the Royal Scots abandoned Intermediate Trench:

That order [to withdraw] never reached our platoon. We stood there battling for our lives. By chance I happened to look back. My eyes nearly popped from my head for behind us I saw the Germans. On both sides of us were Germans; in front of us were Germans. Eight of our fifty men stood there alone, surrounded. Retreat was impossible. It was every man for himself, and the devil stood a good chance of getting us all. I called the attention of the other men to our predicament and each began to look out for himself. I decided my best chance was to go forward. I saw a little clearing, leaped out of the trench and made for the open space between the second- and third-line German trenches. Of course I was in as great a danger of being hit by British shells as by German bullets. I made for a near-by shell-hole. In it lay a dead German. 'You shall be of some use in the world, although you never were before,' I said. Into that shell-hole I crawled and pulled that corpse over me as if we had both died there fighting. Shrapnel from British guns fell all around us – the dead German and me. None hit us, fortunately.

The battle line moved back as the Germans regained the lost ground. I was left farther and farther in the rear, yet British shells never ceased to rain on all the territory around. I heard voices – German voices. Quickly I closed my eyes and held my breath. A German officer, I took him to be, and a soldier passed the rim of the shell-hole. They stopped and looked at us. That the man would come into the shell-hole and stick a bayonet into me to make sure I was dead, I was certain. They stood there talking. Then the talking ceased. I strained my ears for the sound of their approaching footsteps. I had a vision of them standing above me, bayonet poised and ready to strike. It was only by an effort of will that I refrained from curling up as I knew I would when I felt the steel. I suffered all the pain of the wound so certain was I that it was coming. When I heard them talk again and knew that I was safe once more I almost screamed. Their voices were growing weaker. They were moving away. The tears started, as once more I opened my eyes and knew they had gone.[2]

Lance Sergeant Robert Edwards, 7th Battalion Border Regiment, who was killed in action on 7 August 1916 in an attack from Delville Wood towards enemy positions near Longueval.

A short time later, from sheer exhaustion and nervous strain, van Putten fell asleep. How long he slept for he was not sure. He continues:

When I opened my eyes I found it was dark. I looked at my watch. It had long ago stopped. I lay a while and thought. I couldn't remain here. I must make a try to get back to our own lines. The worst I could get was a bullet, a bayonet or perhaps capture. I might get back, although, realizing I had to cross two lines of German trenches, the chances seemed mighty slim. I was hungry and terribly thirsty. I had had nothing to eat since we entered the fight at two-thirty the morning before. My water-bottle was gone and I was suffering greatly. I threw off the dead German and searched him. First I wanted to know what time it was and thought perhaps he might have a watch. But he had none. Neither had he water-bottle nor anything about him to eat. But he had saved my life so I suppose I should not have complained at these little oversights. I began to crawl. Carefully, inch by inch, I made my way in what I supposed was the direction of the second-line trenches. Shells from British guns fell occasionally in the area through which I crawled and one fragment fell so near me that I reached out my hand and touched it. It burned my fingers.[3]

After spending another night in the open, van Putten managed at last to regain the British lines. His highly emotional state having narrowly avoided death on a number of occasions is understandable:

Men of the 46th Battalion, Australian Imperial Force, photographed in 1916. This battalion, from Victoria, was part of the 4th Australian Division and was in action at Pozières in early August.

I made myself known as the men crowded around me, plying me with questions and filling me with tea. I took one big cup of it boiling hot, then I sat down and cried like a baby. My nerves at last had cracked under the strain and it was necessary to take me to the rear. Lieutenant Sutherland took me in charge and gave me a pull at a flask. Then he opened some cans of sardines, gave me hard biscuit and a cake of chocolate. No finer banquet was ever served by the Lord Mayor of London.[4]

Heavy fighting was also still taking place around Pozières, with the OG lines only fully consolidated in the first days of August. On 6 August the 4th Australian Division came into the line here in order to relieve their countrymen in these positions. Among the division's members was Corporal Robert Kewley, who was to receive his third wound on the Somme, having previously been injured at Gallipoli. Kewley served with the 48th Battalion AIF, and wrote home to his sisters of what he had seen and experienced. As well as the awesome scale of destruction, which almost defied description, there was also increasing evidence that the Germans were willing to surrender:

Woods that were one time are now nothing but skeletons torn up by the roots, and every yard of country for miles was torn up as if by volcanic eruptions. We passed big shell holes, in which a wagon and horses could hide, or a platoon of men. We were told we were passing through the village of Pozières, but not a trace of a village could we see. We moved along a sap, trampling over dead and wounded on our road. We got to a certain point, and we were told to occupy the front trench. We went out over the parapet into the open country, several falling by the way. It is almost inconceivable to believe that humanity could face such an ordeal. The enemy artillery was turned on us, and shells were falling thick and heavy all around, and we had to make short rushes and get into shell holes for safety. Some lay in these shell holes all night. Under cover of the black smoke of bursting shells some of us rushed further forward, but no trench could be found; it was absolutely blown to smithereens by our heavies, so men had to take cover wherever they could. Five men and myself found ourselves in a most advanced position, in a little section of evacuated German trench, and we were safer there than anywhere, so decided to stay the night. Before daybreak next morning we decided to look round under cover of the dense haze that covered the ground. We had just started to move when we spied a Boche. We covered him with our rifles, and took him prisoner. On turning round, four more Huns were coming scrambling over the debris; we also covered them and took them prisoners. We disarmed them, and handed them over to HQ ... That day we got hell from the enemy guns; in fact our Battalion was nearly annihilated; terrible slaughter. One platoon officer had just buried another when he got killed himself. I had just bandaged the Captain's wounds; he had a hole through his shoulder; and both legs smashed to pulp, and got him away on a stretcher, when I got buried by a shell. I wriggled out and in two minutes I got plugged through the right thigh making a great gash. I crawled on my hands and knees for quite a few hundred yards to the first dressing station. From there I had to be carried on a stretcher.[5]

Standing on the Courcelette road about 1,000 yards northwest of Pozières lay Mouquet Farm, known to the British soldiers of 1916 as 'Mucky Farm'. It was an important location because it overlooked the rear of the stronghold of Thiepval, still very much in German hands. George Coppard, author of *With a Machine Gun to Cambrai*, was detailed before dawn on 12 August to provide supporting fire to assist Australian troops pushing towards Thiepval from positions near the farm. Coppard was just 18 years old at the time; although he was scared, his account of this incident provides a good illustration of how focusing on the task in hand, together with faith in his equipment, was perhaps the best method of overcoming fear whilst in combat:

Various signal flares lit the sky but were of no significance to us, as our firing had to continue until stand-to. Our job was to assist in pinning the enemy down in his support trenches, and to harass any reinforcements coming forward. We had been told that a sunken road was likely to be used, which also had to receive our attention. I kept up the fire, and, as we had expected, a whizzbang battery began to search for us. Clark and I were apprehensive, although not exactly displeased, as we guessed our fire must be having some effect. If the German infantry asked for assistance from their light artillery, it was on the cards we were causing mischief. The first whizzbang landed about twenty yards to the right. The range was bang on, and a little adjustment in direction was all Jerry needed. The shells came nearer, some a few yards to the left. One hit two yards in front, showering us with dirt and fumes. It looked as if any minute time would stop so far as we were concerned. My stomach rolled in a funk, and I know Clark felt the same. Keeping the gun going was the surest antidote to our rising fears, and that we did. Nobody came and said, 'Pack it up', so we stuck it out and carried on.[6]

Coppard served with the Machine Gun Corps, operating Vickers heavy machine guns. The additional weight of fire they could provide was an invaluable support to the infantry, but members of the MGC were often unpopular because of the destructive German retaliatory fire which their presence in an area might stimulate. Much of this fire would inevitably

Moving up to the French front line on the Somme, August 1916. The sign reads: 'Do not go there without carrying your gas mask.'

fall upon the infantry, frequently after the machine-gunners themselves had moved to pastures new.

That same day the French were also on the offensive, with troops of the I Corps pushing eastwards in an assault which would both outflank Guillemont from the south and also see them finally capture the important village of Maurepas. The *170e Regiment d'Infanterie* particularly distinguished itself by capturing the fortified crest running 1,500 kilometres west of Clery. Elov Nilsen was an American soldier in this unit. He took part in the French assault of 12 August, and wrote afterwards of his experiences here:

On August 11 came the order to leave Etinehem, and off we went toward the front lines. The nearer the front we got, the more signs of actual fighting we saw. Little was left of the villages through which we passed. We saw many British troops, but no civilians after we left Bray, a village five kilometres behind the old first line. The only building there that was not shell-scarred was the church. In all the other bombarded villages I have seen, the church has always been the worst smashed-up of all the buildings. At Suzanne, outside which town the old line, before the offensive started, passed, we made our *grande halte*, had hot *soupe*, and received extra cartridges which made a total of two hundred per man. Each soldier also received four hand grenades. We started off at midnight toward the firing line. At dawn we were up and en route for the first-line trenches, pick and shovel in hand. Our task was to dig communication trenches between the first- and second-line trenches, a work much needed as the existing boyaux were at places only a foot and a half deep.

We had no more than started to dig than the Boches spotted us, and in ten minutes' time shells from their seventy-sevens and one hundred and fives began to fall all about where we were working. Flat on our stomachs we threw ourselves. Now and then I glanced behind me to see how David King was faring, and always I found him too busy with his camera to pay any attention to the bombardment. Every time a shell fell anywhere near us, 'snap' went the shutter of that camera. One large shell landed, I am sure, not more than two metres to the side of us. I thought surely King was done for: then I heard him shout, 'Don't move! Don't move! That's a good one!' And he snapped me there in the new-made shell-hole! To work under such conditions was impossible, and we were ordered back to our first boyaux. We tried to sleep and get fit for the afternoon's attack. At three o'clock came the order to equip ourselves for the charge. We were told to leave our packs behind, to be in as light a condition as possible for marching. Each man took his tent cover and swung it over his shoulders, and with our two hundred cartridges, haversacks filled with two days' emergency food, and a supply of hand grenades, we had all we cared to carry. Then we started off for the first line, all in a happy mood. Every hundred metres of our advance we threw ourselves flat down for a little rest. The din of the battle was terrific, a mad blend of shouting, exploding shells, rifle firing and whatnot from both French and German throats and guns. Then came the turn for us to go out from our shelters and join in the advance. Up we sprang and followed the first wave of attackers. The bombardment was then at its highest pitch, and was the most horrible I had yet heard or seen – worse than either Champagne or Verdun. As we went forward with a rush many lads of my section fell out, killed or wounded. On we went, over the shell-butchered fields, constantly walking over dead bodies or meeting wounded men rushing back to the dressing-post. In groups of fifty and a hundred, prisoners trotted past us, guarded by only one or two French soldiers.

Now the attack in itself ended. We had gone as far as we had been ordered to go, and had reached and taken the foe's second line. My regiment had advanced about a mile and taken more than six hundred prisoners, four machine guns and several trench mortars. Our losses had been slight, but the worst part of the fight was only beginning. We, as reserves, started to dig ourselves in, there in the open field, about four hundred metres behind the newly occupied German position. Shells were falling at a rapid rate, and we hustled at our work, as each man must make his own shell-proof dug-out. Our picks and shovels, which we had never once abandoned, were small, and work was necessarily slow. King and I luckily found a deep shell-hole, and we hastily filled our sandbags and erected a sort of parapet. Then we crept over to the smashed-in German dugouts and found several more sand-bags and an axe. With the axe we chopped up a fallen telephone pole into lengths just right to make a roof for our new home, and, putting on a yard deep covering of earth, we had one of the best shelters in our company. The next night, we had to go up to the front line and work, under a heavy bombardment. Finally the shelling became too intense and we had to run to shelter. I tried to go into a dugout, but it was already full of men. I lay down in the doorway and another soldier ran up and fell headlong on top of me. The position was uncomfortable, but I lay there until things quieted down a bit. Then I told the man on my back to get up, but he did not stir. I got angry and began shouting at him. Still he did not move. Then I pushed him aside and he fell limp on the ground. I examined him and found he was dead. He had a shrapnel bullet right through the forehead and his back was almost torn open by a shell-splinter. If he had not been lying on me, I should have been hit by that very piece of shell. Taking my pick and shovel, I dug him a grave. The One Hundred and Seventieth moved back just behind the lines for a short rest. The regiment was awarded the fourragere and cited for the second time in Army Orders.[7]

French stretcher-bearers bringing back wounded men from the front line on the Somme. (*Library of Congress*)

Serving opposite Nilsen in the same action was Friedrich Georg Steinbrecher, a German officer, who also wrote of his part in this battle. His tone contrasts with the positive, almost cheery tempo of Nilsen's account. Instead, here we find grim determination to hang on:

Somme. The whole history of the world cannot contain a more ghastly word! … At the beginning of the month we left our old position. During the lorry and train journey we were still quite cheery. We knew what we were wanted for. Then came bivouacs, an 'alarm', and we were rushed up through shell-shattered villages and barrage into the turmoil of war. The enemy was firing with 12-inch guns. There was a perfect torrent of shells. The last days had been stiflingly hot. Sooner than we expected we were in the thick of it. First in the artillery position. Columns were tearing hither and thither as if possessed. The gunners could no longer see or hear. Verey lights were going up along the whole Front, and there was a deafening noise: the cries of wounded, orders and reports.

At noon the gun-fire became even more intense, and then came the order: 'The French have broken through. Counter-attack!' We advanced through the shattered wood in a hail of shells. I don't know how I found the right way. Then across an expanse of shell-craters, on and on. Falling down and getting up again. Machine-guns were firing. I had to cut across our own barrage and the enemy's. I am untouched. At last we reach the front line. Frenchmen are forcing their way in. The tide of battle ebbs and flows. Then things get quieter. We have not fallen back a foot. Now one's eyes begin to see things. I want to keep running on – to stand still and look is horrible. 'A wall of dead and wounded!' How often I have read that phrase! – now I know what it means.

Day melts into night. We are always on the alert. We can't establish communication with the rear without casualties. The wounded are in a makeshift dug-out. One has to sit by without being able to do anything for them. Deserters come in. French wounded crawl into the trench with shining faces. In a moment I got to know dozens of men. I had men belonging to three different regiments. I felt then what it is to be in command. It means responsibility, over life and death. The men cling to one like children.

I have witnessed scenes of heroism and of weakness. Men who can endure every privation. Being brave is not only a matter of will, it also requires strong nerves, though the will can do a great deal ... I wish it had all been only a dream – a bad dream. And yet it was a joy to see such heroes stand and fall. The bloody work cost us 177 men. We will never forget Chaulmes and Vermandovillers.[8]

Gefreiter Magnus Anton Frank of Bavarian *Reserve Infanterie Regiment Nr 3*, who was killed on 12 August 1916.

Steinbrecher, a student of theology at Leipzig before the war, was to survive the Somme, but lost his life in April 1917 at Moronvillers in the Champagne region.

As the fighting at Verdun began to wind down, so the French were able to spare more troops for the offensive on the Somme. One such was Roger Cadot, a journalist before the war, who in 1914 was mobilised as a sergeant in an infantry regiment. In mid-August he arrived in the sector near La Maisonette. The hamlet, sitting on high ground and providing good observation, had changed hands several times, and now protruded as a French-held salient into the German lines. Cadot wrote in his memoirs of his time here. To him, the Germans still appeared to be full of fight:

Naturally, I spent the next few days taking note of the new sector, browsing in all directions. Although conquered for six weeks, and upset by the recent shelling to an unimaginable degree, it was already provided with a suitable network of trenches, bequeathed in part, it is true, by the Germans. I visited La Maisonette, an old farm, which its owner Delagrave (an editor), had turned into a country house, but which was now no more than a cellar surmounted by a few walls on which the enemy artillery fired furiously. There *Capitaine* Berthelemot lived serenely and went about his duty with his eternal cigar to his lips.

This first contact with the sector very nearly put an end to my military career. The third day we were there I marked out a trench with Warrant Officer Lheritier through a chaotic terrain, where we unwound the white ribbon as a guide to indicate the position to the night working party, when a volley of 77s warned us that we had been glimpsed. We had just enough time to jump into a crater, where we remained for a quarter of an hour, while scrap metal was raining around us. On the return, close to the communication trench, as I walked along a slope where the stretcher bearers had deposited several corpses into the slime, a 150 fell a few meters from me, surrounding me with an atmosphere of fire and riddling me with clods of earth. On two occasions, in the space of just a few minutes, I had almost met death. She undoubtedly did not want me.

But the harassing firing to which we were subjected, and to which our artillery was responding generously, were insignificant compared to the tremendous bombardments we could hear roaring without interruption on our left, in sectors where the offensive continued ... The German troops defended on the Somme as hard as ours had done at Verdun ...[9]

Another recent arrival on this front was Louis Mairet, a *sous lieutenant* with the French *8e Regiment d'Infanterie*. Mairet's notes and letters were published after his death, and in one notable passage before arriving on the Somme, he comments on the outlook of the French soldier at this stage of the war for whom fighting had become simply a routine, stating perceptively that:

The soldier of 1916 fights not for Alsace nor to ruin Germany, nor for his country. He fights with honesty, through habit and strength. He fights because he cannot do otherwise. Thus he fights because after the first enthusiasm, discouragement arrived after the first winter, and with the second came resignation. What was hoped to be only a temporary state ... has become a stable situation in its very instability.[10]

Mairet also wrote of his experiences on 16 August in a reception camp behind the lines, situated between two squadrons of Royal Flying Corps aircraft and their attendant personnel. For him rest was truly that: peaceful, undisturbed and untroubled by enemy fire:

Facing to the northeast, between the wood of Celestines and the 43rd [Regiment], one vast plateau opens out. We undertake exercises there in the morning; after midday, come sports. These sports are official, which the authorities deign to honour with their presence. The game of association football, which is popular in the north, draws 2–3000 spectators. The 127th is only just beaten by a very strong team of the 43rd. Our neighbours, the English aviators, jump for joy at the sight of the ball, and solemnly come to ask us for a match; their wish is immediately granted. The 127th and 43rd form a joint team, and we cheer for them. The Englishmen are smaller, but quicker than our players. The captain of the squadron, playing at centre-forward, has marvellous spirit. However, after the first half, we gain the upper hand; and we win 2–0. 'Hip! Hip! Hip! Hooray for the Allies!' Thank you, Mister Englishmen![11]

Mairet had been a brilliant student before the war, but, as with so many promising young men of that generation, his potential would never be fulfilled. He was killed in action during the Nivelle Offensive in April 1917. In marked contrast were the experiences of Ehrenfried Tschoeltsch, a junior officer with the III Battalion of *Infanterie Regiment Nr 133*. On the same day his battalion was also in reserve, this time at Warlencourt, some 4 kilometres behind the German front line, occupying a school building. Their rest, however, was constantly disturbed by searching British artillery, which left them with little or no peace, and the men were under regular observation from the air. Indeed, one of the principal reasons for the fraying of German nerves and declining morale in August was the difficulty in getting troops sufficient rest out of the line. Tschoeltsch tells us that:

> An English airman directed the firing. The church with her massive tower seemed to receive special attention from the Englishman. Shot after shot struck nearby. But it was as if God himself protected the sanctuary that had once been built for Him by a pious farming family – not a shot hit it. Towards evening the shooting subsided more and more. There was a ceasefire of about one hour here. The transport column, of which I have already spoken, began. Again, there was hustle and bustle. Silent, quiet, columns and squadrons moved forward – towards death. Sudden thuds. They sound like duds. Again and again a dud? We notice this. Run – the eyes begin to tear already – it is obvious now: gas. Quick, out with the mask. Now the enemy can fire as much as he wants. The gas alarm signals resound through the village and warn of the threatening danger.
>
> In the evening we sit in the school – with the battalion staff. All young lieutenants. The talk is of war and peace, and thoughts of our comrades fallen in the last days – the popular Rudolf Fikentscher, the first we lost here. The conversation moves to bygone school days and holidays, and we paint an idealised picture of how it must have been in those times – times nevertheless when mankind shot one another only with the bow and arrow – the golden, indestructible humour of the young officers breaks inexorably through all the grief and discontent. At night I went again into my cellar. It took me a long time to fall asleep. Finally I was there, but my dreams were bad ones. Gruesome in fact. I felt as if I was touched on the forehead by the pale, cold hand of the dead. I woke up. I put my hand to my head and touched something cold – a snail had crawled across my forehead. For me sleep was now over. The usual vermin, they have long since become socially acceptable, and did not bother me – but snails? Ugh! The cellar was spoiled for me. I decided to move the next morning. Yet heavy thuds did not let me go back to sleep. The cellar shook and trembled. Are those wretches shooting again? I jump up and go out. There I see the state of affairs. Two of our 21cm mortars are positioned in the bushes directly in front of my house. They are shooting behind Pozières. Now I know what the shots in the afternoon were aimed at, and what the airmen wanted. It is hot in support! For if the guns were discovered, the cellar would probably be destroyed by shells along with them.
>
> The next morning I took my field kitchen away from here. The village was bombarded all day, the old houses burnt down. Throughout the day it was necessary to take shelter in dug outs. In the evening it was quiet. I used the hour of the cease-fire for a stroll through the village with my sergeant [Arno] Bauerfeind, an old soldier, who was in the twentieth year of service. He had long been eligible to go to the reserve battalion, but he did not want to leave his company. A few gentlemen of the battalion join our walk through the village. We speak of vacations and peace; yes the soldier always speaks most fondly of that which lies outside the range of possibilities. Suddenly, there is a familiar buzzing in the air. We throw ourselves down where we stand. In the next instant a crack and burst – the wall of the cemetery crashes down. Again a whiz. Aha – this we owe to the mortars, the airman has recognized them for sure! A new crack and burst. We're moving. We want to run away, when we see on the street the collapsed figure of the sergeant. We hurry there. He still lives. We pull him into the roadside ditch, then we take him to the doctor. He shakes our hand weakly – then he is taken to Villers au Flos hospital.[12]

Arno Bauerfeind, the long-serving sergeant, died of his wounds two days after this incident. Tschoeltsch was later to be wounded on the Somme, but after his recovery he transferred to the German air service, flying as an artillery observer. He survived the war, later becoming a general in Hitler's Luftwaffe, and died in 1979. For troops like him who were in reserve on the Somme, the journey up to the forward positions was equally dangerous. Hauptmann Friedrich Oehme went into the line at Martinpuich on the night of 17 August. He wrote home afterwards of the confusion as he and his men approached the front line without a guide and no clear idea, amid the destruction, of where the position which they were to relieve actually was:

> Quite apart from the bombardment, the mere appearance of utter devastation everywhere is enough to make one shudder. Not a house is left standing. Everything is completely destroyed – beams, bricks, and blocks of stone lie in the street. One shell-hole has filled up another. The chalky mud

Ehrenfried Tschoeltsch, seen between the wars in the uniform of the Weimar Republic.

> is splashed far and wide over everything. Trees, wagons, corpses, knapsacks, horses, rifles, tins, wire, bits of equipment, lie all about on the trampled paths between the craters.
>
> Under the fiercest shrapnel and shell-fire the company dashes forward – leaping over obstacles, tumbling into shell-holes, stumbling over bodies, or falling, wounded and unable to continue, still we go on till at last we are obliged to halt, and we lie, grinding our teeth, upon the road. When shall we get on?
>
> At last the mad chase is resumed. We reach the end of the village. There, close by, is the beginning of the front line. The opening is on the left of the main road. [We] plunge in and find a shallow trough which was once a trench. A few men are already lying in the holes which are all that is left of the dug-outs. They look dully at us with cowed and desperate faces.
>
> Now the men are divided up, one here and one there. They are simply crazy with fear. The shells keep falling. Splinters and filth fly through the air.[13]

The next part of Oehme's account is the most telling, for in some units at least the iron discipline of the German army was clearly now breaking down:

> At last all the necessary dispositions are made and I can sit down for a moment … Day now begins to dawn, and I hurry along the trench to see after the men. I realise with horror that before I had been walking over bodies, which were lying about in the water. The men are absolutely demoralised. They had been ordered to fetch bombs, but

Destruction in Martinpuich, August 1916.

if I hadn't finally done it myself they wouldn't have had any. It kept getting lighter and lighter. Suddenly, just as the sun rose behind us, came the order: 'The 10th company will advance 350 yards and dig itself in!'

We were lying in the second line, the first having been captured by the English, and now we had to dig a new front line close to the English one. I collect my men, so as to lead them forward all together under cover, and spring forward. When I look back not one, not a single one, has followed me. I go back, reason with them and order them to go with me. This time it has to be over open ground, as some parts of the trench have meanwhile been blown in. Now I spring forward again, leap through shell holes for about fifty yards, and throw myself down to get my breath. Two men have come with me.[14]

This is a remarkable indictment of the state of morale in this particular unit. Although Oehme goes on to compliment the work of the men who went forward with him in digging in to link up shell holes into a continuous line, he notes that the remainder of his company, some forty men out of

Private Henry Thomas Phillips, 1st/1st Buckinghamshire Battalion, who was killed in action on 15 August in the attempt to capture Skyline Trench, west of Pozières.

MARTINPUICH (Somme) – Ecriteau Allemand – A German poster

A German directional sign at Martinpuich still standing in August 1916, despite the destruction all around.

the ninety he brought into the line, had to be driven forward by another officer armed with a revolver. The weather had also now turned a little; for three days they hung on here in the rain, without blankets or overcoats and without the means even to make a hot drink, before leaving the line chilled, dead-tired and worn down by shell fire.

For the British 18 August marked the beginning of the battle for Guillemont, and an interesting letter survives from Corporal John Roney of the 3rd Battalion The Rifle Brigade, part of the 24th Division, who was in action here. Again, there is little evidence here of camaraderie or fellow feeling for the German soldier opposite. Roney writes in pugnacious terms of his part in the battle:

Private Frank George Bowden, 4th Battalion Royal Fusiliers, who was killed on 16 August near Guillemont, aged 20.

At 2.45 on the 18th, we got the word 'Go!' and away we went, the Buffs on our left and the Leinsters on our right; and before five minutes to three we were in charge of the Boche front line. We had a little hand-to-hand fighting. Our boys are fed up with this 'Mercy, Kamerade!' business – it's all bosh. We took about 200 prisoners between us, and passed them down the line. Then at 5 o'clock over again we went and took possession of the road where they had their strongholds, for which we had a hard fight, and eventually we got the road. The rest of our boys on the right took Guillemont station. We dug ourselves in there, and lay down to a shelling by the Boches. Then they brought up some fresh troops to counter-attack, but they might just as well have stopped where they were for, although practically wiped out, we held on until the Fusiliers reinforced us.[15]

The British too were suffering greatly in the conditions, and it took every ounce of resolve that junior officers possessed in order to keep going. Captain Andrew Buxton and his brother Arthur were also serving with the 3rd Battalion The Rifle Brigade. Andrew wrote in his diary for 18 August of the terrible destruction he found in the captured German positions around Guillemont, with many dead and wounded lying around. He made his HQ in an abandoned dugout, some thirty feet deep, to the east of Guillemont station (which had been captured without opposition) and was impressed by a German doctor who had remained to attend to the wounded. His company was ordered to hold the station with not less than fifty men. The place was a shambles of German equipment, including field-glasses, revolvers, iron rations, rifles, Very lights, a bottle of brandy and another of Hock, cigars, cigarettes, aerated water, two bugles, flutes and medicine cases. Throughout 19 August the men worked to prepare trenches around the station in case of counter-attack; working through the night there was little opportunity for rest. Heavy shelling caused many casualties. Buxton's diary for 20 August continues:

A little dozing, but practically no sleep. Dug-out full of debris, signallers, orderlies, etc. Bosch shelling very nasty but ours far heavier. Not much on the station fortunately. We have got the Bosch here all right now, I think. Guillemont appears like a ploughed field. Our dug-out has two entrances, both very dangerous. Cleared out the dug-out by a chain of men. In evening put on a working party to dig trench along lines of Bosch front line towards D. Coy. Men very done, but had to be done by dawn. Five men wounded by digging on to a Bosch bomb. Had a Coy. of Fusiliers to help. Pigot sent in afternoon congratulations on work and also saying, 'Now get some rest.' Did not pass on latter part of message as too important to continue work. Men very rattled. Cpl. Hogben killed today, also Wedlock of A. Coy. Arthur turned up in afternoon; so ripping to see him. He asked where Guillemont was! The men remarked, 'He can't keep away from the Front.' From French reports it appears possible Bosch may have evacuated Guillemont, so going to patrol accordingly and snatch the trench east of 'High Holborn'. The idea was we should be relieved on Saturday, but nothing doing, though Sunday was promised. On Sunday Pigot sent round to say we had to be in till Tuesday, 22nd. Men very done and rattled, and greatly depressed at this news.[16]

When the men finally left the line on 22 August, marching away on foot, Buxton notes that it was not until they reached Carnoy that they began to sing. It was a clear sign of their battered morale. Their spirits, however, were buoyed by a hot meal which was waiting for them in billets, organised by an officer who had been out of the line on a course. The same day Andrew's brother Arthur wrote home to their parents, his letter giving an indication of the appalling casualty rate for a battalion in the line:

I know you will have been anxiously waiting for a letter, but I simply could not write till our time in the trenches was over. It has been awful, and the fact that we both are well and (Andrew especially) have come through without a scratch is simply providential and due to prayer. He has been through an inferno! I have only just seen him once since Thursday, so can't say much from him, but about (I mustn't give numbers) of wounded men of our battalion have been through our Dressing Station, so I've heard a good deal of what it was like. I simply can't give a connected account, but just a few facts will show. Out of our mess of 7 Officers, Brown and Venner have been killed and Catchside wounded; Andrew, Vernede, myself and Chamberlain are all right. A's Sergeant-Major and his runner are dead. Last week I went on a walk with three charming young Officers, Henderson, Daly, and Barnard, – today I am the only one left, all the three killed. Out of four Company Commanders only Andrew and Boscawen are left, the other two wounded badly; it's too awful for words. It's marvellous that our Dressing Station is still standing; 2 other Regimental ones are knocked out and a despatching station, and only this morning we had a terrific shelling and of course a direct hit from the big stuff they were sending over would have done for the place and all in it. Two men on Friday were standing in the doorway; both were blown in – one died in five minutes, the other badly wounded. Oh! the loss of precious lives is awful, so are the sufferings of the wounded. The constant danger, the noise, the smells are past words. But if I feel it bad, it's ten times worse for Andrew, and even if he doesn't get some decoration you can believe me he has more than deserved it.[17]

Yet in spite of this awful rate of attrition, even at the height of the battle remarkable resolve was still shown by some on the British side to carry on with the fight. Knowing that there was a high probability that he would soon be killed, Harry Butters wrote in mid-August to the padre of his unit requesting that he inform his sister should the worst happen. He added:

Please reiterate to her how much my heart was in this great cause, and how more than willing I am to give my life to it.[18]

Perhaps it was this type of inner conviction which allowed officers and men to continue to face almost certain death. This kind of resolve was not always confined to the British alone. One of the greatest of all German war writers is widely considered to be Ernst Junger, and his memoir *Storm of Steel* is nothing short of a celebration of war as an exhilarating, inspirational experience. Junger is unusual in that he gloried in his role as a platoon commander with *Fusilier Regiment Nr 73*. On 24 August he was also near Guillemont, and wrote:

The sunken road and the ground behind was full of German dead; the ground in front of English. Arms, legs, and heads stuck out stark above the lips of the craters. In front of our miserable defenses there were torn-off limbs and corpses over many of which cloaks and ground-sheets had been thrown to hide the fixed stare of their distorted features. In spite of the heat no one thought for a moment of covering them with soil. The village of Guillemont was distinguished from the landscape around it only because the shell-holes there were of a whiter color by reason of the houses which had been ground to powder. Guillemont railway station lay in front of us. It was smashed to bits like a child's plaything. Delville Wood, reduced to matchwood, was farther behind.

Day had scarcely dawned when an English flying-man descended on us in a steep spin and circled round incessantly like a bird of prey, while we made for our holes and cowered there. Nevertheless, the observer's sharp eyes must have spied us out, for a siren sounded its deep, long-drawn notes above us at short intervals. After a little while it appeared that a battery had received the signal. One heavy shell after another came at us on a flat trajectory with incredible fury. We crouched in our refuges and could do nothing. Now and then we lit a cigar and threw it away again. Every moment we expected a rush of earth to bury us. The sleeve of Schmidt's coat was torn by a big splinter.

At the third shot the occupant of the next hole to mine was buried by a terrific explosion. We dug him out instantly, but the weight of earth had killed him. His face had fallen in and looked like a death's-head. It was the volunteer Simon. Tribulation had made him wise. Whenever in the course of the day, when airmen were about, any one stirred from his cover, Simon was heard scolding and his warning fist appeared from behind the ground-sheet that curtained his earth.

At three in the afternoon the men came in from the left flank and said they could stick it no longer as their shelters were shot to bits. It cost me all my callousness to get them back to their posts.

Just before ten at night the left flank of the regimental front was heavily shelled, and after twenty minutes we came in for it too. In a brief space we were completely covered in dust and smoke, and yet most of the hits were just in front or just behind. While this hurricane was raging I went along my platoon front. The men were standing, rifle in hand, as though carved in stone, their eyes fixed on the ground in front of them. Now and then by the light of a rocket I saw the gleam of helmet after helmet, bayonet after bayonet, and I was filled with pride at commanding this handful of men that might very likely be pounded into the earth but could not be conquered. It is in such moments that the human spirit triumphs over the mightiest demonstrations of material force. The fragile body, steeled by the will, stands up to the most terrific punishment.[19]

However, for the reasons cited above Junger cannot be considered typical of the German soldier in the line at this point in August 1916, after a month and a half of bitter fighting. Even his contemporaries considered him to be unusual, and his account stands alone amid the pantheon of First World War memoirs.

Mouquet Farm, lying about four miles northwest of Guillemont, was still the scene of heavy fighting at this point in August. The farm was an inconspicuous homestead prior to the First World War, but now the Germans had turned it into a formidable fortress. The capture of Mouquet Farm thus became a key objective for the British and Commonwealth forces. On 26 August Captain E.J. Rule, serving with the 8th Battalion Australian Imperial Force, was involved in an ill-starred attempt to take it:

The arrangements were rotten – the battalion staff-work could not have been worse, and it was more by good luck than good management that any of us came out of the show ... We advanced about half-way and then settled into shell-holes to wait. Every time I looked round I could see the long line of men following behind like a snake. Flares were still going up, and it looked more like daylight than night... . I heard a swish as a Stokes mortar shell came tumbling through the air overhead. When it burst on or near the German post we crept forward again. The bursting shells were a good guide, and they were coming over very quickly – one in every four or five seconds. We crept up until we could feel the force of the explosion, and then lay down. It was a wonder some of us were not hit, but we knew that our only chance of salvation was to get up close whilst the barrage was still on, and then rush in before the Hun could get his head up.[20]

Rule and his men became bogged down in a bombing fight with the German garrison, the defenders having the advantage of the longer range of the stick grenade, though it was not as lethal as the British Mills bomb. Rule continues:

> I ... went out to the bottom of the bank and lit my red flare for reinforcements ... I turned to go back to where the surviving bombers were fighting, and, as I turned, I found that the Huns were coming back, pelting bombs at us. One almost hit my foot, and I had barely moved a yard when the bomb went off. I had the impression that someone had stabbed me with hot pins along my legs, and I felt blood running down my hand. It knocked the breath out of me, and I remember staggering around for a while.[21]

Rule and the survivors of his party were forced to withdraw. The Australian attack here ran into difficulties because the complete absence of landmarks in this shell-battered moonscape caused many of them to lose direction. It was a problem common to both sides. Not far away was Theodore Drexel, a former medical student, who was a *Leutnant der Reserve* in the Bavarian *Infanterie Regiment Nr 23*. He wrote of a trench relief in this wilderness which almost ended in disaster; such was the devastation that any and all points of visual reference had been shot away. Even guides were now sometimes unsure of where the front line lay:

> On the evening of 26 August the trench relief party of the 1st battalion marched out of Grévillers and shortly before midnight reached the G11 command post.

A group of German infantrymen on the Somme, August 1916. Arrowed on the right is the platoon commander Theodore Drexel, author of *Einundzwanzig tage im trommelfeuer an der Somme*.

After a detailed briefing on the situation had been given to every man, a Saxon with knowledge of the area was attached as a guide. It was nearly one o'clock when we marched on. With the guide going on ahead, I followed with three sergeants; initially we remained on a broad track, but which soon became a narrow footpath. The terrain was always uneven, the shell holes grew in number and finally we found ourselves in a churned field, no longer were there any flat pieces of earth to be found. Our footsteps meandered between the edges of the shell holes, however, our progress was haphazard with many stops and starts. The night was dark, only intermittently illuminated by the light of flares.

We came near the zone of the constant barrage. On the right and left shells burst, and shrapnel rained down over us. Constantly we had to duck. I had long ago lost any idea as to which direction we were marching in, any sort of orientation was impossible. There was no post, no tree, no trench, nothing which could serve as a clue. I only knew that the company which I wanted to find was about 300 meters on the right of the forest of Foreaux.

'Do you still know the way?' I asked the guide.

'Yes sir, we are half way there.'[22]

They were now approaching the Switch Line which ran west of High Wood, towards Martinpuich:

We continued on and on, the leader always jumping freshly forward. We could only try to keep up. I was convinced that we were being led the wrong way. According to my calculations, we would need no longer than 30 minutes from G11, and now it was already well past one hour. Finally by the light of a flare I saw in front of us a group of men in a narrow fire trench. I rushed towards it.

'What regiment?'

'_____.'

'Where are the _th?'

'Right of the forest of Foreaux. You are to the left of the wood.'

Clearly I saw by the light of a flare, far to the right, a bald trunk staring Heavenwards. Thus further still, the leader took us on. By sketch and verbal discussion I knew that between the wood of Foreaux and the company which I sought was a gap of maybe 120 meters. Close to the front line, English machine-gun nests were studded here and there, so it was necessary to be careful. With guns ready to fire, we went from shell-hole to shell-hole. From time to time I stopped, whistled, shouted, and listened, but no one answered. Again, we went further, the wood of Foreaux we already had to our left, but still there was nobody to be seen digging in. Only isolated rockets were shot up in long periods of darkness. Pieces of equipment lay around; when we came upon a shell crater built up with sandbags, we shouted in, but there was no answer. The enemy fire was now further behind us. I had no further trust in what I had been told, and when questioned my guide admitted that he himself no longer knew where we were. Probably we had gone through a gap in the line and had been walking around in front of the English positions. Orientation was impossible. I let the men take cover in shell holes and waited for the next flare. Only after long minutes, from behind us, maybe 150 metres, came a high shot, coming from the same direction at the same time as a grenade which struck the ground a little in front of us. Now I knew for certain, we were under our own fire and had to turn back. But we had to beware, not to be shot by our own people. We were lucky and reached the ditch without loss.[23]

Bois de Foreaux, as the Germans knew it, was a misprint of Bois de Forcaux, known to the British as High Wood. By whatever name it was called, this contentious and bitterly contested piece of ground still lay in German hands, despite repeated British attempts to capture it. Indeed, the almost reckless nature of the British attacks now was becoming something of a cause for concern. Louis Mairet of the *8e Regiment d'Infanterie*, positioned as he was close to the junction of the British and French armies on the Somme, had seen much of the Anglo-Saxon way of warfare. At this mid-point of the battle, he gave an assessment of the calibre of his allies in his diary on 27 August:

> My impression of the English, the ones I've seen: … Generally calm and indifferent. The value of their artillery: 5 out of 20, against 15 out of 20 with us. But they fire freely. At Falfemont, on the 24th they failed, why? It is said they were stopped by machine-gun fire. The fact is that they failed. Their fault is that they see war as a sport. They are too quiet, striving to appear unconcerned. At Hardecourt, an artillery lieutenant comes to see where is Combles! There is little consistency in their actions, they attack for any reason and for no reason, failing when they should succeed, and, with a certain firmness of mind, saying, 'Missed it today, better luck tomorrow.' But it is so many shells spent, and men lost. In short, they still lack know-how.[24]

Matters would reach a head a few weeks later when David Lloyd-George, on a visit to France, expressed the view, also held by a number of other MPs, that the British appeared to be losing two men to the French one, for comparable gains in ground. The fact that Lloyd-George put his opinions directly to the French General Ferdinand Foch, and asked for his thoughts on the matter, caused ruffled feathers at British GHQ. Foch, however, was ever the diplomat, and he informed the Prime Minister that the lighter French casualties were because his men (having learned the lessons of 1914) were more cautious in the attack, but he wished that this was not the case. Capture of ground of course was not Haig's primary objective at this point. He was more concerned with using his growing artillery superiority to grind down the German army on the Somme, and one man who had been on the receiving end of this battering was a German artilleryman named Walter Schmidt from Tuttlingen. His battery had been in the Ginchy–Guillemont sector since the beginning of the month, and writing home on 30 August he freely admitted that what he had experienced in that short time surpassed everything that he had seen in the previous year on the Eastern Front. He wrote:

> You will no doubt have learned from the newspapers and other sources about how the English with the aid of their airmen, who are often 1,500 feet above the position, and their captive balloons, have exactly located every one of our batteries and have so smashed them up with long distance guns of every calibre that the artillery here has had unusually heavy losses both of men and material. Our dug-outs, in which we shelter day and night, are not even adequate, for though they are cut out of the chalk they are not so strong but that a 'heavy' was able a few days ago to blow one in and bury the whole lot of men inside. The gun-emplacements are surrounded by a ring of shell craters and every day some heaps of 50 to 100 shells are blown up by a direct hit. When we are firing

This belt, with its distinctive snake-style buckle, is part of a British soldier's 1914 Pattern leather equipment. It was found in Bernafay Wood, where field dressing stations were located, and is stamped inside '8 KRR' (8th Battalion King's Royal Rifle Corps). The battalion was part of the 14th Division, and was involved in fighting near Longueval in August 1916, so it is likely that the original owner was wounded there.

The top part of a Belgian army mess tin, captured in 1914 and subsequently used by the Germans. Riddled with bullet and shrapnel holes, apparently from two different directions, it was found close to Pozières and illustrates the ferocity of the fighting there. It retains traces of the original black paint, and the owner's service number is stamped on the top.

A British army haversack, carried in an attack on Delville Wood on 20 July 1916 by Private William Jones, 10th Battalion Royal Welsh Fusiliers. On this day the battalion suffered heavy casualties, in part at least because it strayed into a British machine-gun barrage. The pencil illustrates the path of a bullet which passed through the haversack.

This bottle, embossed with the words 'Elliman's Embrocation', was found in a field close to the Guards Memorial at Ginchy. The product was sold as a cure for aching muscles and joints, and it is tempting to think that it was being used in the autumn of 1916 by a British officer, perhaps to counteract trench foot or rheumatism caused by the wet conditions.

This is part of the folding mechanism of a British army stretcher. The standard issue stretcher folded in half along its length for easier transportation when not in use. The loops allowed the stretcher to be loaded into an ambulance or hospital train. It was found at Thiepval, and may be a relic of the capture of the strongpoint in September 1916.

The barrel and breech of a British SMLE MkIII rifle, found at Pozières. It appears to be loaded, with a round in the chamber, but the safety catch is on. No British or Empire soldier would abandon his rifle unless he was dying or seriously wounded. Many thousands of rifles were recovered by salvage parties during the Somme battle, but many more remained lost.

A British Webley and Scott No. 1 Mark 1 flare pistol. This would have been used to signal the position of forward troops to aerial observers, to call for artillery support in an emergency, or to illuminate No Man's Land at night. It was found near Trones Wood, which was captured on 14 July 1916.

An Australian soldier's shirt button. Bearing the word 'Commonwealth', it was found at Pozières, between the OG lines, where Australian troops attacked in July and August 1916. A tiny item about the size of a penny piece, it none the less reflects one of the most ferocious actions of the entire Somme battle, where Australian dead lay thicker than in any other place.

A spent German 9mm cartridge. It was probably fired by a Luger pistol, possibly carried by an officer, and was found on the line of Regina Trench, close to Courcelette British Cemetery. Many spent 7.92mm rifle or machine-gun cartridges were found nearby, testifying to the stubborn German defence of this position in the face of repeated attacks.

A German fork and spoon set, found near Courcelette in the remains of a shallow dugout in the side of a bank, which may perhaps once have been an artillery position. It is an intensely personal item, and other 'domestic' items were found nearby, including a water jug and drinking vessels.

A British soldier's spoon. Stamped '9698 E.K.', it is believed to have belonged to Private George Burt of the 6th Battalion East Kent Regiment. Burt was wounded in action on 16 October 1916. The spoon was found near Albert; assuming that he had not previously lost it or given it away, it may have been left at a casualty clearing station.

Fragments of German stick grenades found near Ginchy. The grenade (or 'bomb' in the language of the time) became the weapon of choice in the close-quarter fighting on the Somme. Although the German stick grenade had greater range than the British Mills bomb, its black powder charge was less deadly.

Part of a British soldier's boot found near Flatiron Copse Cemetery, probably at the site of a dressing station. The cemetery is located in a valley which was used as the main supply route during the attempts to take High Wood, some two miles away. The location was known initially as Happy Valley, but the sobriquet changed to Death Valley as the fighting intensified.

A German HZ 14 howitzer shell fuse, found south of Delville Wood close to the cemetery. This weapon would have had a short range, and the shell was probably fired from close proximity, perhaps around 22 July 1916, when the British 8th Division held the front line here. The fuse was made by AEG in 1915; later in the war, when brass was scarce, German fuses were made of inferior metals.

A British soldier's jack-knife, found near Bazentin le Petit, on the site of the German front line as it was on the morning of 14 July 1916. It was probably lost by a soldier of the 6th Battalion Leicestershire Regiment, which attacked here. If he survived, he would no doubt have regretted the loss of such a useful item.

A British army enamel mug, found in Flatiron Copse. The lie of the land protected the copse from direct observation from the German lines, and thousands of men and large quantities of supplies passed through it on their way to and from the front. A number of dressing stations were located in this area and it is probable that the original owner passed through here when wounded.

The remains of a German ammunition pouch found in Bernafay Wood. Bearing a Stuttgart maker's stamp and a date of 1916 on the reverse, this pouch would have originally held cartridges for a German 7.92mm Mauser rifle. German wounded also received treatment in British dressing stations, and this item probably belonged to one such casualty.

A pair of British wire cutters, found in what was once No Man's Land close to Devonshire Cemetery near Mametz. They were almost certainly lost in the attack made on 1 July 1916 by the 9th Battalion Devonshire Regiment, which sustained heavy casualties from German machine guns in Fricourt Wood. A sister battalion, the 8th Devons, attacked over the same ground later the same day and also suffered heavily.

A French army grenade, found in a barn on the Somme battlefield. Sometimes called a *Petard Raquette*, in its earliest form it consisted simply of a detonator from an artillery shell wired to a piece of wood. This model dates from 1915.

Front-line barbed wire from Beaumont Hamel. Those familiar only with modern agricultural barbed wire may not appreciate the fact that the wire used in German front-line defences was considerably thicker, with longer barbs spaced at shorter intervals. Large stretches of it remained undamaged on the morning of 1 July 1916, causing many British casualties.

A collection of British army food tins found at White City, a reserve position near Beaumont Hamel. The circular cans may have contained jam or condensed milk, the more angular tin contained Bully Beef. The British made extensive use of tinned food or 'iron rations', and it was essential for survival on a battlefield upon which it was often impossible to transport cooked food.

a barrage the men have to cross a stretch of open ground to get to their guns and then, without taking any notice of falling shells, we have to fire as hard as we possibly can. A few days ago the whole detachment of an NCO and three men were killed by a direct hit during the barrage. As nobody else wanted to fire a gun covered with corpses, the *Fahnrich* and I took on the job, and there, in the midst of dead bodies and blood and in full view of death, I was filled with a feeling of profound happiness because the attack had been frustrated. We have carried out our task if the enemy fails to break through, even if thousands of us have been killed. What does an individual life matter on such occasions, and can one spend it to greater advantage than in offering it up as part of a general sacrifice? There are perhaps banalities and platitudes, but one often realises their truth and value when one is put to the test. Death may be bitter, but we can conquer it in advance, and then the object of it – the salvation of the Fatherland – shines through all the blood and horror and one no longer dreads it.[25]

Patriotism and belief in his nation's cause still motivated this young man to continue willingly to risk his life, despite all he had been through. Many others were not so fortunate, and the relentless artillery fire crushed their mind and spirit; this, after all, was the object which the allies were seeking by this stage of the battle. At the beginning of September the French Tenth Army launched an assault towards Deniecourt and Vermandovillers which would result in the capture of some 2,700 German prisoners. At the same time pressure was increased in other parts of the French sector, with the Sixth Army attacking on its front as well. Leutnant Messerschmidt of *Grenadier Regiment Nr 89* recorded the effect of this ceaseless pounding on the men of his platoon, who were holding positions facing the French between the Roman road and the River Somme. Messerschmidt himself was in the stone quarry at Barleux when a tremendous artillery barrage began, directed by tethered

The crew of a German 21cm *Langer Mörser* artillery piece prepare to fire, on the Somme front.

balloons and airmen, cruising at an altitude of 400–600 metres, who also dropped bombs. The heaviest shells were of 22 centimetre calibre, and later these were joined by the fire of 15-centimetre Rimailho howitzers with their distinctive 'crack-crack' and their black smoke. Messerschmidt describes how some of his men were driven to madness by the bombardment:

> Leutnant R____ fell on the 1st September, in the evening at 11 o'clock, killed by a direct hit in the upper stone quarry. Another four men were hit by the same shell: Noncommissioned officer W_____, who was deafened and mentally disturbed, and three young, not yet 19-year-old grenadiers who were only eight days with the company. I will not quickly forget the screams of one of them, who had a ragged right forearm; he trampled around on the bloody bodies of the other two, so that we had to hold him down by force. I have also repeatedly observed during these days the same or similar effects on mind and spirit from the dreadful artillery and mortar fire. H___ broke down and had lost his memory and the power of speech; I had to let a vice sergeant bind the upper part of his body in a sandbag jacket, because he had torn his own clothes off his body and in a naked state, hit and ill-treated the wounded. Other men rolled around on the ground howling or chanting … A young 89th soldier jumped up towards me, in his hand a rifle with a full magazine, madness flickering in the eyes, shouting: 'Herr Leutnant, you must save me, you must save me!'[26]

The following day the barrage grew even more in intensity:

> … wuuuum! The first heavy went in our stone quarry itself, in the upper part, and two others immediately followed. The survivors with pale distraught faces and wide staring eyes rushed down to the lower part; but also here was a dreadful crashing and banging. My little handful of men melted away alarmingly fast; to hold on any longer here would be pointless, and would have been sheer murder. I ordered the evacuation of the stone quarry to the right and to the left; four groups remained as a security measure in three available dug outs. Towards evening the fire achieved incredible power, from 7 o'clock it beat down in a way which cannot possibly be exceeded. We all feel it and say to ourselves: now they will come! Quickly a check of the faithful rifle, a test of whether the bolt still closes, equipment belts are more firmly strapped, hand grenades, spades, and entrenching tools assembled, the hand grips the handle of the knife!
>
> Yet they did not come. But also there was no rest at night. The enemy covered the entire area with a rain of projectiles, with shells from the heavy artillery, and with shrapnel. This made it impossible to get reinforcements to the forward-most troops, and prevented the bringing up of ammunition, food and the so necessary water; [it impeded the] strengthening and repair work on the bullet-ridden trenches, and the evacuation of wounded. Our comrades came forwards in a thin trickle, but they brought what we needed: ammunition in bandoleers and hand grenades in boxes, bread and rations in bags, coffee in canteens and special carriers of soda water in crates. It was laborious work. In the impenetrable darkness the front was not easy to find, but soon they found any number sheltering in foxholes to protect themselves from the flying pieces of the shells which continually rained down, or taking cover from the light of countless luminous flare cartridges which were as bright as day. The issue of the supplies took place in complete silence; here our people stood, pressed close to the front

wall of the upper stone quarry, here and there stumbling against it and clattering their mess tins. Then the work of cleaning up and preparing began ...[27]

This tremendous barrage was the prelude to an infantry attack, which Messerschmidt also describes in considerable detail. His disparaging remarks about the calibre of the French infantry are perhaps to be expected, but equally should be taken with a pinch of salt, for the Germans were on the back foot by this stage of the battle:

The 3rd September came and with it the attack, the redemption. It was the seventh day of the barrage, drum fire such as one had not known it till then ... Little by little the storm troops of the French had also become more clearly evident: from the hollow beyond the sunken lane and the height before it to the left.... .

These were hideous hours, and the highest demands were made on body and soul. Now it would demonstrate of what spirit we were children. Closely pressed against one another we crouched in the dug out which had only one exit; no word was spoken, each one of us in his thoughts counted the seconds up to the explosion of the next shell. Every half or whole minute came shells of the heaviest calibre in salvoes of three. The last grenadier also knew this: that if such a beast landed directly on a dug out, then no angel could help those sheltering in it. These were moments of the highest tension, [and] they remain with him who endures them, in the memory for ever.

At four o'clock in the afternoon the sentry, Grenadier Vetter, noticed it first and shouted: 'Out! They are coming, they are coming!' Already one also heard infantry and machine-gun fire. Advanced patrols felt their way ahead, behind them complete battalions seemed to be on the parapet, of mixed white and black French troops. A feeling of relief and joy went through our ranks. Fighting spirit glowed again in the eyes of my people. Now there was work to be done, but nevertheless, this was something else than idly having to endure the maddening barrage. And we peppered them with as much as our rifles could give. The first hand grenades flew over, and already we jumped out of the ditch to go forwards to meet the enemy, in the usual way with a cheer. We always finished quickly with the French infantry, as soon as we were eye to eye with them. In the face of this most robust defence, our 'brothers' again also did not stand firm here; as soon as our first steel helmets appeared from the shell holes, the rest of them made a hasty escape to their trenches, and in spite of his cries of, '*En avant!*' their leader could not bring them forward any more.

Only at two places in the company sector had hostile storm troops come through the smoke and dust up to our trench, and then, when German rifle fire started, they had run with upraised hands over here to surrender. On the left it was worse. Here the French lined up steadily and well, and advanced also at first well, then only in disjointed groups, then in disarray. 'Half left of the hill! Range 400! Rapid fire!' The poor fellows stumbled through our steel hail, began to fall and were pushed away to the left of the hill to avoid the flank fire. The foremost trench of the 89th was thereby saved; the few survivors of the defenders had taken refuge with us.

They laughed and cried to each other, although nothing or not a lot was understood: the uninterrupted crash of the shells, the heat of the shrapnel bursting at low height which almost singed our heads, the rattle of infantry and machine-gun fire, the cracking of the heavy and light mortars had excessively attacked one's hearing. Towards Barleux a cloud of smoke had blown up on a gust of wind. In the sunken lane German infantry with fixed bayonets fought man to man. From the rear our reserves approached in groups, in spite of the barrage.

I saw Frenchmen jumping into the depths of the ravine; now where we also wore the steel helmet, the eye had to get used to distinguishing friend and enemy; these were only prisoners. However, what was this? From the left rear, behind the sunken lane, there came about forty French running with levelled rifles; because they did not want to surrender, they were bayoneted; they belonged to an Alpine Chasseur battalion and the 2nd regiment of the Senegalese Tirailleurs. One whose paybook I saw came from Picardy. Thus the information I found here also confirmed that they employed elite troops for the liberation of their homeland.[28]

In the same action, near Barleux, was Major Walter Caspari, a German officer serving with *Infanterie Regiment Nr 75*, the Bremen Regiment. The Germans held the British and French in particular disdain for bringing colonial troops to the Western Front to use against them, and Caspari's own account of the fighting here betrays his personal dislike for the French Senegalese soldiers who were captured by his regiment in a counter-attack; he even implies that they were specially singled out to be bayoneted:

In the foremost trench the advance goes well. We hear from returning wounded that the enemy has been forced back by hand grenade troops on the left. The enemy aircraft observe this clearly, and the heavy enemy fire swells once again. Our artillery answers them. Machine guns hammer in between. It is an infernal amount of noise, an uninterrupted whirl of discordant kettle drums and lighter percussion. Schneider is right next to me. We can only roar our observations in each other's ears. Lieutenant Klauß comes over, seriously wounded in the arm.

Along the road the attack has faltered, no longer are we moving forward. Enemy machine guns stand fast before the approach of the foremost shock troops and pepper the road. The leader of the forward troops has apparently been killed.

We intervene, Schneider at the head – the shock troops move forward – grenades fly – and the crews of the enemy machine guns raise up their arms. Now, with a loud 'Pardon, pardon, bon camerade', French and blacks come up to us in masses, waving both arms high in the air. On the road, the prisoners organise themselves into a single file, and without delay head towards the rear.

Schneider and I receive – without us actually wanting it – a strange parade. We must have met these men with such a stern gaze that while passing, just before they reach us, their right hands fly up to the helmet in a military salute. A very irregular society passes us. Callow youths, old, grey-haired Poilus, the thin and the very stout, tall and short, white and black. On average, however, they are powerful figures wearing good, new equipment. We feel no hatred. Only the very tall, apparently inebriated blacks disgust us. We suspect that the 5th Company have a short time before thoroughly 'cleaned' their trench with their long bayonets! We have taken a large haul of machine guns, rifles and ammunition. Schneider and I have done our duty here and go with Wagschal by the 'middle way' back to the steep slope. We pass a Frenchman sitting quietly. Blood trickles from his left arm. Behind the slope, huddled together, are the prisoners. In fox holes and tunnels German and French wounded are mixed together. When there is a small break in the fire we push the prisoners to the rear.[29]

Many Senegalese prisoners, particularly those who were wounded, were shot out of hand by their German captors in the First World War. Nevertheless, it appears from Caspari's account that this particular group of Senegalese at least were treated reasonably well as prisoners in German hands. Certainly they were treated better than those of a later generation who were captured in the fighting of 1940, large numbers of whom were subsequently murdered by the German army. Caspari for his part had fought against the British in the opening actions of the First World War in 1914, and would go on to command a *Freikorps* unit in the chaos that reigned in Germany following the close of hostilities. He later became a commander in the Bremen police force.

Major Walter Caspari, of *Infanterie Regiment Nr 75*, the Bremen Regiment.

But what of the West African perspective on the fighting on the Somme? Did soldiers from the French colonies identify with the allied cause in this battle, or were they simply dupes, beguiled by their colonial masters into becoming cannon fodder? We are fortunate to have at least one answer to these questions. One of the Senegalese soldiers who took part in the September fighting was Nar Diouf, a *tirailleur* who had volunteered to join the French forces upon the outbreak of the war. Interviewed in the early 1980s, he recalled both the nature of the fighting on the Somme and his own identification with the allied cause:

When we arrived on the Somme on September 4, 1916, we dug some holes [in the ground] – some trenches. And the Germans too did the same thing. And we started to shoot one another. And from time to time, the officers – the French officers – sent some soldiers to attack the Germans in their holes. And we dug a very big hole [deep redoubt] and protected it with some tree trunks to avoid [being hit by] the shells ...

We spent one month on the Somme. But sometimes, the fighting stopped. And a few days later the Germans would make an attack and we fought with them. Or sometimes, we made an attack toward the Germans. But we spent one month fighting ...

But throughout this time, it was the French who [were] trying to push the Germans out of France. So it was the French who used to attack the Germans [most of the time]. And the Germans were on the defensive. And it was very dangerous for us to make an attack – to attack the Germans. But we succeeded in pushing them back from the Somme ...

I was not afraid of dying because I went to France to fight with the Germans – to help the French. So, at that moment, my only thought was [whether we would] win or be defeated. So, I was not afraid at all about the prospect of dying. It was a matter of indifference to me [whether I] lived or died ...

I had no idea at all about [what] the war [would be like] ... because I had never been told about [it] ... The most unusual things I discovered during the war were the artillery and the machine guns, the airplanes shooting down on us and all the shells falling everywhere. But I wasn't afraid of dying. What counted for me was the fact that we should win [the war] … I can't tell exactly what [was] the proportion [of survivors in our battalion from among those sent to the Somme] because every time [we fought] many soldiers died and they brought in other soldiers to replace them … [But] the worst fighting was on the Somme; it was where we lost the most soldiers.[30]

Slightly to the north was French officer Louis Mairet. He was close to the boundary with the BEF, and was part of the Sixth Army's efforts to advance in conjunction with the British on their left. In this sector the French had driven the Germans from the line between Cléry and Le Forest, and were now about to attack again in an action which would bring them to Anderlu Wood, northeast of Le Forest. Mairet could see the continuing battle for Falfemont Farm to the north, and was full of admiration for his British allies:

A typical French Senegalese *tirailleur*. Recruited in France's West African colonies, many of these men none the less identified with the French cause.

2/3 Sept: It's cold. The battlefield is silent. One of the biggest fears of my life: no artillery preparation for our attack. Finally the hour approaches. Last words, last preparations. The British come at 9 o'clock. These men are Scottish. But what carnage! They do not get half way to the farm. Although earlier, we were ready to attack, we also return. Although we certainly catch it! The fourth section is mown down by a machine gun: the captain is injured. Until noon, attack and counter-attack with grenades follow. The losses of our section number seventeen, approximately 50%. Around 3 o'clock, the English attacked Falfemont again. What a horrible sight! So they decide to attack by the left, and then advance to Leuze Wood. Throughout the day, we cannot see what is happening. Through the smoke we drop grenades on the Boche runners. Apart from that, some

The grave of a Somme casualty: Hans Hahn, a *Kriegsfreiwilliger* in a Bavarian artillery unit, was killed on 5 September 1916.

Two French soldiers in discussion at Becquincourt in the autumn of 1916. Note the shell-shattered trees.

alerts, large shells that fall close by. No orders. All that we know is that we are to be relieved and go into reserve at nightfall. The order has just been received to go for a trench in front of Savernake wood where we will be relieved by the 201st.

4 September: I am dying of cold and fatigue. As refreshment: a quarter of wine to ten men. Certainly we will die here. There is talk of relief for tonight, which would make it a fortnight here, but nothing official. The company is in the following situation: down to half of its strength, a lost section and no communication with the commanding officer; what a mess! At noon, word reaches us that the English will attack Falfemont at 3.30am, and that the 201st has been ordered to stand ready to follow the movement, [and] we must do the same. Misery! In the physical state we are in, and with men who can barely walk! And after a fortnight of deprivation! We are hardly ready, when the English attack. It is 3.00am. What courage these people have! They go over the top, and by 6.00am they have reached the outskirts of the farm. But the 201st does not move, and we remain where we are. At 7.00, the English attacked again from another direction. They come to 300 meters, but stop in the open. We ourselves are relieved by the 10th.[31]

The grave of the artist Auguste Ravenel, who was killed in action in September 1916 near Belloy en Santerre. (*Courtesy of Jori Wiegmans*)

The Germans attached great importance to the Peronne–Bapaume road, and as the French drew nearer they fought desperately to hold this line. However, on 3 September the British finally took Guillemont, and this time held it, despite the difficulties posed by rain, gas shells and night attacks. This in turn enabled the French to advance and threaten their objective. Another French soldier in action at this time was Auguste Ravenel, a noted painter and artist before the war. He was killed in combat on 5 September 1916 whilst serving with the *128e Regiment d'Infanterie*. He was, however, not the only French artist of note in action that day. Jean Louis Lefort, born in Bordeaux in 1875, was a member of both the Committee of Independent Artists and the French Society of Watercolorists, and was president of the Society of Modern Painters of Paris and of the Salon of the Tuileries. Lefort had arrived on the Somme at the end of August with his regiment, the *360e Regiment d'Infanterie*, and went into the line between Biaches and Barleux. During this time he produced a number of works depicting scenes of fighting or captured positions, such as *Ravin des Colonels*, the interior of a *Baraquement à Méricourt*, *Le canon de 37 à Cléry*, next to the railway, and *L'arrivée d'un renfort* during the attacks in September 1916. Other works were *Le coiffeur de la Compagnie à Froissy*, *Train blindé au camp 59* and the *Entrée du boyau de la Choucroute* near Herbecourt. The celebrated writer Pierre Mac Orlan was serving in the same vicinity and mentions a number of these locations in his memoir *Les Poissons Morts*. Mac Orlan, who was with the *269e Regiment d'Infanterie*, describes moving up through the congested communication trench known as Boyau de la Choucroute (literally 'Sauerkraut Trench'), which ran parallel to 'Sausage Trench', on his way up to the position known as the 'Ravin des Colonels':

Around us – we have been walking for about one hour – concealed batteries fire incessantly. Each burst shakes us and hurts our ears. Imprecations follow. We continue to march forward. Here before us is a crossroads of trenches. There is a hesitation at the head of the column, the lieutenant, by the beam of a flashlight, reads a muddy sign on the parapet: Boyau Choucroute. We are here. We follow on. The equipment chafes the shoulders, the bag weighs on the neck, one swaps the rifle to the other shoulder. With oversized haversacks we block the narrow passages. Here are the machine gunners with their boxes and their parts. It is a squeeze. The two columns are trying to pass. One flattens oneself against the walls as much as we can to let the machine gunners through. They are pleased to see the relief party coming up the trench.

– 'Are there many of you?'

– 'No, this is the last, do not worry, is there much further to go?'

– 'Good luck in the line.'

We resume our march. A subtle fresh apple scent, like English sweets, takes us by the throat. Tear gas is still standing in the shell holes. We ensure that our gasmasks are close at hand. By chance the night is as cloudy as can be. We tramp on without seeing our feet. From time to time one of us slips and falls on his hands. Despite the fatigue, some laugh at this.

– 'Have you got water in your bottle?'

– 'Yes, I got some at X.'

– 'Pass me some, I'm thirsty and plonk does not refresh you; if you want you can have some of the booze I have.'

A brief halt, I stoop to put my lips to the can. Fresh water revives me.

– 'Who has water,' asks the *Sous Lieutenant*.

– 'Me, lieutenant.'

– 'Would you give me a little, that would be very kind.'

We stop for a moment to breathe. The liaison officer who, as one of the first occupiers, knows the sector well, warns us: 'It is better not to linger here, the trench passes the intersection of the road-X and X. This is frequently shelled. The area is quite unhealthy.'

One picks up the bags once again, and the more one feels the end must be near, the more fatigue encircles your loins and shoulders, and the more you walk fast. One has the impression that the upper part of the body is really too heavy in comparison with the lower part.

– 'Well,' comes the voice of my friend from behind, 'we complained when we were in Artois, but this time it will beat that record.'

– 'There is the ravine held by the brigade,' said the guide, 'is everyone following?'

The trench passes down through a steep slope. We paddle with muddy knees. We need to make long strides; water splashes us: 'Go carefully, dammit! Or you will be going for a swim!'

On the other side of the ravine we climb back up, and the trench becomes almost dry.

– 'Put out all cigarettes, extinguish your cigarettes ...'

– We do not see why.

– 'Put out your cigarette, do you hear me! it's unfortunately necessary.'

The man carefully extinguishes his cigarette and puts it back in his pocket.

– 'We will go over the parapet,' said the lieutenant, 'the dug out of the Colonel is to be found a few hundred meters on the left.'[32]

Back on the British front preparations now began for the Battle of Ginchy, planned to follow on from the taking of Guillemont and required in order to complete the capture of positions which would give observation over the German third line. This was in readiness for a general attack in mid-September, for which the Anglo-French armies had been planning since early August. As a diversion, attacks were launched against German positions on the Ancre, opposite Beaumont Hamel. Arthur Adam was a captain in the 1st Battalion Cambridgeshire Regiment, and he wrote home on 7 September describing his brigade's role in this supporting action. His letter reveals a grudging respect for the German soldier as a fighter:

Again we have I hope a few days' repose after a most extraordinarily strenuous fortnight, culminating on the 3rd in a big battle, in which we took part, in the case of my company a rather subsidiary part, but quite unpleasant enough. It has been an extremely interesting period, some of it horrible beyond description so I won't describe, some of it rather amusing than otherwise; and our regiment ... did everything it had to do (which is it is true not a tremendous amount) quite well. I feel greatly tempted to talk more than I should,

The French war writer Pierre Mac Orlan, who wrote of his experiences on the Somme.

but mustn't. Anyhow my respect for the Bosche as a sticker and efficient soldier has gone up, but as a gentleman I think less of him than heretofore. Anyway he knows quite well that it is better to kill than to wound; and maybe he should be respected for it. It was a very enormous battle, but by no means wholly successful, and I suppose probably these shows never are completely so. But the whole business was extremely strange to me, and as a sort of introduction to the business of war as opposed to sitting in trenches … quite good; only it didn't make me think the job any less difficult or less unpleasant than I imagined… . We are now in a wood, in tents and huts and at last it isn't raining; so life is very cheerful; but it generally does.[33]

On 10 September he wrote of his quiet pride in the fact that he and his men had been tested in battle and had not been found wanting. Again, the mutual bonds of respect within the battalion are evident:

We are all feeling rather pleased with ourselves as the result of the war, and I shall go up next time with a very great confidence in my gallant fellows. And the CO is still extraordinarily good, especially in times of war, and becomes more and more a delightful man as the battalion grows more to his liking. I find him always most affable and sympathetic.[34]

The British also had what might be termed 'subject' peoples in their ranks. Let us not forget that the Easter Rising in Dublin in 1916 had, for the first time in this war, raised a serious question mark over the loyalty of southern Irishmen to Britain's cause. How would their loyalties be expressed during the Battle of the Somme? Captain Thomas Kettle of the Royal Dublin Fusiliers was a leading Irish Nationalist. He had joined the Dublins in 1914, when Belgium was attacked, to fight, in his words, not for England but for small nations. Like Adam, Kettle expressed sentiments of pride in regard to his own men, and his loyalty to them was his first concern. He wrote of moving up into the line on 8 September, prior to the Battle of Ginchy:

We are moving up to-night into the battle of the Somme. The bombardment, destruction and bloodshed are beyond all imagination, nor did I ever think the valour of simple men could be quite as beautiful as that of my Dublin Fusiliers. I have had two chances of leaving them – one on sick leave and one to take a staff job. I have chosen to stay with my comrades. I am calm and happy but desperately anxious to live… . The big guns are coughing and smacking their shells, which sound for all the world like over-head express trains, at anything from 10 to 100 per minute on this sector; the men are grubbing and an odd one is writing home. Somewhere the Choosers of the Slain are touching, as in our Norse story they used to touch, with invisible wands those who are to die… .[35]

Educated at University College, Dublin, a Barrister, a Member of Parliament, poet, journalist and Professor of National Economics at the National University, Dublin, Kettle was to be killed in action on the following day, 9 September 1916, at the age of 32. If nothing else, his death illustrates the calibre of young men which Great Britain was losing in this dreadful conflict; men who were potential future leaders of their country, men who would be difficult to replace, and for whose loss the post-war world would be all the poorer.

Second Lieutenant Arthur Conway Young was an English officer in the Royal Irish Fusiliers, like the Dublins also part of the 16th Irish Division, which was raised in the south. In spite of the inevitable question marks over its loyalty, the division proved it was one of the best the British had on the Somme, and its fighting quality was superb. Young writes with frankness in a letter home of his own personal fears and doubts when ordered into the attack, but yet at the same time the letter illustrates how his depression vanished at the moment of the advance, to be replaced by the exhilaration of being part of an enormous common enterprise:

It was about 4 o'clock in the afternoon when we first learned that we should have to take part in the attack on Ginchy. Now, Auntie, you expect me to say at this point in my narrative that my heart leapt with joy at the news and that the men gave three rousing cheers, for that's the sort of thing you read in the papers. Well, even at the risk of making you feel ashamed of me, I will tell you the whole truth and confess that my heart sank within me when I heard the news. I had been over the top once already that week, and knew what it was to see men dropping dead all round me, to see men blown to bits, to see men writhing in pain, to see men running round and round gibbering, raving mad. Can you wonder therefore that I felt a sort of sickening dread of the horrors which I knew we should all have to go through? Frankly, I was dismayed. But, Auntie, I know you will think the more of me when I tell you, on my conscience, that I went into action that afternoon, not with any hope of glory, but with the absolute certainty of death... .

We were ordered to move up into the front line to reinforce the Royal Irish Rifles... . The bombardment was now intense. Our shells bursting in the village of Ginchy made it belch forth smoke like a volcano. The Hun shells were bursting on the slope in front of us. The noise was deafening. I turned to my servant O'Brien, who has always been a cheery, optimistic soul, and said, 'Well, O'Brien, how do you think we'll fare?' and his answer was for once not encouraging. 'We'll never come out alive, sir!' was his answer. Happily we both came out alive, but I never thought we should at the time. It was at this moment, just as we were debouching on to the scragged front line of trench, that we beheld a scene which stirred and thrilled us to the bottommost depths of our souls. The great charge of the Irish Division had begun, and we had come up in the nick of time... . Between the outer fringe of Ginchy and the front line of our own trenches is No Man's Land – a wilderness of pits, so close together that you could ride astraddle the partitions between any two of them. As you look half-right, obliquely along No Man's Land, you behold a great host of yellow-coated men rise out of the earth and surge forward and upward in a torrent – not in extended order, as you might expect, but in one mass, – I almost said a compact mass. The only way I can describe the scene is to ask you to picture five or six columns of men marching uphill in fours, with about a hundred yards between each column. Now conceive those columns being gradually disorganised, some men going off to the right, and others to the left to avoid shell-holes. There seems to be no end to them. Just when you think the flood is subsiding, another wave comes surging up the beach towards Ginchy. We joined in on the left. There was no time for us any more than the others to get into extended order. We formed another stream, converging on the others at the summit. By this time we were all wildly excited. Our shouts and yells alone must have struck terror into the Huns, who were firing their machine-guns down the slope. But there was no wavering in the Irish host. We couldn't run. We advanced at a steady walking pace, stumbling here and there, but going ever onward and upward. That numbing dread had now left me completely. Like the others, I was intoxicated with the glory of it all. I can remember shouting and bawling to the men of my platoon, who were only too eager to go on.[36]

Young's experience of combat was paralleled by that of countless others, not just on the Somme but in warfare of different generations – fear, anxiety and tension before the event were replaced by calm efficiency and even in some cases enjoyment once battle had actually been joined. Young was the son of pacifist parents, and made no secret of his own dislike of war, stating that the Somme had proved the American General Sherman's adage that 'War is all Hell'. Yet at the same time he was fiercely proud of his own men, and of his regiment's part in the battle.

Second Lieutenant Edward Falby, 1st/4th Battalion Loyal North Lancashire Regiment, who was killed in action on 9 September 1916 in Hop Alley, between Delville Wood and Ginchy.

Another British officer in action near here was Captain Gilbert Nobbs, who on 9 September was serving with the 6th Battalion London Regiment when he was seriously wounded and taken prisoner in the battle for Leuze Wood (known as 'Lousy Wood'). His account neatly captures both the furious adrenaline rush of battle, and the moment of realisation when finally he was hit:

I jumped into a shell-hole and found myself within ten yards of my objective. My three remaining runners jumped in alongside of me. They were Arnold, Dobson and Wilkinson. Arnold was done for. He looked up at me with eyes staring and face blanched, and panted out that he could go no farther, and I realized that I could count on him no more. I glanced to the left, just in time to see three Germans not five yards away, and one after the other jump from a shell-hole which formed a sort of bay in their trench, and run away… .

I yelled to the men: 'Get ready to charge, they are running. Come on! Come on!' I jumped out of the shell-hole, and they followed me. Once again I was mad. I saw nothing. I heard nothing. I wanted to kill, kill! Pf-ung! 'Oh, my God! I'm hit! I'm blind!' I was wounded! I was blind! But the moments that followed are clear in my memory. The brain shocked by a blow works quickly and actively in its excited effort to hold its own. I was quite conscious and thinking clearly. I knew what had happened and what would happen. I remembered every detail. My head at the moment was inclined to the right, for I was shouting to the men. Like a flash, I remembered that about fifty yards to the left of me there was a 'German strongpoint' still occupied by the Germans. A bullet had entered my left temple; it must have come from a sniper in that strongpoint. The bullet had passed clean through my head. I thought it had emerged through my right temple. I was mistaken on that point, for I found some days later that it had emerged through the centre of my right eye. I remember distinctly clutching my head and sinking to

Officers and sergeants of the 59th Company Machine Gun Corps, out of the line following the Battle of Ginchy. The company was commanded with great gallantry on 9 September by Captain Herbert Mason (*seated second nearest the camera*), who was subsequently awarded the Military Cross. After the war he would go on to become a noted film and theatre director. The machine gun is a captured German trophy.

the ground, and all the time I was thinking, 'So this is the end, the finish of it all; shot through the head, mine is a fatal wound.'[37]

Nobbs, like Ian Fraser in the preceding chapter, would need to make a new life for himself after the war, without his sight, but in the present for him came the immediate challenge of survival in a German POW camp. His next of kin meanwhile had been told that he had died, and had received a telegram of condolence from the War Office. It was a month before they learned the truth. Captain Nobbs was eventually repatriated to England in December 1916.

South of the Somme, the French had made such good progress that General Micheler had ordered the Tenth Army to extend the offensive south from Barleux to Chilly. The front south of the river moved eastward in pace with the line to the north until it pushed across the railway from Peronne to Roye and got near the main road to Roye and Noyon. When the forces fighting on the north bank reached the Bapaume road, they were within range of Mont St Quentin, due north of and protecting Peronne, which now became the French objective. On both banks of the river there was terrific fighting. On 10 September Paul Dubrulle, another officer in the French *8e Régiment d'Infanterie*, went into the attack for the first time on the Somme, near Maurepas. He moved up through country which had already borne witness to bitter fighting. On his way through the village he passed the château, the once splendid building now an utter ruin. Moving beyond it, worse sights were to meet his eyes:

I am finally out of this heartbreaking chaos. My heart relaxes and breathes. But soon I encounter a horror even more intense. At the end of the village, a grim picture presented itself to me. In this village, the ruins hid the most poignant horror, the sight of corpses; they were spread across the ground. The fighting had been atrocious, everywhere Germans lay sprawled. On the right I take a dirt road, and arrive at the famous sunken lane. Upon leaving it, a vision of horror stands before me. Taking advantage of this natural defensive position, the enemy had put up a fierce resistance: our soldiers had to capture its bays one by one, in a fight with grenades. The terrain had not yet been cleared. At every step, by the edge of the road and in the holes, lay corpses, horrible, blackened, swollen, and mutilated by terrible injuries; here and there, detached limbs and heads added further to the tragic tableau. The ground was covered with war materials in huge quantities: rifles, machine-guns, boxes and bandoliers of cartridges, grenades, tools, knapsacks, coats, helmets and berets lay scattered in a heartbreaking mess. I contemplate for a moment the field of horror, and I pass on, diverting my gaze away.

We advance through the trench named Boyau Dorme. This trench was conquered step by step, and displays the same tableau of horror. To this painful feeling, soon an

Dead German soldiers litter the ground in the position known as Le Chemin Creux, after a French bombardment.

intense fatigue was added. Walking became difficult. The trench narrows, we crouch at every step, it is not deep and forces us to walk doubled over; it is crowded: a company of the 33rd is held in reserve here. The men loiter or lie sleeping, and we do our best to step over them amid indignant protests.

We arrived before Moltke Trench. A new difficulty stops us for a moment: we must capture Brody Trench, and yet more trenches in this direction. So now it is a race to see who will prevail, under the rain of bullets and shells. But we had such troubles in the narrow defile that this problem seems minimal, with satisfaction we go up into the free air and forward, by the grace of God![38]

Now Dubrulle came upon evidence of new German tactics, a sign that they were beginning to try to hold their front line more lightly. A few weeks earlier, at the end of August, the German commander von Falkenhayn had been replaced by Field Marshal Paul von Hindenburg and his subordinate Erich Ludendorff. It was a vote of no confidence in von Falkenhayn's policy of attempting to win back every piece of lost ground at whatever the cost. Ludendorff's tactical doctrine was to be more flexible in defence, and Dubrulle describes what this meant on the ground:

Always the same horrors: war material, corpses and human remains lie scattered around. We cross Moltke Trench. Immediately my attention was attracted by a new spectacle. In front of Brody Trench, the terrain is dotted with a multitude of rectangular holes, arranged randomly and looking vaguely like a series of lines. I wondered what this could be, and our guide gave me an explanation. This is a new Boche tactic. Now, when they occupy a defensive line, they place these outposts intended to break up our attacks or at least to slow their progress. For this to succeed, they rely especially upon surprise. They avoid digging continuous trenches which would easily be discovered by aerial photographs. They replace them with a series of small, isolated holes: one to two meters long, half a meter wide. They also take all possible measures to keep them hidden: the holes do not have a raised parapet, the excavated earth is scattered over a wide area, and their opening is covered with a tent, the colour of which blends beautifully with the grey earth. They have infantry and machine-guns, and these, in absolute stillness, lie slyly awaiting the big moment.

These lines of holes were the outposts of Brody Trench. Did they cause us a lot of trouble when we removed the enemy from that position? I do not know, but I could see that their new scheme was costly to the Germans. Each hole was occupied by one, two, three corpses. And there were hundreds and hundreds of these holes. I did not prolong my inspection, for the horror of these holes was too great, and then, it was necessary to move on. I climbed the ridge, I crossed Brody Trench and after crossing the plateau, I arrived safely at the first line.[39]

The next major effort on the French front was to come two days later, on 12 September, and it witnessed another significant success with the capture of Bouchavesnes. The French here were confronted by two parallel lines of trenches, the first position running through Frégicourt, Le Priez Farm and Marrières Wood, and the second running along the Peronne–Bapaume Road about two kilometres behind the first and linking Rancourt, Feuillancourt and Bouchavesnes. Dubrulle was again in action here, and recounts how the morale of the Germans in his sector was completely shattered, and the survivors made for

This photo is a trophy of war. A note on the reverse states that it was found at Le Kazino, a German command post captured by the French *21e Régiment d'Infanterie* on 8 September 1916.

pathetic figures in their abject surrender, some offering pipes or waterbottles as trophies to their captors, others kneeling and begging for mercy in broken French. The French line was pushed out now beyond the Peronne–Bapaume road, and the advance left Combles isolated as a German salient, with ground to the north held by the British and to the south by the French. One French soldier, writing fifteen years later, remembered this action:

On September 12th the usual scenario came up: regulating watches, communicating the H Hour, partially breaking the parapet, designation at aims: for my section 1800 meters roughly the left horn of Anderlu Wood, or what remained of it, and then 'bayonets ready' and 'go ahead'! Two big shells burst out in the air in front of us, it was the agreed sign, it was H Hour, the jump towards the unknown, for some of us towards death.

From a glance on the right and on the left, I was glad to see my section following me at five or six meters exactly as if they were at drill. On each side, the rest of the company drew its line that other units prolonged indefinitely. Whatever you think of the war, it was a real show to see three divisions attacking at the same time, thousands of bayonets shining above human waves and their columns in an intense roar. The bullets struck here and there in front of us, taking off a little dust like a light wreath of smoke [which] quickly disappeared. A few comrades fell down, the whole of a group vanished in the explosion of a huge shell. The enemy artillery reacted a little, our artillery barrage lengthened. The sacks were heavy, the ground difficult with shell holes. However, the progression was fast, the enemy trench could now be seen from the place where a few gunshots sparked off, the machine guns stopped. We were going to cross the trench and keep on; the cleaners armed with knives, revolvers [and] handgrenades were going to do their work. A great big German stood in front of me on his levelled trench, the extreme point of my bayonet was less than 50 centimeters from his chest, he was raising his arms, begging for his children, I took my rifle down and ordered the enemies surrendering to go to the back lines. They hastened unequipped, with their hands on their necks, between our columns, one by one. Some of our men, whom I had no time to watch, finished, with one bullet, the capture of a neutralised enemy.[40]

Louis Botti was an officer in the *1e Regiment de Marche de Zouaves*, which was allotted the task of attacking positions south of Combles on the same day. Botti was badly wounded in this incident, and wrote of his experiences afterwards:

Paul Ménard, *25e Régiment d'Infanterie*. Wounded near Chilly, he died in hospital at Hargicourt on 14 September 1916.

We are within 20 metres of a perfectly buried defence, unknown to us, which covers our first objective, across the width of the plateau, the Tranchée de l'Hopital.... A hiss; a pain in the thigh: I am hit ... The tirailleurs, stopped by the barrage of grenades, lay down ... The Boches see them and fire at this target ... Three times I try to gather the tirailleurs; three times they get up again; three times the fire of the enemy immobilizes them.... Larue, the second lieutenant of the company of Billeron, eyes fixed on me and hand held high, devotes himself to the same efforts....

Boches emerge from the Tranchée de l'Hopital, bareheaded, without equipment, without weapons, and with hands raised and run across our line.... We are not dealing with anything more serious than a line of skirmishers' holes in front of which we are held up. Without being ordered to do so, Lachaise and I leave for a reconnaissance, circling round not a few of the enemy, with neither caution nor haste ... Any sense of danger had certainly not settled upon us. The position does not extend beyond the south slope of the plateau: it is covered, against any action from the flank, by a vast hole established at right angles to its axis.

At our approach, the five Boches who occupy this hole raise their arms. With a revolver in the fist, and great bawlings of 'Heraus!' we indicate to them to leave their entrenchment; they are hesitant in their attitude and move no more than if they were statues, however, their neighbours continue fiercely answering the fire of the tirailleurs ... It is necessary to finish it, for those who seem to want to surrender as much as with the others, and we decide on the field to send for the grenadiers, to take the position from behind, and for machine guns, to cut down all those who emerge from the holes ... In the centre of the position, an officer, bare headed, fires carefully with a carbine. I empty a cartridge from my revolver at him, 30 metres away, it is too far and completely out of my range.

I see Berthelot: I search for his section ... The second wave debouches on the rear quarter: bayonets held high, at a walking pace, they are stopped at 80 metres short of the tirailleurs. A grenadier, the only one remaining or the only one who answers the appeal of Lachaise, throws his grenades with force: alas! They do not burst ... I have little hope for my guns ... I retire to choose an emplacement for them ... I see one of the Boches who had shouted 'kamarade' plunge his arms, one after the other, into the hole, pull out a grenade, prime it and throw it down in front of him, two steps from Lachaise who remained above him …

I shout: 'Lachaise, beware!'

Some fire, and some smoke; I spring up, I unload my revolver four times point-blank in their faces: with the final shot, the man slides into his hole, bulging eyes, dead before I fired …

Lachaise is there … How? I cannot explain it!

I move back to wait for my machine guns …

My team, kneeling in the rear behind me, are under the fire of the machine guns from the Bois de l'Hopital … Roux shouts to me that he is mortally wounded …

… A great shock runs up the left leg … I roll into a shell crater … That's it … Relief and fear… .

Bertrand howls: 'My Lieutenant, I have a bullet through the chest but I will bandage you all the same!'

I pass him my packet of dressings … He undresses me … and he is worried, I am afraid that he will bandage me badly … Lieutenant Bonnet comes into sight with a rifle, charging alone over the shell holes. I call out: 'Come here and bandage me, Bonnet!'

I cannot do any more than think of being taken away. I call for stretcher-bearers. Two black men come, they hesitate to take me… .

I see, now, white handkerchiefs rising from shell holes … too late, and tirailleurs springing frantically down into them with the bayonet.

Now we descend by the opposite slope under the fire of machine guns and under the barrage that the Boche has unleashed; the vision of shattered trees: the shells which burst so near that it seems to me that their explosions are going to pulverize us …

And then my two wounded stretcher-bearers halt, at the departure point of the attack …

The men go down into a hole – like a freshly dug grave, just big enough, in doing so making me suffer dreadfully …

I feel I am slipping away …

I wake up, covered with earth, waiting resignedly, under the full fire of the barrage, for a shell to close this pit over me for ever …

And this was the calvary common to all the wounded: the shaking of the stretcher carried for miles through the shell holes; the appalling transport over the dilapidated roads, in the mule cart on the way to the rear; toward life rediscovered, with its joys – and its sorrows.[41]

From testimony like this, there can be little doubt that by mid-September the morale of the German units opposite the French in the southern part of the Somme sector was crumbling, following blow after heavy blow. The French for their part were in buoyant mood. Another Frenchman transferred to the Somme from Verdun was Lieutenant Fonsagrive, who was serving with a heavy artillery battery. Fonsagrive's first impression of the Somme battlefield was one of wonder at the sheer scale of the destruction and at the incredible number of mangled, fly-blown corpses of German soldiers, which he encountered in large quantities as he moved up through former enemy strongholds to his new battery position. The French clearly believed that they had scored a crushing victory over the Germans at Verdun, and were now about to do the same thing again here. So rare

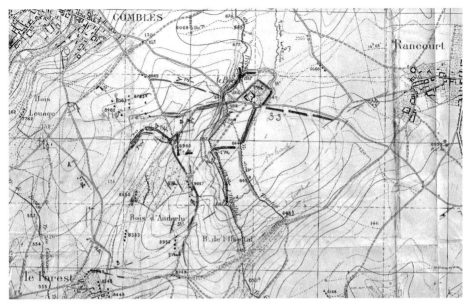

A French army trench map showing the position of the *Tranchee de l'Hopital* ('Hospital Trench').

was combat fatigue or disillusionment in Fonsagrive's unit that he goes out of his way to describe the single individual affected by it, and to point out that the incident was an isolated one:

> The battery is going through a period of good fortune. It has suffered no loss either of gunners or drivers. The task of the latter is neither convenient nor free of dangers. The crossing of Maurepas is particularly daunting and the area around Louage Wood is not a place of pleasure, especially at night. To get up to our position, the ammunition wagons must avoid serious obstacles: trenches filled with slime or deep shell holes. The track, since it often rains, is but a cesspool where the poor horses wear themselves out pulling wagons and the limbers loaded with artillery shells.
>   – 'You see,' comrade S. told me one evening, 'I can not stand it; this is not the place of a father who has three children.'
>   – 'You have only two since the third died.'
>   – 'But I had the third; it must count!'
>   – 'If you say so! Why are you telling me this?'
>   – 'Because you have to help me get satisfaction; I want to go to the regimental train; I am the oldest: it is my right.'
>   – 'What do you want me to do, man?'
>   – 'It is necessary that you talk to the officers; I can not go on with replenishing, I'm tired and I am miserable.'
>   Yet he had no right to be demoralised. Fortunately the young, those of the gun battery, hold good.[42]

For Fonsagrive and other French troops on the Somme, morale undoubtedly received a major boost in mid-September from the news of the recapture of Fort Douaumont by their

A German army locomotive peppered with bullet and shrapnel holes, pictured after its capture by the French army on the Somme.

compatriots at Verdun. It also had a commensurate demoralising effect on the Germans, as a conversation which he reports with a captured enemy officer confirms. Fonsagrive was also shrewd enough to realise that the spirits of the average French soldier rose and fell according to the barometer of more mundane issues than, for example, the progress of the war. Later he writes:

> The shelter of the NCOs is close to the kitchen and the passage of infantry that are in reserve. Sometimes poor devils stop, tired. A quarter of coffee or a bowl of broth restores them. Morale often depends upon the state of the stomach. When it has received adequate treatment, morale returns. The men of the battery also urge the cooks not to neglect their work. But in general our men do not have too much to complain about. They have a sufficient standard of food and most receive packages which contain highly enviable supplements of food.[43]

Thus by mid-September there was mounting evidence of a sense of crisis in the German army in the west. The French crossing of the Peronne–Bapaume road caused considerable disquiet, and the enemy response was to bring three new divisions into the line here in order to shore up his positions. Visiting the Somme late that summer, Ludendorff, who had replaced von Falkenhayn, had criticised the inflexibility of the defence there. Without doubt, he stated, the Germans had fought too doggedly, clinging too resolutely to the mere holding of ground. The question now, as the allies tightened the screw on the Germans on the Somme, was which side would break first. Would the British, who were able to bring increasing material pressure to bear, and the French who were growing in confidence with each new victory, succeed in forcing the Germans to make a mistake, or would new German tactics mean that the defensive battle could be prolonged, thus increasing the likelihood that the allies would be worn out by the effort?

Chapter Five

The Terror of Flers

The battle of wills on the Somme was now reaching its denouement. Which side would crack first? Undoubtedly the Germans had been badly shaken by the fighting of the previous two months, but to a lesser extent so had the British. Only the French remained relatively buoyant by this point. Mid-September found the allies on the Somme preparing for a major new offensive. There were a number of reasons for this. Firstly, some evidence from German prisoners suggested that morale on that side might be weakening, to the point at which a breakthrough (eschewed by Haig earlier in the summer) might now be possible. At the same time there was a growing quantity of photographic evidence to show that the Germans were engaged in the construction of new, stronger positions in the rear of their front line; increasing the pressure might disrupt this. Additionally, new troops were now becoming available on the allied side. Fresh British formations such as the Guards Division had arrived on the Somme for the first time, and new Commonwealth battalions further strengthened Haig's hand; with the winding down of the battle at Verdun the French were also able to bring fresh troops to their front. Finally, for the British there was the tantalising prospect of using a new secret weapon, as yet untried, but which promised great things.

Thus the third and final general offensive launched by the British on the Somme – the Battle of Flers-Courcelette – was to begin on 15 September. For the fresh troops moving up to take their positions for the attack, there could be no doubt of what they were about to become involved in. A stark scene met the eyes of George Everitt, a Suffolk man serving with the 1st/24th Battalion London Regiment, who recalled going up through Mametz Wood, verdant green and in full leaf when the Welsh attacked it in July, but now just a collection of shattered stumps pointing skywards:

> I remember going through Fricourt on our way to Mametz. That was a sight. I don't think there was a brick or stone left in that village. There was rubble everywhere, and not a sign of life, except for our own stuff on the roads. The bricks and stones from the battered villages were used to make up roads, but it was no sooner done than there were shell holes all over the place again … Beyond was the wood, if you could call it a wood. The land here was sort of rolling upwards, and there wasn't a leaf to be seen on the trees. There was scarcely a tree. They were just like a lot of huge splinters sticking up in the ground. Everything else was grey and bare and a mass of craters and wire entanglements. The rims of the shell holes reminded me of grey waves, rolling down towards you.[1]

Everitt was a typically stoical British tommy, and his simple philosophy would stand him in good stead in the terrible days which were to follow:

I do remember a feeling of comradeship, of all being in it together … When I first went in, I thought of what my father used to say: 'We're here today, boy, and gone tomorrow.' But I can't honestly say I felt afraid. I used to think to myself: 'Well, that wouldn't do to be nervous.' I knew we were out there to do a job, and there wasn't any alternative. So I just got on with it. I don't think I was ever very nervous. 'Tis true, that was not a nice feeling, and all sorts of things would go through your mind when I thought about home. I used to wonder whatever would happen if I got popped off. Still, I thought to myself: 'What is to be will be. If you get hit, you get hit.'[2]

The forthcoming battle was significant for a number of reasons. Canadian and New Zealand units joined the fighting on the Somme for the first time here, but more importantly the action will live in history as bearing witness to the first use of tanks in warfare. Haig's objective, as with the previous major British offensives on the Somme, was to break the German line and allow the cavalry through to exploit the opening. The line of the new attack ran from Pozières windmill in the north to the fields south of the village of Flers, and it was here that Haig hoped for his breakthrough. In the end it was not to be, and the offensive became merely another attritional struggle. Anticipation beforehand, however, was extremely high, due mainly to the presence of the tanks, which had for so long been a closely guarded secret. These new mechanical inventions were part of the recently formed Heavy Section Machine Gun Corps (later known as the Tank Corps). Their crews, drawn in the main from the Army Service Corps (drivers) and Machine Gun Corps (gunners) were in buoyant mood and were filled with an eager desire to put their training into practice. They were, on the whole, proud of their machines and wanted more than anything else an opportunity to demonstrate exactly what they were capable of. Robert Tate, a tank driver from the northeast of England, was one of those about to go into action:

The spirit was marvellous … The spirit among the men, and the comradeship was absolutely marvellous. The morale – you couldn't wish for anything higher, amongst

A group of tank crewmen pose proudly for the camera. Although this photograph was taken in 1917, there is a good chance that some of these men were veterans of the action on 15 September 1916. All have been wounded at least once, all wear the sleeve badge of trained tank crew, and one is wearing the ribbon of the Military Medal.

everyone. Of course the point was we didn't know what we were coming up against, we'd never been in action and we were all in very good, high spirits.[3]

The buzz which surrounded the arrival of the tanks was difficult to suppress, and the infantry who were about to accompany them into action were desperate to know more. Second Lieutenant G.P.A. Fildes of the Coldstream Guards was among those troops on the southern flank of the British attack whose ultimate objective was the hamlet of Les Boeufs. The news of the arrival of the iron monsters, the day before the battle, was initially greeted with disbelief in his mess.

Lunch-time found us all ready for a speedy departure from Carnoy, with kits prepared and every preparation made for a strenuous period in the line. With the announcement that lunch was ready came the arrival of an unexpected guest, a subaltern from a sister battalion in our vicinity.

'Come in, come in! We're just dying of boredom. Have you any news?'

The President, acting as host, manoeuvred an empty box into position with his foot. John, the new-comer, gazed round portentously; evidently his manner was intended to impress. One by one we feared the worst.

'Well, I don't know whether you folk will call this news, but it's 24-carat fact,' he announced. 'The hush-hushes are here.'

A groan went up from the assembled party.

'My poor fellow,' exclaimed The President, 'if that's all you can tell us, clear out and report yourself to your MO. We are accustomed to lies these days, but stale ones aren't popular with our battalion.'

At this outburst John grinned benignly, since it denoted the atmosphere he so much desired; then, leaning forward across the table, and emphasising his words with a tattoo from his fork, he delivered his news: 'I may be first cousin to Ananias and all the rest of 'em, but what I tell you is sober fact. I've seen 'em.'

Five pairs of incredulous eyes contemplated him in grave silence.

'Where, if I may ask?' inquired The Captain, in his suavest tones.

'At their depot, not three miles from this dugout. Oh, you may smile! But grinning like a beauty chorus won't alter facts. I've seen 'em and I've had a long talk with one of their pilots.'

'You aren't rotting, are you?' The President's manner showed signs of irresolution.

'Never more serious in my life! They absolutely beat the band. There's two sorts, male and female. The gent carries light quick-firers; the lady, being naturally more talkative, spouts machine-gun bullets. They are said to be proof against anything but a direct hit from a shell, and do four miles an hour along a road – caterpillar driving bands, you know. The crews are priceless; try to make out they are sort of land marines, and jaw about 'His Majesty's Land Ship *Hotstuff*'. They might have been pulling my leg – probably they were – but the Admiral in charge told me they could stroll through the walls of a house or snap a two-foot tree-trunk like a match.'

A long pause greeted this narration, for the news seemed utterly incredible.

'John!' exclaimed The President at last, 'either you are the greatest liar in the British Army, or ...'

'Or?'

But The President remained dumb, his imagination still failing to realise the marvellous alternative. The ensuing pause was ended by the judicial tones of The Captain: 'The yarn would have been quite good enough without your telling us you had seen them.'

'But I have, yesterday afternoon. Come and ask our Adjutant; he was there too.'

'You've seen them!'

'As near as I am to you now. You've my word for it.'

Something in the speaker's tone compelled belief. Then the amazed silence which had fallen upon the party was shattered by a crash upon the table as Raymond sprang up with a terrific yell.

'My godfathers! The Bing Boys are here!'[4]

It was an exclamation redolent of the times in which these young men lived; in referring to the tank crews as 'the Bing Boys', the Guards officer was using a cultural reference guaranteed to amuse and delight anyone of that generation – the comedy *The Bing Boys Are Here* opened in 1916 in the West End, and ran for 378 performances. It was one of the most important musical hits of the London stage during the First World War. Its music remains intensely evocative of those years even now, and its most famous song, *If You Were the Only Girl (in the World)*, is still widely known and recognised today.

That same evening, American NCO Robert Holmes and his men, serving with the 22nd Battalion London Regiment in trenches somewhere near the front line, were startled by a deep and menacing rumbling noise. So afraid of it were they that they cleared their fire bay in anticipation of an attack:

It was getting a little light though heavily misty. We waited, and then out of the gray blanket of fog waddled the great steel monsters that we were to know afterwards as the 'tanks.' I shall never forget it. In the half darkness they looked twice as big as they really were. They lurched forward, slow, clumsy but irresistible, nosing down into shell holes and out, crushing the unburied dead, sliding over mere trenches as though they did not exist. There were five in all. One passed directly over us. We scuttled out of the way, and the men let go a cheer. For we knew that here was something that could and would win battles. The tanks were an absolutely new thing to us. Their secret had been guarded so carefully even in our own army that our battalion had heard nothing of them. But we didn't need to be told that they would be effective. One look was enough to convince us... . the tanks passed beyond us and half-way up to the first line and stopped. Trapdoors in the decks opened, and the crews poured out and began to pile sandbags in front of the machines so that when day broke fully and the mists lifted, the enemy could not see what had been brought up in the night.[5]

The following morning a new chapter in the history of warfare was to be written, but Holmes felt anything but inspired by the prospect of involvement in such a momentous occasion. His account, however, offers a valuable insight into how the role of the padres of the Royal Army Chaplains' Department in battle extended far beyond mere Holy Communion, and also into the weight of responsibility felt by NCOs as well as officers. The objective of the attack was one which had figured in British plans several times before, and which had a grim reputation:

Day dawned, and a frisky little breeze from the west scattered the fog and swept the sky clean. There wasn't a cloud by eight o'clock. The sun shone bright, and we cursed it, for if it had been rainy the attack would not have been made. We made the usual last preparations that morning, such as writing letters and delivering farewell messages; and the latest rooks made their wills in the little blanks provided for the purpose in the back of the pay books. We judged from the number of dead and the evident punishment other divisions had taken there that the chances of coming back would be slim. Around nine o'clock Captain Green gave us a little talk that confirmed our suspicions that the day was to be a hard one. He said, as nearly as I can remember:

British officers waiting in a trench for the order to advance.

> 'Lads, I want to tell you that there is to be a most important battle – one of the most important in the whole war. High Wood out there commands a view of the whole of this part of the Somme and is most valuable. There are estimated to be about ten thousand Germans in that wood and in the surrounding supports. The positions are mostly of concrete with hundreds of machine guns and field artillery. Our heavies have for some reason made no impression on them, and regiment after regiment has attempted to take the woods and failed with heavy losses. Now it is up to the 47th Division to do the seemingly impossible. Zero is at eleven. We go over then. The best of luck and God bless you.'

We were all feeling pretty sour on the world when the sky pilot came along and cheered us up. He was a good little man, that chaplain, brave as they make 'em. He always went over the top with us and was in the thick of the fighting, and he had the Military Cross for bravery. He passed down the line, giving us a slap on the back or a hand grip and started us singing. No gospel hymns either, but any old rollicking, good-natured song that he happened to think of that would loosen things up and relieve the tension. Somehow he made you feel that you wouldn't mind going to hell if he was along, and you knew that he'd be willing to come if he could do any good. A good little man! Peace to his ashes. At ten o'clock things busted loose, and the most intense bombardment ever known in warfare up to that time began. Thousands of guns, both French and English, in fact every available gun within a radius of fifteen miles, poured it in. In the Bedlamitish din and roar it was impossible to hear the next man unless he put his mouth up close to your ear and yelled. My ear drums ached, and I thought I should go insane if the racket didn't stop. I was frightfully nervous and scared, but tried not to show it. An officer or a non-com must conceal his nervousness, though he be dying with fright.

The faces of the men were hard-set and pale. Some of them looked positively green. They smoked fag after fag, lighting the new ones on the butts. All through the bombardment Fritz was comparatively quiet. He was saving all his for the time when we should come over. Probably, too, he was holed up to a large extent in his concrete dug-outs. I looked over the top once or twice and wondered if I, too, would be lying there unburied with the rats and maggots gnawing me into an unrecognizable mass. There were moments in that hour from ten to eleven when I was distinctly sorry for myself. The time, strangely enough, went fast – as it probably does with a condemned man in his last hour. At zero minus ten the word went down the line 'Ten to go' and we got to the better positions of the trench and secured our footing on the side of the parapet to make our climb over when the signal came. Some of the men gave their bayonets a last fond rub, and I looked to my bolt action to see that it worked well. I had ten rounds in the magazine, and I didn't intend to rely too much on the bayonet. At a few seconds [before] eleven I looked at my wrist watch and was afflicted again with that empty feeling in the solar plexus. Then the whistles shrilled; I blew mine, and over we went.[6]

Holmes survived the battle, and the war, to return home to the United States. He published his memoir of his service in the British army as *A Yankee in the Trenches*. Interestingly, one of the warmest reviews to appear on its dust jacket came from fellow American Somme veteran – and rival author – Arthur Guy Empey.

Although the tanks allotted to the 47th Division failed to make a great impact in this part of the line, the unit made good progress none the less. Also in this division was Private Leonard Wilkinson of the 15th Battalion London Regiment (Civil Service Rifles), who likewise went over the top on 15 September near High Wood. Wilkinson remembered the tension in the hours leading up to zero hour (for him it was at 6.30am) and the fact that the men had had no sleep as they awaited the order to attack. The rum ration was passed round, and Wilkinson's substantial portion was further augmented by that from men who had abstained. He freely admitted to having had 'plenty', and that this had more than put him in the mood for killing Germans. He wrote of the advance which followed:

We soon reached a crater which was occupied on one side by some German bombers who showed fight but we soon silenced them with a few 'Mills'. As arranged, our companies [sic] advance took us outside the wood whilst the other three companies continued the advance straight through the wood, so luckily for us we were soon in the open and found it much easier going.

Suddenly about 40 yards in front of me I saw a German trench with a machine-gun position on the parapet [and] at the same time some Jerrys came running along the trench to the gun in order to bring it into action. I shouted to the fellows near me drawing their attention to the gun and at the same time I dropped on one knee and fired, the first round missed, the second found its mark, the force of the bullet knocking a German's tin hat off as he sank backwards into the trench, the third also found a billet and the unfortunate man dropped beside his comrade.

By that time our fellows had reached the trench and downed the rest of the gun team so that the gun never fired a shot at us. I reached the trench and jumped in to see the result of my firing and found that I had hit both men in the head and killed them instantly. I had done this with no more feeling than a boy firing with an airgun at a target in the garden, but now I had seen those dead Germans I sobered somewhat and began to take things more seriously.[7]

The issue of rum in the front line was controversial at this time; the temperance movement was strong in Britain, and many civilians abhorred the thought of their soldiers being even slightly the worse for alcohol. Wilkinson continues his frank account with another incident which would have raised eyebrows at the time and which even today has a resonance with controversial recent events in Afghanistan:

> We still moved slowly forward and came upon another trench which held some Jerries; they had already dropped their rifles and offered no resistance. I wanted to use the bayonet but could not bring myself to do it, so I fired a couple of rounds at two yards range into the two nearest to me. This was nothing else but murder, I don't know what made me do it as they could easily have been taken prisoners. I shall never forget the looks on their faces as I pointed my rifle at them, such sickly grins which showed fear, they shrank back before they were shot.[8]

There can be few who would disagree that this is a powerful account, and it begs the question, had excess alcohol played a part in this incident also? Whilst recuperating in hospital later, Wilkinson was remorseful and remembered feeling sorry for the two Germans he had killed out of hand, as well as for their families. It must be added, however, that his diary shows that his feelings towards the enemy hardened once again when he was eventually posted back to the front line.

The greater part of High Wood was still held by the Germans at this point, and the 47th Division's initial objective was to capture the remainder of the wood and its section of the Switch Line trench. After suffering heavy losses, by mid-morning those battalions

After continuous bombardment by both sides, by September the woods on the Somme were little more than ruins.

desperately fighting for possession of the wood had called for and finally received sanction for an artillery barrage on the west and northwest parts. Additionally, a hurricane bombardment by Stokes trench mortars, in which 750 shells were fired in fifteen minutes, was made on the eastern part. The Civil Service Rifles attacked once more after this, and the Germans at last started to surrender. By 1pm the British finally held High Wood. However, although the heavy fighting had died down by mid-day, it was found that remnants of the 140th and 141st Brigades were holding only isolated portions of the German support line. These brigades were not in touch with one another, and between them lay 300–400 yards of trench still strongly held by the enemy. The 21st Battalion London Regiment (First Surrey Rifles), which had been in reserve, was ordered to form a link between these two brigades. At 4.45pm the battalion went forward from behind High Wood, and advanced from the eastern corner in a northeasterly direction in artillery formation, with a fighting strength of 19 officers and 550 other ranks. However, arrangements could not be made for artillery support or adequate covering fire, and as the leading platoons came under observation they were subjected to an intense enemy artillery bombardment and later to heavy rifle and machine-gun fire. Within an hour, and having advanced less than a mile, the First Surreys would lose 134 killed and 373 wounded. The only crumb of consolation for this battalion and others like it was the fact that this thorn in the British side had finally been wrested from German hands.

Captain R.L. Bradley of the 22nd Battalion London Regiment, writing to his mother about his part in the capture of High Wood, gives a good illustration of the power of religious faith in battle conditions. The positive influence of a good padre on the men of his battalion was noted by Holmes (and indeed by other writers who served in the First World War). Although for him this was a result of the charisma of the individual rather than his message, for others sincere religious conviction was very much an adjunct to morale, as Bradley states:

> Now it's all over and we are back I can think a bit which is what one can't do in a show and it strikes me how little during it all one thought of and lived in God. There seemed to be so much to do, keeping cheery and bucking up and steadying the men that somehow one didn't live quite enough in Him. Of course He knows there's not much time for a prayer and doesn't expect them … [the men were] positively anxious for the Bosch to come over so that they might show him just about how far he'd get if he tried it on. Oh it was a wonderful exhibition of a spirit running right through a company and it's a time I shall remember to my dying day with real gratefulness.[9]

Captain Quentin Walford, 21st Battalion London Regiment. He led his company in the attack on High Wood on 15 September 1916, his servant being killed there that evening. Walford wrote later to the boy's parents: '[He] was a splendid little chap … we all miss him – or rather those remaining in the Company do – very greatly.'

Tanks roll past a watching New Zealander on the way to the front, September 1916.

Even though religious belief was very much a matter for the individual, in those days rates of attendance at church or chapel were far higher than they are today, so we may assume that there were considerable numbers of other men like Bradley (and indeed Hope Bagenal in a previous chapter), who were sustained in battle by their religious convictions.

This was also an important day for the New Zealand Division, in its first major action on the Western Front. This division was one of the smartest in France and as the war progressed it came to be regarded as something of an elite formation. Advancing on a front stretching between High Wood and Flers, the New Zealand Division was tasked with capturing the heavily defended Switch Line. Major C.H. Weston was serving as a company commander with the 1st Battalion Wellington Regiment on the New Zealand divisional front, and provides us with a good description of the scene here, as the news reached him of the formation's successful advance:

Good news began to filter back with the wounded, and that welcome sign showed itself of German prisoners being escorted down the road past our bivouac. The Taranaki Company was to be in Battalion Reserve for the first part of the Battle, and early in the morning was called upon to provide two parties, one of twenty-five other ranks under Lieutenant McIsaac to carry grenades, and the other of forty to assist in making a new road from Mametz to Longueval. Then at 1pm the remainder of the Company received orders to move to Green Dump near Longueval and there provide more Carrying Parties. It was, however, to retain its organization, so that it would be ready to fight on the following day if required. A Dump is a spot where food, water, stores or munitions of any kind are collected, and to Green Dump, on the British side of the Crest that looked down the slope to Flers, we wended our way.

Marching as on a road was, of course, impossible across fields or in shell-pitted country. The Dump was a scene of activity, with a big Dressing Station close by to add to its importance, and not long after piling some of their gear and having something to eat, two parties of fifty-seven and fifty-one, under Second Lieutenants Gray and Farrington, disappeared over the hill, laden with barbed wire and other R.E. Stores, to build Strongpoints beyond Switch Trench.

As I had nothing to do after lunch, I followed in the direction they had gone. The high ground, by Advanced Brigade Headquarters in Carlton Trench, gave a clear view of the Battle Ground, Delville Wood on the right, Switch Trench and the ill-fated High Wood on the left. Flers itself was hidden in the fold of the ground, but the ridge between it and the village of Eaucourt l'Abbaye to the west showed up plainly. The German communication trench, Goose Alley, ran back along this ridge from Flers Trench to the uncompleted Gird Trench that the enemy had partially dug to protect the village of Gueudecourt. I walked over part of the country we had just won. The tide of battle had ebbed, and in front of me a sullen, angry barrage from the German Howitzers was playing on the trenches that the enemy knew by now he had lost. Here and there were laden parties in single file threading their way through the barrage, and, as one could see through the glasses, paying the toll of thoroughfare as they went. In smaller numbers were stretcher-bearers and wounded men painfully struggling back. But the ground itself caught and held one's attention. Shells from our largest guns had burst in it for weeks past, and so closely had they fallen that two men could not walk abreast on unbroken ground for more than a few yards. In the captured trenches lay German dead side by side and in heaps, while scattered everywhere were unburied corpses. Above all floated the stench of carrion flesh.

Later in the afternoon, Company Headquarters moved a little way down the hill from Green Dump into Check Trench. Thence I was summoned to Battalion Headquarters to stand by for orders. A wonderful cup of tea and forty winks carried us Company Commanders on till midnight, when the Commanding Officer came back from Brigade. The [New Zealand] Rifle Brigade, with some English troops and a Tank, had captured Flers village and, reinforced by some Companies of the 2nd Battalion of our Regiment, were holding on. Our Battalion had to continue the advance at 9.35 a.m. and take Grove Alley, another German communication trench from Flers Trench to Factory Corner and Gird Trench. Grove Alley lay between Flers and Goose Alley, and its capture would assist a further advance against the latter trench. Hawke's Bay and Ruahine were to attack, with Wellington West Coast in Support and Taranaki in Reserve.[10]

Tanks also supported the 15th (Scottish) Division's successful attack on Martinpuich, at the centre of the battle line. One of its members, Private Edgar Robinson of the Royal Scots, was clearly not yet familiar with the term 'tank', when he wrote:

We had a lot of trouble with the Germans at Contalmaison before we got them out, and then we took a village called Martinpuich, about a mile from our firing line, on the 15th September. We went over the top and it was 'Hell' all the way, but those motor machines helped us a lot. The Germans were fairly astounded at them, as they could not damage them, however hard they tried. They started throwing bombs at them, but that did not affect them, so they were thrown off their mark, and we were giving them something for running, only their machine-guns played on us terribly. But when we get the Germans from behind they don't half get along. We had just reached Martinpuich, and were digging ourselves in for safety, when a machine-gun turned on us, and as luck would have it I got one just above the left knee.[11]

A German officer named Friedrich Frerk provided a graphic account of the fighting at Flers from the German perspective. Frerk undoubtedly served on the Western Front with the German army, and gained the Iron Cross for his bravery. His book about the Somme offensive, published just as the battle was closing, suggests that he was a participant in it, yet oddly he ascribes the wrong date to the attack on Flers. Was Frerk truly an eyewitness to the events he describes? If he was not, then he certainly knew someone who was, for his account contains a remarkable amount of detail, even down to the weather conditions that morning which are confirmed by other sources:

Private Archibald Nugent, 1st Canterbury Regiment, New Zealand Expeditionary Force. He was badly wounded in the right knee on 16 September, and his right leg was subsequently amputated.

> … white, flowing fog was lingering in the positions of friend and enemy alike when the new day dawned. The early sun tried to penetrate the wall of mist, but she lacked the strength, she only coloured it, and bathed it in luminous magenta. The immense barrage had not decreased, the iron hurricane roared continually. In the trench outposts, the drowsy German heads lifted to stretch themselves a little whilst still under the protection of the fog, and to look to see what new thing the 'Tommy' would probably bring forth. The barrage had abated a little bit, but the veil of mist is too thick, the eye cannot penetrate it, even now. But, nevertheless, in the end, the sun won; she struggled through the humid smoke to the ground and flashed beaming about the furrowed, exhausted land, shone in every hollow, the corner of every trench, every hole, as if to wish everyone good morning. The approach was free again, the fire of the hostile artillery had become quite weak.
>
> The sentries there in the trenches suddenly rubbed their eyes, shook their heads to convince themselves that they really still lived, and stared with big eyes again forwards, shuddering with bewilderment. There it crept, rumbling and wheezing over shell craters and ditches, around obstacles and enemy corpses and fluttered and swung like a drunkard, closer and closer. It directed its two great staring eyes upon our troops, who lay as if frozen there in a ditch, and did not know what to do. All at once the staring eyes flashed red with lava, and vomited shells.[12]

Frerk writes so fluently that even in translation his words have an almost poetic ring to them. He captures well the sense almost of resignation to their fate – coupled with grim determination – which often characterised German soldiers in this battle. There is also interesting detail here about one tank in particular, which he calls the *Spuk von Flers* – the 'Terror of Flers':

Also a sharp volley of lead hammered into the ditches of the unsuspecting men. And not one, but two of the fabulous creatures wobbled closer and sowed death and downfall in the German ranks. However, those in the trenches had forgotten the fear of the previous ghastly days and nights. Such a monster with superhuman strength could probably surprise them, but never put them to flight. A mad fire pelted down on the colossi, which swayed, however, freely on their way. And the machine guns hammered, and hand grenades roared, but the ungainly cart was invulnerable, his mass fire drumming down all around. However, behind him the English storm waves surged near, around, by, finally to break through. The colossi rolled further on their terrible journey through the devastated area. Nobody held them, because nobody could hold them. Since communication with the artillery was lost, no one was able to inform them. Thus after clearing the first German position, the devil's cars rumbled in to the village of Flers to clear the way for the English infantry. And they cleared the way and took Flers and wobbled along the wide road which leads through Ligny-Thilloy to Bapaume. But, 'it's a long way to Tipperary'; they did not reach Ligny and certainly came nowhere near to Bapaume as some maybe had thought they would. Finally, immediately behind Flers they discovered the German artillery, which dealt immediately thoroughly and affectionately with the horrific machines. Howling German shells whizzed through the air, ploughed with a crash into the hard armoured skin, they smashed and scattered them like matchwood, until the monsters – wrecked and blazing – gave up their 'breakthrough journey'. Only one man, just one, poor mechanic arose at the right time from the inferno and was captured by our men, the others burnt in the blazing gasoline. Such was the grisly end of the 'Terror of Flers'. These were the armoured cars of the 'English Motor Machine Gun Corps' upon which such fantastic hopes had been placed by those beyond the Channel. Not only at Flers,

A rare German photograph of the wreckage of Mk1 Male tank, C1 *Champagne*. On 15 September C1 supported the Canadian attack on Courcelette until it became ditched in a German communication trench.

[but] wherever they appeared, after the modest initial success – caused by surprise – these 'land battle cruisers' became pitiful wrecks. One got stuck helplessly in the German wire barrier, instead of continuing on through it, a second and third reached up to possibly thirty meters on the Guillemont–Combles road to the German trenches nearby and was stopped there by a well-aimed hand grenade. A fourth crept into Leuze Wood and after a short time was on fire, and just the 'Terror of Flers' reached … the first German position only to find an inglorious end behind Flers.[13]

It appears from the detailed work undertaken in recent years by a number of historians that only one man from the Heavy Section was captured on 15 September. He was a member of the crew of tank number 747 (otherwise known as D6), so this may be the true identity of the 'Terror of Flers'. This tank, under the command of Second Lieutenant Legge, passed the eastern edge of Flers and was engaging two German batteries in Gird Trench and Gird Support when it was hit.

One of the most successful of the British attacks on 15 September was made by the Guards Division, setting off from Ginchy and also attacking the eastern side of Flers village. Future British prime minister Harold Macmillan, serving as a subaltern with the Grenadier Guards, would be seriously wounded here. One of the officers of the Irish Guards, Valentine Williams, wrote up his memoirs of this day's action in 1917. Williams writes in the third person, referring to himself as 'the Ensign':

The German shell fire had greatly increased in intensity. They were now laying a barrage over the whole scene of the advance. Our young man found that walking alone over heavy, shell-swept ground is a very different thing from sweeping forward with the advancing line, with courage and resolution running, like an electric fluid, from man to man. So he bent his head and started to get over the ground and out of the barrage as hard as he could. Strange and manifold are the encounters of the battlefield. A brief half an hour before, the brown and furrowed slope, up which our Ensign was painfully making his way to the farther ridge beyond which the Guards had disappeared, had been No Man's Land – the desolate tract at which, from the front trenches, one would peer furtively through a periscope. Now it was the highway of the battlefield, strewn with the wastage of the fight, traversed by the lagging steps of the wounded.

There is this vision in our Ensign's memory … an officer with half his tunic torn to ribbons, one bare arm wrapped in bandages protruding from his shirt, bareheaded, livid of face, besmeared with mud and blood. He staggered like a drunkard as he walked straight ahead, falling into shell-holes, heedless of the enemy fire. On one lapel of his tunic the small grenade of the Royal Engineers had survived intact.

'Blown up with some sappers,' he said thickly to our young man, 'lookin' for dressin' station … terrible … terrible, …' and he reeled onward over the broken earth.

Then came a hurrying, stumbling herd of German prisoners, abject, dishevelled, hands above their heads, four strapping Guardsmen, each with a helmet hung to his belt, driving them before them, broad grins on their faces. Now our Ensign had reached the first of those hidden trenches which had brought a burst of unsuspected fire to bear on the advancing Coldstream. The khaki was pretty thick amid the trampled and riven wire, but beyond the Feldgrauen lay in heaps, many still wearing the little round caps and the greatcoats in which they had been sleeping, their arms outspread, waxen-faced, limp, and where they lay the brown earth was stained a deeper hue.[14]

Later, Williams was himself blown up by a bursting shell, after stopping to assist a fellow officer who was wounded. He continued:

'So long! I hope you'll be all right,' said our Ensign, and once more started to clamber up the slope after a glance at his compass to assure himself that he was bearing in the right direction. He kept a sharp look-out ahead to see if he could discern any signs of his own Battalion. He thought he must soon be catching up with them now.... . Then, without any warning, he was flung headlong into a shell-hole amid a foul reek of black smoke and a thick cloud of dust.

'That's done it! I'm dead!' was his first thought; but he found himself unwounded at the bottom of the hole, his throat and nose full of dust and his ears singing. He scrambled out in a panic and dashed on. He caught up with a Guards officer, whose face he seemed to know, leading a party of heavily laden men.

'Are you machine-guns?' he asked the other, as he drew level ... his voice sounded very faint in his ears. The other made no reply. Our Ensign repeated his question, and still he got no response. Our young man was feeling dazed and rather cross, and was about to shout his question for the third time, when he observed, greatly to his surprise, that the other officer was speaking to him – that is to say, his lips were moving, but our Ensign heard nothing. Then the officer put his hands to his mouth and bawled: 'I'm ... Stokes mortars ... you know me ... you dined with us the other night!' Our Ensign explained that he had just been blown up ... and realised that he was almost deaf. Presently their ways parted, and our Ensign was once more trudging on alone. He crossed a trench where Guardsmen were digging in furiously among a lot of German corpses, passed a Tank on the extreme left, apparently stranded and looking forlorn but intact, met other troops of German prisoners, each bigger than the last, shuffling along at their brisk, characteristic amble, reached the top of the ridge, and plunged into a network of broken barbed wire. There the bullets were humming, and men were shouting and shooting furiously from a crowded trench just in front of him, while in the distance he heard the 'tack-tack' of machine-guns and the reverberating explosions of bombs. Bending low, our Ensign pelted through the wire, and sprang into a dense throng of men in the trench.[15]

Williams found himself once again with the Guards – Grenadiers, Coldstream and Irish. The remains of half a dozen battalions were there, in the deep and narrow trench, packed close as herrings in a barrel so that it was impossible to force a passage. As for officers, at that moment there was no trace. The trench showed abundant signs of the appalling pounding it had received during three days of incessant artillery fire. The British shells had blown whole segments bodily out of it, so that here and there the parapet or the parados, or sometimes both, was blasted clean away. Williams continues:

In its time it had been a good specimen of a German fire-trench – in point of fact it was the German main third line – with a neat fire-step, solid traverses, and deep, timber-lined dug-outs with many steps leading sheer down into the bowels of the earth. But now the fire-step was broken and crumbling, the traverses were nearly all blown in, and in many of the dug-outs part of the framework had collapsed, leaving the entrance either sagging or completely blocked up by fallen earth. The place was a shambles. There were shapeless masses of field-grey trodden down fast into the soft mud bottom of the trench, and sprawling forms, both khaki and grey, lay all over the place. In a yawning rent in the trench, at our Ensign's very elbow, was the dead body of a lad wearing the black buttons and badges of a Rifle regiment, – a mere boy, with a round bullet-hole in the temple. At his side a figure was sitting, knees drawn up, head resting on the hand, in an attitude of contemplation. Our Ensign recognised a sergeant of his own Battalion … an oldish, steady man whom he had known well…. So tired and utterly weary was the look on his face, that for the moment the young officer fancied that the man had fallen asleep. But the waxen features told a different tale…. Our Ensign's heart sank a little within him as he gazed on the two listless figures: all the morning they remained there, and every time he passed them he felt himself shrinking with horror.

The trench was strewn with 'souvenirs' – German helmets and caps and rifles and greatcoats and ammunition pouches, boxes of cigars, loaves of bread, tins of meat and sardines, empty bottles, letters, pay-books, littered about among the prostrate forms. The men in the trench were turning these over; many had rank German cigars in their mouths. But our Ensign had no time to waste in poring over these things – as the only officer present, he felt that it devolved upon him to try and bring a little order into the chaos.[16]

Williams succeeded in rallying the men, and survived the battle. He had been a journalist before the war, and in its aftermath he travelled widely as a reporter, covering events such as the Versailles Peace Conference and the discovery of the tomb of Tutankhamun, as well as happenings in America. It was during this period that he began writing thrillers and around 1926 he gave up his post as Foreign Editor of the *Daily Mail* to pursue a full-time career as an author. He later moved to Hollywood to become a scriptwriter.

On the northern part of the Flers battlefield there was also success, with the men of the Canadian Expeditionary Force (CEF) capturing the village of Courcelette. Among the Canadians going into action this same day was Joseph Smith of the 29th Battalion, who had been a cowboy on a ranch in Ontario before the war. Smith's unit, part of the 6th Brigade of the 2nd Canadian Division, advanced parallel with the Albert–Bapaume road directly in front of Courcelette. Much has been written about the importance of comradeship in war, and of the intense emotional bonds formed between young men who experience extreme danger together (the bonds of mutual loyalty among Second World War bomber crews are another good example of this), and although Smith's account was written for propaganda value and consumption by a domestic audience whilst the war was still in progress, his description of the emotional stress of combat and the importance of having his close friend beside him in battle is still a valuable one:

As we went forward into their second line, I missed Tommy. His cheery little face was gone. I couldn't stop to look for him; that was absolutely against orders. So on I went, thinking about him, and getting madder and madder every second. He had been knocked out, I supposed, as it was the only thing that would take him very far away from my side. The dirty swine had killed him! So I began to see red. I wanted to go look for him, but I couldn't! It was this thought that obsessed me as we jumped into their second line, and from there on I remember very little. Things were vague and unreal. Some incidents were impressed on my mind for the moment, but as I look back on it now, it all seems impersonal. The person who doesn't drink may not understand the simile, but when a man is on a drinking bout he will remember everything up to a certain point. From then on everything is a blur. The next morning the boys at the office will tell him of some weird thing he may have done the night before and he may have a hazy recollection that something of the kind did happen, but he never can be sure. So it is with the soldier in an attack. He goes along for a certain length of time with a clear mind on which is registered vivid impressions. Then the impressions grow dimmer and dimmer until there is no surface left on which they can place themselves.

In the second line we had fighting, fairly stiff for a moment. There were grunts and groans, then silence, except for the never ending crash of the cursed barrage … Why the hell didn't the barrage move on and let us get out of the stinking place? … Just then someone shouted in my ear. I shouted in answer, but I have no idea what I said. Someone offered me a cigarette; I remember that. I lit it, wondering if my hand would shake. It didn't, and I remember how pleased I was over it. Outwardly, then, I was calm. But on the inside every nerve in me cried for action. This standing, waiting – it was torture. The prisoners moved off to the rear. Another hour, and for them the war would be over. While lighting another cigarette, something cracked me on the back. 'Got one at last,' flashed through my mind. I wondered why I didn't fall over, when in front of me bounced Tommy. I fell on his neck and we had another cigarette. He yelled in my ear: 'The concussion of a blinkin' Boche shell blew me about ten feet. Couldn't find you again until daylight.' Sure enough it was daylight. I had never noticed the change. My mind had been on other things than day and night. I had realized I could see easier than before, but I hadn't put it down to daylight. The barrage slackened for a few seconds, then increased its intensity again. It was the signal to get ready for a forward move. So we gave our equipment a hitch and prepared for the last spasm by creeping a little closer to the barrage. It was movement we wanted to relieve the strain of standing still. Three lines were all we had to take and take them we did.[17]

A German field gun and its crew, dug in on a sunken road on the Somme, autumn 1916.

Frederick Howard meanwhile was with the 11th Canadian Mounted Rifles, a unit which, despite its name, was fighting as infantry. Howard was an extraordinary man: an Australian, he already had two years' service with the Australian Light Horse (including at Gallipoli) under his belt when he was discharged, only to enlist for a second time in Canada in June 1916. His memoir is interesting not least because it sheds light on British infantry tactics, which, since the beginning of the battle, had been revised and improved in the light of the more successful methods being employed beyond the army boundary to the south:

> It was on September 15th, at the taking of Corsalette [sic], that the British tanks made their first appearance on the battlefields in France and it was because of these that the Germans reeled under the spell of surprise. The troops accompanying the tanks marched behind them in a new battle formation perfected by the French, and as the deadly machines waddled along over the shell torn ground the boys behind watched carefully the effectiveness of the new instrument of death designed by the British. The character of the ground over which they were traveling saved them from shell fire because they were first high in the air and later were almost out of sight as they were crawling along the bed of a huge shell crater – but never did they stop in their course no matter what obstacles were placed in their path. On reaching the barbed wire I personally thought that the tanks would be in difficulties but to my surprise the camouflaged monsters just went ahead as if all was well, and when the first German trench was reached the tank ahead of me crawled over it and halted in the midst of a multitude of frightened Germans and bursting shells. The whole atmosphere was full of smoke and a general haze seemed to envelop the work of the tanks. Germans in great numbers would now attack the tank and adopt all kinds of methods in order to stop its work but when the machine guns had cleared the immediate surroundings of Huns, the crew on the inside left-wheeled the tank and down the trench she went spitting death to every German in sight from the various guns operated by the crews. The sight of dying and dead Huns after the passage of the tanks is something to remember even to an old hand in the game of killing. Any Germans who escaped death from the fire from the tanks were immediately taken care of by the boys following in the new walking formation.
>
> The Germans, realizing the hopelessness of their efforts against the tanks, were all excited and yelling in their strongest voice 'Kammerad' but I feel that little mercy was shown them, as they adopt Red Cross and surrendering capers every day in order to catch the soldiers of the Allies. On the aerial men observing sufficient evidence to show that a general surrender was really meant, word was sent to the artillery and the raining of our shells ceased in this particular section of the Hun trenches. The objective in this move was Corsalette and just as we were reaching our goal I reeled over with a dizzy singing noise in my ears and I found myself actually lying on the ground and unable to get up, but I could not for the moment ascertain exactly the cause of this. I did not have to wait long, however, for I immediately felt the flow of warm blood over my chest and on looking down I observed where a bullet had pierced my uniform and entered my shoulder. On realizing my position I felt disappointed in not observing the fall of Corsalette under the good work of the tanks, which will ever remain in my mind as the greatest surprise the German soldiers ever will get prior to their Kaiser suing for peace sometime in the future.[18]

Armine Norris, another Canadian, writing home to his father in September 1916, was positive that the allies now had the upper hand on the Somme, and was confident that the superiority in British firepower would carry the day. He was, however, equally aware that the worsening autumn weather could only work to the advantage of the Germans, as it became harder and harder to get reinforcements into the line, rations up and guns moved into new positions:

> The German army in the West front is trying to do what the British did for the first year, and Fritz doesn't like it. Every day our shell fire gets a little stronger and his a little weaker, and his infantry cannot hold us back. For a year the British troops fought against his big guns with rifles and outnumbered three to one without adequate artillery support they stuck to their ruined trenches and the German infantry could not turn them out. Now it's our day and no rifle fire greets us; not that it would stop us, but our artillery is so predominating that our advances cost us often no more than ten per cent, in casualties. It's rain and mud that's helping Fritz at present.[19]

Lieutenant Armine Norris was a 21-year-old University of Toronto student when he attested for the 50th Battalion Canadian Expeditionary Force.

Norris had been a student at the University of Toronto before the war. Now he was an officer in the Canadian Machine Gun Corps, having first enlisted in the ranks of the 50th Battalion in February 1915. Again, in a letter to his mother he gives us valuable insight into the sense of loyalty which motivated many of those soldiers from the dominions to volunteer for active service – and the very real feeling that the British family of nations was endangered by the German threat:

> We've lost a lot of our 'Originals' but on the whole we've been very lucky, and as for myself, I feel, to put it in plain English, that God has been very good to me. I do not expect to be in as dangerous a spot again for a while, but, Mother, if my turn comes, we won't grudge it, will we? For so many have died, and so many must yet die. At any rate I've lived to know that the worst is over and that victory is certain. England is winning now and the triumph is going to be complete. Of course I've always known we'd win, but it's a great thing to have been spared to see at least the beginning of the end. I haven't, I think, told you about the captain's will. He left all his kit and personal things to the men in the section. He wished to have inscribed on his cross, 'I believe that I am but one of countless thousands who died happy that England might live.' For a man holding that faith it wouldn't be hard to die, would it? All of us are willing to die for England, but in acute danger when shells fall close one is sometimes apt to forget. It is really pride of race that keeps men steady. It is traditional that British soldiers do not run and do not

surrender, though we have to do both at times. Fritz, however, runs like a rabbit, when he might win if he fought, and he is quite eager to surrender when a safe chance offers. I am referring to the ordinary German infantry men we meet. The men of some of the crack regiments will not do either and are just as steady as our men, but (for which we should be thankful) there are not many of these, and, poor devils, what they have to face is awful. We'd have lost this war if our infantry of 1914 had been as poor-spirited as the German infantry, generally speaking, of 1916, but our fellows faced the music and 'hung on.' We're feeling rather proud of ourselves for you know our division had never been in a real advance before and we gained a lot of ground.[20]

As Norris astutely observed, the German army was composed of men from many races and nations, not all of whom shared the same level of fighting ability and spirit. Prussian regiments, and the Prussian Guard units in particular, were noted as doughty fighters, but many of those regiments recruited in eastern Germany contained ethnic Poles and others with far less regard for the Kaiser's cause. As the allied policy of attrition wore German numbers down, they could less afford to pick and choose, and the overall quality of their troops declined as well. Given the almost limitless reserves of manpower represented by the British Empire (and of course by the French overseas territories as well), it was a contest the Germans could not win. Wilhelm Bruns, by way of a parallel to Norris, was a man also deeply motivated by national pride. The former Rector of the famous boarding school at Pforta near Naumberg, Bruns was serving as a reserve officer in a German regiment near Courcelette, and has left a gripping account of this phase of the battle from the enemy perspective. In his chapter of the anthology *Das Deutsche Schwert* ('*The German Sword*'), he wrote:

14th September was a day of heavy fire on all trenches, [and] we noticed that behind the enemy positions his troops had gathered. At 5:30pm with my reserve I occupied the position assigned to me north of Courcelette, on the road from Pys halfway to Le Sars. Grenades greeted us. In the evening at 8 o'clock we were ordered to bring forward help. All three battalions were already in front, the left wing was utterly vulnerable because contact with the regimental headquarters had been lost. So here was a hole. Would the enemy advance here, and break through before we could plug the gap? … I was [now] about 900 meters north of Courcelette on the road to Pys, I was sitting there with three of the telephone line repair troops and relayed some of the commands and messages between regimental headquarters and fighting troops. My dwelling was an open hole in the mud, partially boarded, in which I lived for two days and three nights. I had a very good view because this shelter was on the flat crest of a ridge, from where I could see the features of low lying Courcelette well. A frightening artillery duel developed at dusk on the 15th September, enveloping the area in dust and powder smoke…

Above us hovers, cheering, the god of war. With us, as with the enemy, the frontage is quite sparsely held: it is not exactly known where the enemy line runs – their 'line' in fact consists of craters, poorly connected to each other by rough spade work. Here crouching and kneeling, the men are without shelter from the rigors of the weather, small-arms fire, or the destructive effect of the heavy guns. Vigilance and diligence, loyalty and patriotism range among our comrades here, on the border between life and Death's hand. The shrapnel bursts in the air with an exciting, tormenting crash. The shells churn up the ground, tearing gaps in the barbed wire through which infantry can spill.

At any moment the enemy can come. This morning he was present in dense masses in shell holes, old shelters and battered trenches. He attacked in four waves, in spite of our barrage. Behind, more attack troops were massing ... Now the scene is half-lit by moonlight. Open your eyes! Ears! wake up! listen! Are you tired? hungry? thirsty? Oh, the thirst that is generated by excitement and dust! Initially it was possible to bring up hot food by creeping forward at night. Now in these days of heightened struggle that is over. Only coffee, tea and soda water are our companions in the first line. The night lasts a long time. The British crouch in shell holes ready like cats to attack. Can not you hear them creeping forward? A flare goes up! In its pale light the terrain appears ghostly, without life. Your excitement has fooled you into imagining things. The landscape appears horrible: it is completely tumbled, there is a wild tangle of shattered undergrowth, all kinds of debris smashed by shells, infantry bullets, shattered houses with shutters lying around, the rubble of masonry walls, broken tiles in countless amounts, old equipment, furniture from the time of peace, pouches, broken rifles, empty tins of meat – all this proves the terrible nature of the struggle. There is no grass, no flowers, no animals. How frightening is the

FOR KING AND COUNTRY.

In Memoriam.

Lance-Corporal WILLIAM LEONARD ELMS,
1st Buffs,
Killed in Action, September 15th, 1916.
Aged 27.

A memorial card for Private William Elms, 1st Battalion East Kent Regiment, who was killed in action on 15 September. In 1921 his body was among fifty-nine exhumed from a mass grave and reinterred at Guards Cemetery Les Boeufs. As the individual soldiers could not be identified, he is now commemorated on the Thiepval Memorial to the Missing.

impression of this tortured country, at night as painful as in daylight! The half light of the moon will see the end of this madness ... midnight comes without success for the British, and gradually the thunder of the guns at Courcelette dies down.

The hot gun barrels also wish to be left alone again, to cool off and again to be able to deliver new destruction. But the sentries have no rest, the outward calm creates in them inner excitement: are the enemy gathering in this silence to prepare a surprise attack? If you were elsewhere, you would suffer no scarcity or hardship. Shame on such a thought! Here you stand, a part of the living wall protecting the Fatherland and Freedom. Home! You precious word, you most beautiful treasure of the earth, like a jewel I learned to love you now, now I have come to know your worth! Think of your loved ones in your faithfulness. Each evening before bedtime they pray for you, and when they wake up wrap you in their caring, loving sentiments. During the day, their loyal thoughts and desires are focused upon you. Is this not so? Through that you create new courage, new strength and new joy! That makes your life in spite of all the heavy toil, hardship and danger doubly worth living. Ssst! a grenade rushes over you to the rear area and there stabs its victims with a hundred jagged splinters. Do not dream of fairytales and the

The destructive force of a barrage on the Somme, 1916.

peace of home! The battlefield is a different world, a great, haunting presence. Already there is light in the east, the morning is breaking, radiant. The night was long? Or was it short? You do not know: the prospect of death kills even the concept of time. Over there you see medical orderlies, under the protection of a white flag they scour the battlefield for dead and wounded. We do the same. Meanwhile the remainder continue the fight, before death and wounds bend friend and enemy to mutual service and helping love.[21]

Bruns was undoubtedly a patriot, who admired the bravery and the passion of his compatriots in combat (writing of them in the battle for Courcelette, he stated that 'fighting is their zest for life'). Yet in spite of the determined resistance of some Germans, there was a sense now within the BEF that the front line was really moving forward, and this did much to inspire morale. A Canadian gunner officer, Arthur Chute, wrote of this in his memoir of his time with an ammunition column on the Somme:

Suddenly in the Somme push there was experienced a change of spirit throughout the entire forces. While we sat still in one place month after month our spirits steadily descended, but when we were once advancing we were un-dismayed by cold, or hardship, or lack of food, or ceaseless toil, or added dangers, or increasing death. None of these things mattered so long as we were going ahead. The first time we advanced the guns of our battery in the Somme last fall was the happiest moment of all my eighteen months' fighting in France. That was what we all went to France for, and at last, after ceaseless and apparently ineffective sacrifice, we began to realize the end of our existence ... Two hours before the time ordered found us on the road. At the battery position there was a thrill of excitement, not common among old soldiers in France ... As soon as all the guns were hooked to the limbers the order was given, 'The battery will advance in column of route from the right. W-a-lk – march.' How many times had I given that order for mere maneuvers, but now for the first time it sounded with a thrill. Gunners and drivers alike were dead beat, but there was no lagging back. With a gusto the guns and limbers swept over the crest onto the road. Once on the road, the whole column swept forward at the trot.[22]

As the battle progressed, the need for aerial observation of the enemy dispositions never lost its importance. In the French air force it was sometimes the custom to take infantry officers or NCOs into the air on an ad hoc basis in order to act as observers. In the second week of September French *poilu* Adrien Henry was on his way back to rejoin his regiment on the Somme front, after a period of convalescence from wounds. Before he could reach it, a spell of this type of duty awaited him, but such was Henry's warlike nature that he could not resist using this opportunity not just for reconnaissance but also for offensive operations. His personal attempts to take the

Adrien Henry, the French private soldier whose aggressive attitude was out of step with that of the pilot of his reconnaissance aircraft. (*Courtesy of Frédéric Henry*)

fight to the enemy did not, however, find favour with the regular pilots, and as a result he was soon back on ground duties:

The division asked for an observer from the infantry to ride in an aeroplane. I volunteered and for a week I went up in the 'chicken coop' to see where our lines ran. But I did not get on very well with the fellow aviator who flew the 'plane. I recognise that, technically, I myself did not have much authority. I considered myself to be the traveller, with the pilot as the coachman, whom I had to obey. I wished to descend closer to the ground, in order to see clearly and thereby fulfill my mission. But the pilot would not do this, claiming that if we went lower into the zone of shell-shot and rifle fire, the aircraft would surely be brought down. I was replaced by a more docile companion, who was less demanding. I remember my last flight. We had made a fairly large circuit, and passed over Albert and behind Sailly Saillisel, which I recognised from before. On starting this last mission, I wanted to achieve a very personal satisfaction. I carried in my pocket half a dozen percussion grenades, about which I said nothing to the pilot, then once I had completed my mission, did I direct my equipment towards the enemy lines.

In this flat region, we could see roads scrolling away out of sight. They were barren. Not a single human being seemed to use them. I went to throw my grenades at random on the German lines, when I saw a small grove, of a dozen trees at most, under which I could easily distinguish several vehicles. It was a fine target, [and] I shouted to the pilot where I wanted to go, because it was difficult to hear over the engine noise. We arrived above the grove, where I threw my grenades. I had hit the mark because I saw, a few moments later, two horses, having broken their ties, flee out of the trees. I was pleased with myself that day, for I am pretty sure that many of my shots were on target. Turning towards our lines we were greeted by numerous shells, but not one burst less than a hundred meters from us. I could clearly hear the explosions, but they did not stop us from returning.[23]

Nevertheless, by the autumn of 1916 bad weather and heavy cloud cover was rendering aerial observation increasingly difficult. Aircraft were either grounded altogether, or their view of the enemy lines was obscured. A French staff officer named Jacques Civray, writing in his diary in September 1916, was mindful of the caveats which came with information gleaned from aerial observation at this time:

This fact proved to me that the information provided by aviators must sometimes be subject to caution. Without denying through this the merit of our pilots, whose boldness and audacity are the admiration of all, I think their recognition powers are often incomplete and may only in some cases give accurate results, if they are confirmed by observations of the cavalry. If the pilots fly in any weather, they do not always see what is happening below them, because they face significant barriers, clouds, rain squalls or snow, and in these cases any observation is prevented.

The intelligence of the aviator is precious when it is positive. If he saw columns of troops in motion, or an enemy camp, then there is no doubt he saw it, and he can estimate the troop strength observed by using landmarks familiar to him. But even in clear weather, airmen may not be aware of what they see. Batteries are often hidden under sheaves of straw, tree branches or hidden in a copse of fir trees. Infantry can only work at night, and shelter in the day in sheds, houses, and churches ... That is why an airman sometimes said that there is nothing there, when there is something he has not seen.[24]

Things were slightly different in the British service in that infantry observers were generally attached to Royal Flying Corps squadrons on a considerably longer-term basis, in fact for the duration of the war. The offensive spirit in the RFC was also much more prevalent. As evidence of this we have the account of Alan Bott, a second lieutenant with a commission in the Royal Garrison Artillery, who flew as an observer with 70 Squadron RFC operating from Fienvillers in the autumn of 1916. Bott flew on patrol work over the Somme battlefield and wrote:

Punctually at five o'clock the order, 'Start up!' passed down the long line of machines. The flight-commander's engine began a loud metallic roar, then softened as it was throttled down. The pilot waved his hand, the chocks were pulled from under the wheels, and the machine moved forward. The throttle was again opened full out as the bus raced into the wind until flying speed had been attained, when it skimmed gently from the ground. We followed, and carried out the rendezvous at 3,000 feet.

The morning light increased every minute, and the grey of the sky was merging into blue. The faint, hovering ground-mist was not sufficient to screen our landmarks. The country below was a shadowy patchwork of coloured pieces. The woods, fantastic shapes of dark green, stood out strongly from the mosaic of brown and green fields. The pattern was divided and subdivided by the straight, poplar-bordered roads peculiar to France.

We passed on to the dirty strip of wilderness which is the actual front. The battered villages and disorderly ruins looked like hieroglyphics traced on wet sand. A sea of smoke rolled over the ground for miles. It was a by-product of one of the most terrific bombardments in the history of trench warfare. Through it hundreds of gun-flashes twinkled, like the lights of a Chinese garden.

Having reached a height of 12,000 feet, we crossed the trenches south of Bapaume. As the danger that stray bullets might fall on friends no longer existed, pilots and observers fired a few rounds into space to make sure their guns were behaving properly.[25]

The squadron operated Sopwith 1½ Strutters, two-seater aircraft with a forward-facing Vickers gun operated by the pilot, and a Lewis gun operated by an observer in the rear cockpit. Bott soon became involved in a dogfight, and the fickle nature of both aircraft and armament are made clear:

I looked down and saw eight machines with black Maltese crosses on their planes, about three thousand feet below. They had clipped wings of a peculiar whiteness, and they were ranged one above the other, like the rungs of a Venetian blind. A cluster of small scouts swooped down from Heaven-knows-what height and hovered above us; but C. evidently did not see them, for he dived steeply on the Huns underneath, accompanied by the two machines nearest him. The other group of enemies then dived on us.

I looked up and saw a narrow biplane, apparently a Roland, rushing towards our bus. My pilot turned vertically and then side-slipped to disconcert the Boche's aim. The black-crossed craft swept over at a distance of less than a hundred yards. I raised my gun-mounting, sighted, and pressed the trigger. Three shots rattled off – and my Lewis gun ceased fire.

Intensely annoyed at being cheated out of such a splendid target, I applied immediate action, pulled back the cocking-handle and pressed the trigger again. Nothing happened. After one more immediate action test, I examined the gun and found that an incoming cartridge and an empty case were jammed together in the breech. To remedy the stoppage, I had to remove the spade-grip and body-cover. As I did this, I heard an ominous ta-ta-ta-ta-ta from the returning German scout. My pilot cart-wheeled round and made for the Hun, his gun spitting continuously through the propeller. The two machines raced at each other until less than fifty yards separated them. Then the Boche swayed, turned aside, and put his nose down. We dropped after him, with our front machine-gun still speaking. The Roland's glide merged into a dive, and we imitated him. Suddenly a streak of flame came from his petrol tank, and the next second he was rushing earthwards, with two streamers of smoke trailing behind.

I was unable to see the end of this vertical dive, for two more single-seaters were upon us. They plugged away while I remedied the stoppage, and several bullets ventilated the fuselage quite close to my cockpit. When my gun was itself again, I changed the drum of ammunition, and hastened to fire at the nearest Hun. He was evidently unprepared, for he turned and moved across our tail. As he did so, I raked his bus from stem to stern. I looked at him hopefully, for the range was very short, and I expected to see him drop towards the ground at several miles a minute. He sailed on serenely. This is an annoying habit of enemy machines when one is sure that, by the rules of the game, they ought to be destroyed. The machine in question was probably hit, however, for it did not return, and I saw it begin a glide as though the pilot meant to land. We switched our attention to the remaining Hun, but this one was not anxious to fight alone. He dived a few hundred feet, with tail well up, looking for all the world like a trout when it drops back into water. Afterwards he flattened out and went east.[26]

Among the Germans flying on the Somme at this time was Oswald Boelcke, now notching up an impressive tally of kills, as he wrote in a letter to his parents:

> Yesterday you read of Number 30, but even that is a back number. Number 31 has followed its predecessors. On September 17th came Number 27. With some of my men I attacked a squadron of F.-E. biplanes on the way back from C. Of these, we shot down six out of eight. Only two escaped. I picked out the leader, and shot up his engine so he had to land. It landed right near one of our kite-balloons. They were hardly down when the whole airplane was ablaze. It seems they have some means of destroying their machine as soon as it lands. On September 19th six of us got into an English squadron. Below us were the machines with lattice-work tails, and above were some Morans, as protection. One of these I picked out, and sailed after him. For a moment he escaped me, but west of B. I caught up with him. One machine gun jammed, but the other I used with telling effect. At short range, I fired at him till he fell in a big blaze. During all this, he handled himself very clumsily. This was Number 28.
>
> On September 27th I met seven English machines, near B. I had started on a patrol flight with four of my men, and we saw a squadron I first thought was German. When we met southwest of B., I saw they were enemy 'planes. We were lower and I changed my course. The Englishmen passed us, flew over to us, flew around our kite-balloon and then set out for their own front. However, in the meantime, we had reached their height and cut off their retreat. I gave the signal to attack, and a general battle started. I attacked one; got too close; ducked under him and, turning, saw an Englishman fall like a plummet.
>
> As there were enough others left I picked out a new one. He tried to escape, but I followed him. I fired round after round into him. His stamina surprised me. I felt he should have fallen long ago, but he kept going in the same circle. Finally, it got too much for me. I knew he was dead long ago, and by some freak, or due to elastic controls, he did not change his course. I flew quite close to him and saw the pilot lying dead, half out of his seat. To know later which was the 'plane I had shot down (for eventually he must fall), I noted the number – 7495. Then I left him and attacked the next one. He escaped, but I left my mark on him. As I passed close under him I saw a great hole I had made in his fuselage. He will probably not forget this day. I had to work like a Trojan. Number 30 was very simple, I surprised a scout above our front – we call these scouts 'Häschen' (rabbits) – fired at him; he tilted, and disappeared. The fall of Number 31 was a wonderful sight. We, five men and myself, were amusing ourselves attacking every French or English machine we saw, and firing our guns to test them. This did not please our opponents at all. Suddenly, far below me, I saw one fellow circling about, and I went after him. At close range I fired at him, aiming steadily. He made things easy for me, flying a straight course. I stayed twenty or thirty meters behind him and pounded him till he exploded with a great yellow flare. We cannot call this a fight, because I surprised my opponent. Everything goes well with me; healthy, good food, good quarters, good companions, and plenty to do.[27]

Boelcke's victory number 31 was a Nieuport Scout which crashed near Morval. The aircraft which a few days previously had flown on like a ghost ship, despite having a dead pilot, was a Martinsyde G.100 of 27 Squadron RFC. As Boelcke had predicted, it crashed later on 27 September behind enemy lines, the pilot, Second Lieutenant Stephen Dendrino, being buried at Beurains German Cemetery.

That same month an experienced British pilot returned to the fray after being wounded the previous year. He was Second Lieutenant Frank Courtney, posted to 20 Squadron (operating FE 2 aircraft), another British squadron which was to gain the 'Somme' battle honour. Courtney had interesting observations to make on the relative merits of British and German aircraft and on British versus German tactics. He makes the point in his memoirs that almost all the air fighting on the Somme took place over German-held territory because this was a deliberate choice by the Germans. Courtney points out that the great Boelcke (who he describes as the only German airman truly respected in the RFC) was the only enemy pilot prepared to cross the British lines, and yet even he was not ashamed to proclaim the uninspiring slogan of the German air service: 'Let the customer come to us.' Courtney further adds that this situation, and the aggressive attitude of the RFC of which he was so proud, was all the more remarkable when one considers the great

The German ace Leutnant Wilhelm Frankl of Jasta 4, who brought down his thirteenth victim, a French Caudron, near Rancourt on the Somme on 26 September. (*Library of Congress*)

inferiority in machinery which the British possessed. For more than a year the RFC battled on as underdogs against the German Fokker *Eindecker*, and their aggressive policy could only be sustained at a high cost in casualties (culminating in the 'Bloody April' of 1917). Courtney continues:

But we did have a number of planes, such as the F.E.s to which I was now assigned, that could at least fight back when they were attacked, even though they were much too slow and unwieldy to take the offensive. With them we carried out our so-called fighter patrols by cruising around over hostile territory with chips on our shoulders, defying the enemy to attack us. When they did, they had all the advantages of the initiative, but they did not always escape lightly, and occasionally they fared very badly … The F.E.2 was a remarkable airplane – which is not intended as a compliment, because the most remarkable facts about it were that it was ever called a 'fighter' and that it was retained in service for so long and in such numbers. It was a ponderous, 2 seat pusher biplane of nearly 50 foot span, as compared to the 28 foot monoplane span of the Fokker. Its great size and rocklike stability made it as manoeuvrable as a cathedral, and it was impossible to dive it: at anything much over a hundred miles an hour with nose down, the elevator control would overcome the pilot and the stick would push itself hard back into his lap whilst the plane levelled off. I had devised a trick method of diving it by first hauling it up into a stall and then holding it down when it fell off into a dive, but enemy fighters were not disposed to wait around while I performed this ceremony. It had twenty-eight exposed struts and booms for its wing and tail structures (and eleven more for the landing gear), with endless fathoms of connecting wires. With these built-in head winds, no amount of power could give it any useful speed, so when our F.E.2d's acquired the 250hp Rolls Royce engine, as compared with the 120hp of the original F.E.2b, the increase in speed was almost negligible. The extra power did, however, give us a generous improvement in climb – and we needed it.

Fighting on the F.E.2 was like no other kind of fighting. The gunner's field of fire was an entire, unobstructed hemisphere of air space ahead, whilst the sometimes painful stability of the plane gave him a solidly steady platform to work from. On the other hand, anywhere below and behind the plane – and that was a lot of space – an enemy was completely safe from the F.E.'s gun, and the F.E. control was much too sluggish to evade attack from the rear. So a single F.E. could be sunk in short order by a fast and nimble enemy with the ability to get quickly behind it. This fact fooled the Fokkers for a long time into the belief that the F.E. was naturally easy meat. But a formation of F.E.s was a very nasty unit to attack. Our procedure, when attacked, was to break formation and swerve off in all directions, milling around and trying to keep as close together as reasonably possible. The Fokkers didn't like this at all, because an F.E. was in danger only when lined up squarely with a Fokker's fixed gun, whereas a Fokker was in danger any time it got at all in front of an F.E. and with several F.E.s weaving closely around, there was almost no time when a Fokker might not find itself heading the wrong way under the gun of at least one F.E.[28]

The view through the tail struts of a De Havilland DH2 'pusher' over the Somme battlefield in September 1916. The white puffs are exploding anti-aircraft shells.

To some extent the aggressive attitude of the RFC forced the Germans to introduce new aircraft types in order just to maintain their advantage in equipment, and the arrival of new types of fighter, the Halberstadt and Albatros, on the Somme in September may be taken as evidence of this. Needless to say, the struggle to maintain air superiority over the battlefield, which was already proving costly to the allies, would become still more stern. Whatever the dangers faced by airmen (of either side) when on patrol or in combat over the Somme battlefield, they could at least return after a mission to a warm, dry and reasonably comfortable billet. For those on the ground below them, as summer turned to autumn the conditions deteriorated even further, to an extent not previously seen thus far in the battle. Lieutenant John Glubb, a Royal Engineers officer, had arrived on the Somme battlefield in late July, and was tasked first with repairing and building roads, and latterly with constructing a light railway. He wrote in his diary for 19 September:

> The weather has been bad for the last two days and has made the operations much more difficult. Just two days after the attack when the infantry were done to the world under constant fire and had neither time, men, stores nor energy to dig in properly, the weather broke. On the 18th, it poured all day, and the north wind made the cold bitter. The troops up the line looked as if they had been dipped in a swimming bath. Their sodden khaki, looking almost black, clung to their bodies all over like wet bathing dresses.[29]

Glubb observed that many of the wounded men lying out in shell holes must have died of exposure, as the rain fell relentlessly on the night of 18 September and most of the following day. On 23 September Glubb was up beyond High Wood, surveying the new No Man's Land between the wood and Eaucourt. He wrote in his diary of the way in which he personally rationalised the enormous losses sustained so far in the battle:

> The area is thickly dotted with specks of black and grey, lying motionless on the ground. When you approach, the black patches rise into a thick buzzing swarm of bluebottles, revealing underneath a bundle of torn and dirty grey or khaki rags, from which protrude a naked shin bone, the skeleton of a human hand, or a human face, dark grey in colour, with black eye holes and an open mouth, showing a line of snarling white teeth, the only touch of white left. When you have passed on again a few yards, the bluebottles settle again, and quickly the bundle looks as if covered by some black fur. The shell holes contain every débris of battle, rifles, helmets, gas-masks, shovels and picks, sticking up out of the mud at all angles.
>
> One cannot see these ragged and putrid bundles of what once were men without thinking of what they were – their cheerfulness, their courage, their idealism, their love for their dear ones at home. Man is such a marvellous, incredible mixture of soul and nerves and intellect, of bravery, heroism and love – it cannot be that it all ends in a bundle of rags covered with flies. These parcels of matter seem to me proof of immortality. This cannot be the end of so much.[30]

Glubb goes on to note that his men had now been taken off road repair and were laying track for a Decauville light railway, in order to get troops and supplies up to the front line over the cratered ground more effectively. He also observes that a broad gauge railway was constructed at the same time, from scratch, right up to the old British line, though his statement that it was constructed by Indian labourers is an intriguing one since the Indian Labour Corps did not arrive in France as a unit until 1917.

Also present on this part of the battlefield was an American nurse named Alice Fitzgerald, serving with the 2nd/2nd London CCS. Her letters serve as a useful reminder that numbers of women were serving on the Somme, and were often close enough to the fighting to experience real danger. She writes of the physical hardships which she experienced, but also of the sense of satisfaction which she derived from her work:

I am in the thick of it, as this is the nearest Clearing Station to the Front. I assure you I am all but in the trenches! We are situated in a horse-shoe, with the firing line on three sides. We can only walk a short distance in all directions for fear of getting shelled. Our quarters (nurses') are in small Bell Tents. I have a nice little one all to myself. Two days of pouring rain have made everything disappear under inches of dirty clay mud. My costume these days consists of rubber, knee-deep boots, rubber coat, [and] a sou'wester. Going in and out of tents, and even in the tents, which leak, nothing else is possible. The shelling is continuous, air fights going on. We are advancing splendidly. German prisoners tell me they are very tired of the war, and have had so little to eat! I think the end is in sight.

We are on ground formerly occupied by Germans, and see the trenches, the empty shell cases, of the old scene of fighting. When I first came, there were no floors to the tents, only the bare ground. It rained for three days; and I got out of bed into a puddle every morning. The mud was something awful. The work is of course of a most active sort. We get the patients by ambulances from the field hospitals, and we sort them. The operative cases are operated upon; those too ill to travel are settled comfortably; and others are dressed, fed, and sent on by train to the base. They pass through our hands by the hundreds. I could not imagine that men could live with such awful wounds; in civil life they would die of fright alone.

I am right in the thick of it now; and the shells whizz by our ears in great style. It is queer that, where there is such real danger, one does not think of it. I have charge of two tents which hold from 60 to 70 wounded each, and they have been so covered with stretchers that I had to crawl in and out to get through. It is awfully hard work nursing a patient on a stretcher which only stands about 6" from the ground; and I sometimes wish I were not so tall! We are in the wilderness; even newspapers do not come regularly; and as for mail, I have not seen any since I came. I was able to get money on my letter of credit at Abbeville where I stopped over, so I am settled for three or four months …

I am just as happy as the day is long, working in my little tent-ward, and trying to help the poor fellows. Soldiers are really wonderful. They go to fight with a smile; they come back half dead with a smile. The least we can do is to make them as happy and comfortable as we can. Nothing is too good for them. I went through the wonderfully interesting spot quite lately, German dugouts, shell holes, craters, etc., etc. As far as noises are concerned, I do not believe there are any which I have not heard. If noises could kill, we should all be corpses. It is roar, roar, roar, day and night, – guns nearer by with their louder reports, aircraft fights, anti-aircraft guns, bombs exploding, German shells whizzing over our camp. And with it all, it is a blessing to be busy.[31]

Alice had been sent to the front by an American society in Massachusetts, which was raising funds in memory of Nurse Edith Cavell, demonstrating that even if the US was not yet officially in the war, it had moved beyond strict neutrality and might be termed by the allies as a friendly non-combatant. Other American resources were finding their way onto the battlefield beyond nursing skills, for US-made shells were also pounding the German lines in increasing numbers.

Thus the breaking of the weather, though not unexpected, would bring a new dimension to the battle as it entered its final two months. Late September, October and November would for many soldiers – British, French and German – be months of unalloyed misery as they struggled to stay warm and dry. The autumn of 1916 was particularly cold and wet, and even though British military capability was beginning to reach its zenith, the weather would now begin to play an increasing role in dictating the course and conduct of operations on the Somme. The battle had also, it is fair to say, become one increasingly dominated by technology – aircraft and, more especially, tanks were now playing a role the extent of which scarcely anyone had envisaged on 1 July. More than this, however, the battle was becoming one of resources, and the preponderance of one form of technology above all others – artillery – might well tip the balance as the endgame on the Somme came into view.

Chapter Six

The Battle of Resources

By this stage the Battle of the Somme had evolved into what some German writers have called 'die Material-Schlacht'. The enormous industrial potential which Great Britain possessed was finally beginning to be harnessed effectively towards the war effort, and it was becoming a battle of material, weaponry and manpower. For example, just in terms of the number of artillery pieces at their disposal, the BEF had some 800 more on the Somme front at the end of the battle than at the beginning. Even though many of their individual soldiers still fought bravely, the German high command was beginning now to feel the pressure of the potentially limitless military resources which the allies were bringing to bear upon them. As well as their own industrial strength, the British and French had the limitless munitions production capacity of the United States upon which they could draw; in terms of manpower, both had sizeable overseas territories from which trained men were beginning to feed into the conflict on the Western Front. As autumn turned to winter the morale of the German troops in the front line was being steadily worn down by this material battle. The question was, would British and French morale continue to hold out, in the equally trying conditions of mud and cold which all sides now faced on the battlefield?

The next objective for the British was Combles, which lay at the junction between the British and French armies. As with so many other villages on the Somme, the Germans had turned Combles into a miniature fortress. It was hidden from view in a natural depression, and its garrison was sheltered in quarries connected by tunnels to the concrete defence works protecting the village. The battle for Combles and for Morval was launched on 25 September, in a joint operation between the British Fourth Army and the French Sixth Army. In fact, the assault had been postponed for several days because of rain, which had affected operations with increasing frequency during September. The worsening weather made artillery observation difficult, and the thick soupy mud made for transport difficulties to and from the front line, as well as rendering shell fire less effective as the projectiles sank deep into the mud before exploding. The Fourth Army's advance on 25 September was to be its furthest since 14 July, and despite some resistance in places it left the Germans in severe difficulties, particularly in a salient which developed to the northeast of Combles. Only exhaustion on the part of the attacking troops and lack of reserves prevented the Fourth Army exploiting its success further. The French made slower progress near the inter-army boundary, due to the obstruction presented by St Pierre Vaast Wood to their attack north towards Sailly and Sailly-Saillisel.

Again we have an account by a German soldier in the line, on this occasion close to Morval, facing the British assault. This man was Johann Anton Geuer, a 23-year-old officer from Cologne. The British on this occasion conformed to the French preference for afternoon attacks, which meant that the final bombardment took place in daylight. (The British preferred dawn attacks, to avoid the attacking infantry waiting for too long in the front line, where they were vulnerable to German counter-bombardment.) Geuer writes:

Again a bright summers day. Reports tell us that the enemy intends to make a big attack. Airmen swarm in circles about our heads. One observation balloon after another rises up. The barrage starts right and left and increases to quite a great fury. The ground behind us looks terrible. For the time being, we are isolated. This must be addressed, since if they break through on the right, we are completely surrounded and cut off. Between midday and 2 o'clock the fire reaches its climax. About 2.15 it moved to the rear, and the enemy goes forward. First thin waves, then thick masses. The commanders proudly lead their columns. Our barrage is well sited, three times the energetically led attack breaks down under our fire. Whole troops of wounded Englishmen pass us at a distance of about 300 meters, helping each other back. They bombard once again, with guns of the heaviest caliber. Again a frantic rush. They break through and come thereby halfway into our rear. I fire into them with machine guns. At the same time, shortly after 3 o'clock, the artillery fire on our trench begins. In a short time the trench looks shattered. Repeatedly the heaviest calibers smash into the wood, and the tangle of the splintered branches hinders all traffic. We lie without shelter in holes, exposed defenselessly to the entire hail of iron. In spite of all that, my people are in faultless condition. The burning wish 'let them come' drowned out all feeling of thirst. Unfortunately, one of my best non-commissioned officers falls here. An entire platoon is entombed in a filled-up crater in the earth. They crawl out, distraught. On the left of us lies Combles, which is full of gas. It is not possible to get through to the rear at all any more. Meanwhile, as well as the Englishmen on the right, the French complete on the left the encirclement. We are surrounded in the semicircle. Gun fire and MG fire from the back and flanks beat in our trench. Strangely, the fire suddenly begins to slacken. It becomes quiet. I look over the position, and put on a cheerful face to encourage the people who stare at me so oddly and questioningly. It becomes evening. Rockets climb up in a circle all around us. Behind us they must think that we are completely destroyed; our own artillery starts to shoot at our trench. The route which is still open behind us amounts at most to 1,200 meters, and three battalions must go by it. It becomes quite quiet. About 8.30 the order comes for the forward-most companies to retreat. I move away at 10.15. In complete silence we go over the terrain, from cover to cover. Some people stay behind in the trench, these latter fire flares, as if the position was still held.[1]

Geuer was to survive the fighting on the Somme, only to lose his life two years later on the Western Front. Further north, on 25 September, the British attack faced Gueudecourt, well protected to the north by Gird and Gird Support Trenches. Dick Read of the 8th Leicesters participated in the attack on Gird Trench on this date and remembered an individual, one-to-one combat:

It seemed to me that one man, particularly, had us spotted, and our first job was to find him. Fatty agreed so, shoving the gun up quickly, I fired several short bursts in the general direction of the Germans in the trench while Fatty took a hurried look around. Two bullets all but struck the gun as I got it going, but after that there were no more. Fatty, shouting gleefully, 'that's made the b... get down,' rose to his knees. Suddenly he pointed. 'Hi – give it to him, Dick. There the b....... is, behind that barrel ... Back of the trench!' Raising myself, I got the butt of the gun properly into my shoulder, peering through the sights and firing short bursts as I endeavoured to spot the barrel. As I saw it, to my disgust the drum came to an end. In the same instant I saw the

German appear from behind the barrel, raise his rifle and steady it against the side to fire at me, but Fatty, bless him, was too quick for him. Unknown to me, he had taken careful aim with his rifle at the barrel and, almost as the German appeared, he fired. I remember well, still looking along the sights, seeing the puff of dust spout from the German's chest as he fell over backwards.[2]

Tanks were used once again in this action, and a German anti-aircraft officer gives a remarkable account of the part played by mobile anti-aircraft guns, mounted on vehicles, in knocking them out. The officer, identified only as Grunow, states:

Dick Read of the 8th Battalion Leicestershire Regiment, who took part in the attack on Gueudecourt.

The British and French had opened a barrage shortly before midnight. Shot after shot howled over, sometimes heavy, sometimes light and medium calibre; a murderous drum-fire. You could see nothing, not a hundred paces! The light Auto-Flak guns, close behind the front line, wait for things that are to come. Telephone lines are long since shot to pieces, but messengers for the most part remain; but they can no longer pass through the barrier of fire. The enemy search in vain for the guns, which can escape the murderous fire rain only by continual change of position. A deep, slow sound as of running engines – Tanks! Tanks in masses wallow near. They must have overrun our foremost infantry outposts in the dense smooth fog. Now it's time to be quick! Commander and men turn the gun to counter the next monster in a feverish haste. A brief command – 150 m, the distance – and now the barrel fires out the shots! – At first too short, then right on top, and now again a shot strikes with full force the lower part of the colossus. A jet of flame sprays out. The fuel tank is penetrated and ablaze. Motionless, the monster lies there. The crew who jump out are done for by infantrymen who have gathered around the flak guns. Slowly, the enemy are driven back by superior force, and repulsed when they venture too near. Tank after tank sinks into the grave, and lies motionless, their wings lame, killed by the German anti-aircraft shells. Agile and fast, the mobile Auto-Flak guns hasten now here, now there, to help the hard-pressed infantry and create a clear path…. . the infantry nestles close to us. There is the support that they need, which keeps the tanks and ground attacks at bay.[3]

The next day, 26 September, was a highly significant date – indeed, it was among the most significant of the entire Battle of the Somme, for it witnessed the fall of Thiepval. This battered western sentinel of the German line on the Somme was effectively outflanked by the gains further east earlier in the month, and after stubbornly resisting all frontal assaults, it was eventually captured by encirclement. Only pulverised masonry now marked the village, the centre of four crossroads. This gloomy hog's-back, bristled by charred stumps of trees, had spat defiance all summer long, and stood unconquered under hundreds of tons of shells. The fine chateau which once stood here was long since destroyed, and the height was now a rabbit warren, tunnelled in all directions. It dominated a wide field of fire, and from the rubble machine guns swept the approaches. There was no dashing assault at the last. Its resistance was gradually crushed after weeks of costly advance, and its garrison, strong in the belief of their impregnability, forced out.

The end came as the attackers closed in, subduing dugouts with bombs; there seemed no key to the main underground system until a tank lumbered along half a mile of redoubt and crushed it. Karl Gorzel from Breslau was a survivor of this action and wrote on 1 October of his experiences there. Again, it was British aerial superiority which, in the eyes of the ordinary German soldier, gave the BEF the advantage:

A German officer poses for the camera at the entrance to his dugout, during a quiet moment.

Now that the horrible affair at Thiepval lies like a bad dream behind me, I will tell you in broad outline how I have been faring on the Somme.... As we were passing through Cambrai we saw Hindenburg and greeted him with exultant cheers. The sight of him ran through our limbs like fire and filled us with boundless courage. We were going to feel the need of him too!

On the evening of September 11th we relieved the 5th Guards (Regulars) in the Thiepval position. The march up was awful. The nearer we got, the more intense became the gun-fire and the flatter the communication-trenches, which at last disappeared altogether. Then we had to advance in spurts through the murderous shrapnel and shell-fire. Even there we had heavy casualties. The next morning the English attack began and the guns were not silent for two hours during the day. At dawn I looked around me: what a ghastly picture! Not a trace of a trench left; nothing but shell-holes as far as the eye could reach – holes which had been filled by fresh explosions, blown up again and again filled. In them we lay as flat on the ground as if we were dead, for already flocks of enemy aeroplanes were humming over us. We were absolutely at their mercy, and with remorseless accuracy they directed the English heavy-guns, shell after shell, into our line, and themselves fired with machine-guns at everybody who made the slightest movement below.

Hour after hour passed. The wounded lie helplessly groaning. The supply of water runs out. The day seems to stretch itself maliciously to twice its usual length. The fire increases to such bewildering intensity that it is no longer possible to distinguish between the crashes. Our mouths and ears are full of earth; three times buried and three times dug up again we wait – wait for night or the enemy! Oh that waiting! – it scorches the brain and drives one frantic. And the bursting shells' dance-of-death becomes ever madder – one can see nothing for smoke, fire and spurting earth. Feverishly one's eyes seek to penetrate the curtain of fire and detect the advancing enemy. Suddenly the barrage lifts – the shells are falling behind us – and there, close in front, is the first wave of the enemy! Release at last! Everyone who is not wounded, everyone who can raise an arm, is up, and like a shower of hailstones our bombs pelt upon the attacking foe![4]

Lieutenant Adrian Stephen of the Royal Field Artillery, a graduate of Sydney University, New South Wales, wrote a particularly interesting and astute letter in the wake of this action. He not only describes events as he saw them, but offers an insightful analysis into allied progress in the campaign so far. What also impresses the reader today is the clear development in infantry tactics which had taken place in just a few months. Rather than walk across in lines to be shot at, men now moved up in smaller groups, one behind the other, in order to offer less of a target. To a large extent, the credit for this must go to the commander of the 18th Division, Sir Ivor Maxse, whose thorough and innovative methods of training his infantry would become the blueprint for those used throughout the BEF (though it was also due in part to the influence of French tactical thinking). Stephen states:

I could see the first wave walking towards Thiepval, and then a second wave sprang up and spread out behind them, then the last wave took shape and followed up in artillery formation; small bunches of men, with an interval between each bunch, or more often six men advancing in single file with a stretcher bearer in the rear. It was a wonderful sight. Never have I seen such a calm, methodical and perfectly ordered advance. It seemed incredible that this parade could be marching on Thiepval, the most sinister of German strongholds, yet hardly a man fell. The barrage was as perfect as it was terrible. The white smoke of shrapnel ran like a rampart along the trenches that were the first objective, as clear as though it were made of tape carefully placed and measured.[5]

By contrast, he also observed that the fighting efficiency of the Germans appeared now to be on the wane. Where once they would have crushed an attack whilst it was still forming up with a devastating barrage, now their response was desultory. The Germans were also demoralised by the appearance of a tank, which was becoming almost a mandatory part of every British attack on the Somme now. In spite of their unreliability mechanically, their effect upon morale was considerable:

Thiepval was now a closed book, though runners would sometimes emerge and dash stumbling to our trenches. The Boche retaliation was feeble and badly placed. His barrage fell behind all our men, and very few shells had burst among them, and even then never did they cause a man to turn his head or swerve out of place – unless he fell. At this stage a tank crawled on to the scene and crept laboriously, like a great slug, towards Thiepval. It disappeared among the ruins, puffing smoke. Subsequently it caught fire. Thiepval now became as stony, as devoid of life, as it was before the attack.[6]

Even though the capture of Thiepval would come to be seen by later writers as only a partial success, with the gilt rubbed off the gingerbread to a greater or lesser extent by the fact that the Germans continued to hold some of their defensive works to the north of the village itself, Stephen at the time was under no doubt at all what this meant. Thiepval had been a thorn in the British side since 1 July and its capture was a major achievement for the BEF, and as far as Stephen was concerned it marked a significant point in the decline of the German willingness to fight:

> When the light failed, our men were still playing hide and seek. We had taken the Zollern Redoubt, part of the Stuff Redoubt on the right, and part of the Schwaben Redoubt on the left. Above all, Thiepval had fallen. Thiepval, the proud fortress garrisoned by one regiment since September 1914, had at last, after three big attacks, yielded. It was a good conquest, for the slopes of Thiepval are surely as tragic and bloody as any in this war, except, of course, Gallipoli, but the battle of Thiepval was significant, not so much for the actual ground gained, as for the sudden appearance in the conflict of an element hitherto unseen. Not only the battle of Thiepval, but the whole battle of the Somme, must be judged from three points of view:
>
> 1. Strategic progress.
> 2. Material progress.
> 3. Moral progress.
>
> Now, strategically, the battle of the Somme is a great British reverse. We had failed to do what we intended to do. The battle was lost on July 1st. The Boche line still held. Moreover, it had taken us months to accomplish what, according to time-table, should have been done in as many hours. Let us not hesitate to confess that strategically the battle was a failure. Of course we are now threatening the communications of Bapaume, Vely and Achiet after four months. We had meant to do that in as many hours. Materially we have turned the battle into a success. We have killed Germans, taken guns, villages and men. Our material progress is as obvious as the map. Morally we have never obtained complete mastery. The Boche morale remained as hard as his line and as unbreakable. But here we come to Thiepval. For the first time I saw Germans surrendering in droves before putting up a fight. For the first time his hitherto faultless military machinery failed to swing reserves where they were wanted. On the 26th September I felt our moral ascendancy. It was as obvious, also, as the map at my elbow or the ground under observation. It was not pronounced, but it was there. Indeed one can compare, rather fancifully perhaps, our whole offensive to a little boy who sets out to climb a big tree. On failing to reach farther than the first bough he takes out a pocket knife and proceeds to cut it down. That is what we are doing. On 26th the tree, after three months of cutting, was showing a little weakness through loss of sap. We must push on – on – on without rest and without mercy, even towards ourselves. Our moral ascendancy, however slight, makes one feel like that. It fires one with fresh enthusiasm.[7]

This is truly a remarkable letter, for without the benefit of hindsight this officer, who was on the spot, had coolly and assiduously assessed the success or otherwise of this battle. Sadly, he was to be killed two years later. More evidence of British resolve comes from Bernard Newman, who was serving as a staff sergeant with the Army Service Corps when in late September he visited an aid post for an anti-tetanus injection, following a minor injury. Finding the post overwhelmed with wounded, he offered to lend a hand. One incident which followed must have been typical of many at dressing stations on the Somme battlefield that summer and autumn:

Stretcher bearers brought in a young officer. The doctor took one look at him – then motioned him to be carried to one side. I knew what this meant: the case was hopeless – the doctor must devote himself to men who could be saved. I squatted down by the stretcher. The young officer was conscious, and far too badly hurt to be in pain. But he was an intelligent man, and knew why he had been placed on one side.

'Well, it comes to all of us,' he said calmly. 'I would like to have lived, but – I wonder what's going to happen when we've won – is this really the war to end wars?'

'I hope so.'

'There's something missing, you know. Conferences, treaties, politics – maybe the solution is simpler than that.'

He was quiet for a while, for his blood and his life were rapidly running out. Then he said, suddenly: 'Can you remember the twenty-third Psalm?'

'I'm not sure.'

'Say it to me.'

It must have been years since I had said the 23rd Psalm. Now, desperately, I fought with my memory – I must give this dying man the comfort he deserved.

'It has the key to everything,' he whispered. 'Say it.'

'The Lord is my shepherd, I shall not want,' I began.

'He maketh me to lie down in green pastures; He leadeth me beside the still waters. He restoreth my soul – '

Here I hesitated, as my memory failed. 'Go on,' he said.

I continued slowly: 'Yea, though I walk through the valley of the shadow of death, I will fear no evil: Thy rod and Thy staff shall comfort me.' This was surely what he meant: the ultimate consolation to a dying man.

'Go on,' he insisted.

Again memory was erratic, and I knew that phrases were missing. 'Thou anointeth my head with oil: my cup runneth over. Surely goodness and mercy shall follow me – '

'That's it!' he interrupted. 'Goodness and mercy! Those are the keys! With them, no treaties are needed. No war – no ugliness – '

For a while he talked, but I was so moved that I could scarcely hear him. When at last I drew the blanket over his face, I moved away humbly, as from the presence of the great, and forgot all about my anti-tetanus injection.[8]

The most revealing aspect of this incident (aside from the apposite nature of the 23rd Psalm, the so-called 'soldier's prayer') is the dying officer's absolute conviction that the allies would win – a belief which sustained the men of the BEF throughout this long and brutal battle. Similar difficult, almost arbitrary decisions as to who might live and who probably would not were taking place in dressing stations behind the German lines, the medical staff at times being similarly overwhelmed. An interesting parallel account exists from Alfred Ihne, a German medical orderly working aboard a hospital train on the Somme front at this time. He writes:

The loading of the train usually took 10–12 hours, perhaps even longer and it was an enormous struggle. After more than 300 seriously wounded warriors had finally been found a place, the orderlies were dead tired, but now began their actual main work, namely the care of the injured. What was really surprising was the active and indefatigable manner in which they went about this during the long journey, and the fact

A burial at a dressing station cemetery near Albert, 26 September 1916. The padre reads a lesson as Major E.L. Knight, commanding the Eaton Motor Machine Gun Battery, Canadian Machine Gun Corps, is laid to rest.

that they would not be overcome by fatigue or sleep. There was no relief. It was demanded of every individual to strive to the best of his ability, and every individual also gave his all. On top of all this were the fearful wounds and mutilation, and the misery which one saw! Even though one had seen, nevertheless, bit by bit already of a lot of this kind of thing and was fortunately hardened a little bit, every now and then one's strength nearly faltered. 'I feel the suffering of all mankind,' as the saying goes, but duty called, and one firmly intended to remain and to work ... on one journey it was a field military hospital which had to be emptied. Here the loading was especially difficult. We were required to bring the wounded from the military hospital tent to our train. No car or other means of transport was available. Thus we laid the wounded on a stretcher and carried them to

Private Frederick Norton Warlow, 7th Battalion Canadian Expeditionary Force. Badly wounded on 25 September, he died on 1 October in hospital.

our train. The way led through a field of stubble (there was no path), and the transport of each wounded man required about 10 minutes. Then in the train the final loading was done.

Several times it happened in these journeys that the poor soul on the stretcher died before they could be placed on the train. Death also demanded his victims from those already loaded on board, either shortly before the departure or soon after this. At the next station we unloaded the dead people, as well as the severely wounded, who could not withstand the journey. Under normal circumstances such cases fortunately seldom entered the hospital train, because only wounded capable of transport should come aboard. But in such hasty clearings of field hospitals, few had time to be concerned as to whether the patient is capable of transportation or not. Yet on other journeys during the Somme battle, the hand of the angel of death also touched our train. One evening thus we were held up at a railway station because the track was crowded with ammunition and troop trains, and we could not leave. There, within one hour three very young wounded gave her their lives. One passed away while we tried to introduce a saline solution to him, the other had a bad stomach injury through which the intestines had already come out, and the third had been shot in the neck; suddenly he jumped out of his stretcher bed and fell to the ground dead. All three found the salvation of their sufferings, but their country was poorer by three brave hopeful sons. Gradually the darkness fell, the guns roared out in the near distance, and the nightly fireworks of war illuminated the heavy clouds hanging in the sky like daylight. Around midnight the lieutenant of a railway company reported to us that we should dim all lights in our train as much as possible, because the station had already been shelled a little. We were the last hospital train which was loaded so far forward. After a nineteen-hour stay in the fire area of the English guns we drove out of this place, and we will not look back soon.[9]

Meanwhile, away on the eastern portion of the British front the Canadian Corps continued to batter away at the Germans near Courcelette. Lieutenant Coningsby Dawson was an

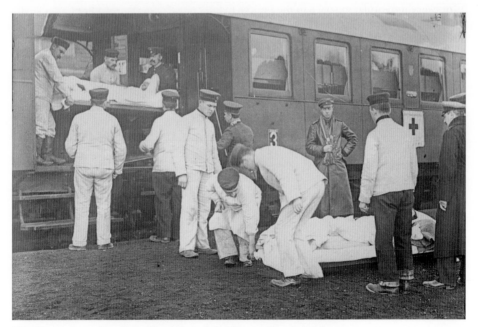

The slow process of loading wounded aboard a German hospital train.

eyewitness as the Canadian Corps pushed northwards from their lines just outside the village, capturing Zollern Trench in the process and bringing them up to face another major German defensive feature: Regina Trench. Dawson wrote to his family:

> I was Brigade observation officer on September 26th, and wouldn't have missed what I saw for a thousand dollars. It was a touch and go business, with shells falling everywhere and machine-gun fire – but something glorious to remember. I had the great joy of being useful in setting a Hun position on fire.[10]

René-Edmond Sergent, a *Canonnier-servant* with the French *13e Régiment d'Artillerie*, killed in action on 22 September near Bouchavesnes.

Dawson was in the thick of the fighting, having guns smashed around him by enemy shells, but this only served to strengthen his resolve that the war must be brought to a victorious conclusion, whatever the price might be in terms of manpower. In spite of his Hun-hating attitude he was not entirely immune to the pathos and misery of war:

> No matter what the cost and how many of us have to give our lives, this War must be so finished that war may be for ever at an end. If the devils who plan wars could only see the abysmal result of their handiwork! Give them one day in the trenches under shell-fire when their lives aren't worth a five minutes' purchase – or one day carrying back the wounded through this tortured country, or one day in a Red Cross train. No one can imagine the damnable waste and Christlessness of this battering of human flesh. The only way that this War can be made holy is by making it so thorough that war will be finished for all time … Don't suppose that I'm in any way unhappy – I'm as cheerful as a cricket and do twice as much hopping – I have to. There's something extraordinarily bracing about taking risks and getting away with it – especially when you know that you're contributing your share to a far-reaching result. My mother is the mother of a soldier now, and soldiers' mothers don't lie awake at night imagining – they just say a prayer for their sons and leave everything in God's hands. I'm sure you'd far rather I died than not play the man to the fullest of my strength. It isn't when you die that matters – it's how.[11]

In the French sector of the Somme battlefield that autumn the Germans were most definitely now at a disadvantage. In retirement after the war, a former German officer named Hauptmann Mentze wrote to a veterans' newspaper, seeking information about the whereabouts of his former runner. As well as illustrating the weakness of the German forces in this sector, the letter offers a revealing insight into officer–men relationships within the German army. Often these relations are categorised by historians as stuffy and over-formal, with little shared sympathy or feeling between officer and man in the archaic and class-dominated Prussian military system, but this letter reveals that a bond of mutual respect and comradeship had in this particular case been forged between officer and enlisted man through the experience of shared danger:

At the end of September 1916, in the terribly heavy fighting on the Somme, I was the commander of 4 Company, *Infanterie Regiment Nr 149*, in the line in front of St Pierre Vaast wood, between Rancourt and Bouchavesnes. The companies were mixed up [and] furthermore it was impossible to get rations to us. Without water, in broiling autumn heat, [and] with frosty nights – we were threatened by shells and bullets. Daily we expected the breakthrough of the enemy assault troops, [and] there under a crushing hail of iron we lay yet for days on end. Great was our worry. What was the use of a machine gun, if its ammunition was not readily to hand? We were aware that it was upon

Georges Marie Joseph Many, a medical orderly with the French *172e Régiment d'Infanterie*, who was mortally wounded on 25 September 1916.

machine-gun fire alone that we mostly depended, to hold off an enemy breakthrough. From number 1 Company, which was also under my command, since there were no longer any of its officers in the front line, I had selected the war-volunteer Muths as the bearer of messages to 'Government Farm' [a headquarters position]. There was no braver, pluckier or bolder young man, he had already multiple times taken the ill-fated path through the tree stumps, thus enabling us to withstand and repel the onslaught.

However, now came the most serious order: he had to get ammunition to us; if he did not, the situation was critical. We looked each other deeply in the eye! For a moment, everything about our loyal comradeship held us in a spell! And then you started out, comrade Muths, on the difficult path to get the necessary machine-gun ammunition to myself and the others. I watched you from behind, as from stump to stump in a zigzag fashion you leaped, until you disappeared into the depths of Pierre Vaast wood close behind us. I lay low, only scrambling around now, as our comrades called: 'Save ammunition! We are out of grenades!' How often my gaze went there, towards Pierre Vaast wood. Where was Muths? Today I still do not know how many endless hours we waited – but he came back with a few reinforcements and wheezing, dragged ammunition behind him – ammunition! I still remember, dear Muths, how I shook your hand, and embraced you. Do you still remember it? But I also remember this: I immediately made you a Gefreiter and recommended you at once for the Iron Cross! You got it, even though your sergeant looked askance at my appointment of a 'front pig' as Gefreiter. What did it matter to us? And do you still remember, how we got stuck then, after such an exceedingly strong enemy attack burst through our barbed wire defences. We were the very last of our troops to withdraw, as by about 7 o'clock in the morning the 'Frenchies' had taken the Pierre Vaast wood with artillery fire? … and then, after nearly two hours of fire, we crept out on our bellies through the undergrowth?[12]

A French artillery officer, Jules Henches of the *32e Regiment d'Artillerie de Campagne*, wrote to his family of the gruelling nature of this kind of warfare amid the cloying mud and incessant rain of late September. He too was impressed by what he saw of his British allies, who were fighting so closely alongside him. For Henches, it was not just the noble attitude of the British but also their technical innovations which were to be admired:

I write in haste. I have spent the night of 28 to 29 [September] waiting for my batteries. The weather was so dark, and the ground is such that having left at eight in the evening, they did not arrive until four o'clock in the morning. We are in holes and in the rain in old trenches. I spent almost twenty-four hours without eating and forty-eight hours without having anything hot.

[I am] amid the English, in a village. It is a terrible life, but so far not comparable to Verdun as a wasteland. Yesterday, going to the observation post with my captains, one of them, who was talking with me, was wounded by a grenade that he or I had burst by walking over it. This mud is total. The ground is covered with dead English that they are only just beginning to bury, and in the midst of all this, in the mud and water, paperwork reigns supreme. We slept on the floor. I did not wash for two days. It seems that we must remain here forty days. The usual situation. The men are tired, but still working. I have just finished a reconnaissance, we are still moving forward. I met Colonel B..., of the infantry, who took me to lunch. All of the landscape is horrible, full of weapons, ammunition, corpses of men and horses. Woods and villages no longer exist. The English possess amazing courage and calmness, they neglect any precaution, are very friendly, and seem to have admiration for us. Their imprudence is the cause of their huge losses. They seem to prefer to be killed than to get dirty and do not 'hide' like us: unlike us, they remain standing; it is very beautiful, but not clever. It seems likely that they equate lying down with cowardice. They make no noise, except with their guns which do not stop, are very numerous and which fire whenever they want.

I saw this morning a [tank] 'Crème de menthe' that had been overturned and remained there. It is perfectly true that they cross even the most improbable trenches and shell holes: the stories about them are correct. We are already tired. What will happen in forty days? One can not imagine what the men endure and how we live. Everything is painful: the ration parties, the marching, the terrain, the fire, sleep itself. They always demand more from us, and also force it from us, if they want to arrive at a result. I have just spent a nervous quarter of an hour whilst resupplying ammunition. All my men and horses congregated behind the batteries, and with the threat of a shell coming over! [Yet] everything ended smoothly.

2 October – My two assistants R... and D... are very good. We work day and night. I do not understand how the Boche hold on. But the horror of all these scenes is terrible. Vehicles roll over corpses. No water to wash ourselves.

4 October – We continue to live in the water and fog, in the mud. One of my men, a runner, returned to me on the pretext that he did not have anything to eat with him. It seems to me that the extra rations which are available to officers are intended for such cases. There should be more respect for men who have such a hard life and are so deserving ...[13]

For Henches, and by extension his men, there was no doubting the righteousness of France's cause, though the sheer practical difficulty of fighting a determined and resourceful enemy in such arduous conditions threatened to subsume idealism:

Maurice Drecq, a soldier of the French *150e Régiment d'Infanterie*, who died of his wounds at a dressing station at Etinchem on the Somme on 29 September, aged 20. He was already a holder of the *Croix de Guerre*.

Musketier Fridolin Schmider, *Infanterie Regiment Nr 114*, who was killed in action on 13 October 1916 near Allaines, in combat with the French.

6 October – I have not been able to have a wash! I have moved my command post further forward, so that I can see better. We strive to see through the chaos, but it is not easy. The guns are so many that it becomes difficult to recognize one's own children. I'm still in a trench. They all look alike, with their dirty, smelly environment, the only precarious protection is that which we can improvise ourselves, and they lack the most basic amenities. I had lunch shivering in the open air. It is incredible that we can withstand this life. I looked at some newspapers: the Crown Prince laments war! There should be no exaggeration and no illusions about what can be achieved in a short space of time. I have given up hope of a quiet winter. Our losses have not been heavy, even very light so far. Clouds of British aircraft cross the sky when it is sunny. I could have done with the help of one of them, but it is now too late in the evening. They have much to do, having few favourable hours. And our paperwork continues, with a sharp reminder if it is not provided on time! It would be hilarious in any other situation …

October 14 – I have just received your letters. I am sorry that you torment yourself so much. I am now much less exposed than I have been before, what I do know is that everything depends on chance … Those who suffer with us understand the ordinary man, and think of those at the front. A 'leader' should not 'order' until he is sure that the command can be executed. I refuse to see in France a spirit which lives for conquest and gain: in my eyes, she lives to bring freedom. All poilus, consciously or unconsciously, think this way.

October 15 – Nothing really new here: our normal work adorned by rain. We received a good communique regarding the situation on our right. I sent a few words this morning to J…, who had written to me. He tells me of the death of an officer of the 4th section of the 46th [Regiment], a very nice boy, killed a few days ago. It is a fierce struggle against the 'beasts' but it is very difficult to gain the upper hand in this kind of combat. We struggle in an inextricable tangle of issues, such as reinforcement and resupply of provisions. It is difficult to achieve everything, and everything is important. It is a real headache, and one must take into account our fatigue, a very natural fatigue. No letter tonight …[14]

Henches and three of his officers were killed in action the following day, one kilometre southeast of Combles. Further north, near the position known as the Pimple, slightly east of the village of Le Sars, was a corporal of the Bavarian *Reserve Infanterie Regiment Nr 16*: a certain Adolf Hitler. He was later to write, in his notorious political tract *Mein Kampf*:

At the end of September 1916 my division was sent into the Battle of the Somme. For us this was the first of a series of heavy engagements, and the impression created was that of a veritable inferno, rather than war. Through weeks of incessant artillery bombardment we stood firm, at times ceding a little ground but then taking it back again, and never giving way. On October 7th, 1916, I was wounded but had the luck of being able to get back to our lines and was then ordered to be sent by ambulance train to Germany.[15]

Leutnant der Reserve Hans Mayer, of Bavarian *Reserve Infanterie Regiment Nr 16*, killed in action on 7 October 1916. Another soldier of this unit, Corporal Adolf Hitler, was wounded the same day.

On this day Le Sars was captured by the British, the Bavarians being attacked by soldiers of the 47th (London) Division. Some historians have claimed that Hitler's wound in this action was serious enough to explain the medical condition which was mocked in the bawdy British song of the Second World War, but it seems unlikely that he was left monorchic given that the wound kept him away from the front for just a few months. Be that as it may, Hitler has this to say about the state of morale within his own unit:

In 1916 several distressing phenomena were already manifest. The whole front was complaining and grousing, discontented over many things and often justifiably so. While they were hungry and yet patient, and their relatives at home were in distress, in other quarters there was feasting and revelry. Yes; even on the front itself everything was not as it ought to have been in this regard. Even in the early stages of the war the soldiers were sometimes prone to complain; but such criticism was confined to 'internal affairs'. The man who at one moment groused and grumbled ceased his murmur after a few moments and went about his duty silently, as if everything were in order. The company which had given signs of discontent a moment earlier hung on now to its bit of trench, defending it tooth and nail, as if Germany's fate depended on these few hundred yards of mud and shell-holes. The glorious old army was still at its post.[16]

Hitler goes on to write that the spirit of the German front-line soldier was still strong, even though those in the rear areas were infected with the malaise of shirking and defeatism. This is perhaps not surprising when one considers that among the lines of communication troops, disaffection could seethe and grow without the direct pressure of the enemy about to descend upon them, which might otherwise suppress it. The rear areas also contained many lightly wounded men awaiting return to the front, or reinforcements moving forward. In such units the bonds of shared peril and mutual interdependence were weaker; the officers would also be unfamiliar to the men, and less likely to have earned their respect through common front-line danger. Writing on 10 October, an unnamed German soldier on the French Somme front provided a remarkable illustration of the morbid fatalism which allowed the front-line soldier to continue to function in this grinding machine:

I arrived here yesterday morning at three o'clock. For how long, no one knows. You may be sitting permanently in the front line, especially in such uncertain days. I was six days in a position at Chaulnes, which is smashed into the ground. You have seen many horrors of war, but I do not think even you have witnessed one like this. Daily, there was raging fire, mostly of the heaviest calibre. A single roar of the earth, a constant fluctuation of the smoke- and gas-laden atmosphere. In

Gefreiter Georg Auer, of the German *3. Marine Infanterie Regiment*, who was killed in action on 8 October 1916 in Regina Trench near Courcelette.

a word: beastly! Towards evening we were always on high alert, but the enemy attack was nipped in the bud by the timely arrival of our barrage. The rainy, cloudy weather which did not allow for observation by aviators and balloons, was convenient for us. Today, unfortunately, sunny weather has re-appeared. Already, the fire also increases. It sounds from afar like the angry roar of a bull, which in vain kicks his head against a wall. When it gets closer it sounds like the splintering of a giant wooden ruler.

Even the poor dead cannot be given a quiet place to rest. On a night lit by the pale moon, and showered by the rain, we buried them behind the firing line. The steel helmets of the diggers blinked hastily up and down as grenades and shrapnel howled constantly around us. In a short time, when even the simple wooden cross is shot away, no one will see the place where these good men rest. Here, one comes gradually to the conviction that the human being is simply worthless. One learns literally to despise life. This conviction also gives one the necessary calmness to face the gruesome death which lies ahead. Death is also not the most terrible thing: rather, that is a serious wound that prevents one from getting to safety, so that one perishes miserably in the mud, as at the beginning of September hundreds fared here. More than anything, I would like to be spared, the other is all one ... [Unfinished].[17]

Corporal Charles Bryan, 11th Field Ambulance, Canadian Army Medical Corps. He was killed in action on 13 October 1916.

Private Nelson Sanguins, 13th Battalion Canadian Expeditionary Force. He was captured on 8 October 1916 in a disastrous attack on Regina Trench, in which his battalion was almost destroyed.

The writer was himself killed on 13 October, and we may assume that some emergency intervened prior to this to prevent him from completing his letter. Yet for some Germans it was still the sense of pride, patriotism, duty, and of course comradeship which kept them going. One German officer, Victor Pruess, writing at the same time as the unnamed soldier above, was also philosophical in his outlook:

My life is the fatherland, my work, my soldiers and my loved ones back home; all that lend themselves to me with their cares, with their suffering, and their joy as friends – and those are many. Their friendship is to me a delightful possession, which helps me through some dull day, you have known this for a long time. Why do you remind me of the fact that danger and death surround me daily out here? Is death something so bad, can a death for a glorious thing be hard? Perhaps it may be that we can reconcile life. I will not deny you your intuition. But I believe that there are probably people who are only reconciled with life by death.

How otherwise could thousands march here with us in the same step, fighting in the ranks with us if they carried the agonizing thought that they could meet the bullet before having found reconciliation? Nevertheless, to give our lives for our brothers is the greatest love, and death is salvation and victory – and I think that we have out here the best opportunity to think about it – it is probably the case that you need to do something out of the ordinary, to 'walk in God's footsteps', that one must wait silently until one is given the deeper knowledge. And so it is to be out here is nothing out of the ordinary, but a duty, a silent action and waiting, and it's not all a sacrifice as you might think, because a victim can not 'like' being such, one is a victim only if one is in pain.[18]

Day-to-day life in the front line was now becoming increasingly dominated by the hardships of struggling to survive, even when not directly under enemy fire. French infantryman Adrien Henry returned from convalescence to the positions held by his unit around 10 October. He found that the practical difficulties of living outdoors in autumn were exacerbated by poor equipment:

> I rejoined the 161st in the ends of trenches at Sailly Saillisel, but I did not participate in any major attack, I merely got my share of German shells, and sometimes those of our gunners firing too short. I remained with my company or rather what was left of it, because the killed, wounded and those with frozen feet were numerous. It was not the cold that had contributed most to freeze the toes and to cause the gangrene, it was spending eight days there in holes where we could not remove our boots. For many, puttees bound too tightly had prevented the free flow of blood and a number of personnel paid with the loss of a foot or maybe more for their negligence or inattention.[19]

Although the French had abandoned their conspicuous red trousers the previous year in favour of the more practical *horizon bleu* uniform, their accoutrements and clothing still left much to be desired, and the front-line French infantryman was much hampered by them. French infantry poilus were also always heavily laden, the same author recalling that:

> [There were] many straps that crossed the chest or were carried from the shoulders. These included the straps of the backpack, always heavily loaded, the two straps of the haversacks, one for rations and the other carrying grenades, the strap of the gas mask box, and then there was the strap of the two-litre canteen. To all these, one could add braces for trousers and the sling of the rifle, which was always there, 4kg 240 which had to be carried around.[20]

Difficulties of a different kind presented themselves to those whose task it was to cross and recross the battlefield in order to bring up supplies. The memory of one such individual encountered during this spell in the line stayed with Henry afterwards:

> I remember a poor infantryman, or rather his corpse. He must have been a cook. His body had fallen there in the dirt, into a large shell hole two meters deep, filled with thick mud through which we could just make out the corpse. However, this man's chest was covered by the belts of a dozen canteens. He must have been the carrier undertaking the chore of fetching wine from the rear, and that was why he was provided with all these vessels. Was he killed by a bullet or a shell? Was he drowned in that cesspool? Nobody will ever know.[21]

Another Frenchman in the line near St Pierre-Vaast, not far away from Henry, was an engineer officer, Pierre Jolly. Jolly's unit of sappers (or *Genie* as they are known in French) went into action on Friday, 13 October. For the French the number thirteen has lucky rather than unlucky associations, and so the sappers of the 15–2 Company were not unduly worried; indeed, Jolly himself perceived the date as a good omen:

> ... we see neither steeple, nor roofs, nor orchards, nor flowers. Our boots crush underfoot a ruddy dust. The remains of Maurepas blend into the earth ... A peasant continues his journey with a wagon of sugar beets ... The shovels of territorial road workers make hurdles for us. Soldiers of every type and service pass them by. Soldiers never get bored of watching others. 'Where are you going?' Fliette looked at the speaker without honouring the question with an answer. I am struck by the silence of our ranks ... 'It is the 15–2!' declares, with a tone of discovery, a captain whose collar is adorned with a mysterious embroidery and who, even more mysteriously, has the good fortune also to be clean. He offers me, I do not know why me rather than any other, a packet of cigarettes. 'Take them, quickly!' They are smart ones: they will please Lefleury. The driver of the sugar beet wagon, a large, ruddy-faced man, gives us the blessing of his heart: 'Good luck boys!' This hardly counted for much, because Maulin, for whom it was enough to know that it was Friday 13th, answers him with a rude word. This evening, when with a noise like hail the ruddy-faced man pours red beans from his garden into his pan, he will tell his friends that the 15–2 is coarse. So are reputations made. Having left Maurepas without our seeing it, we cross the rectangle of its future national cemetery ... We advance through the petrified chaos of the battles of August 1916. Here and there, men, mostly 'enemies', and horses punctuate through the decay of their flesh the chronology of the communiqués: both stated and implied. The country towards the woods appeared completely raked over. From this disembowelled earth, clods of entrails pour out ... Elsewhere, gashes are marked with whitish scars.... . On Friday, October 13th, 1916, I was distracted. I had too much to look at. Firstly, the German sausages. Just like musical notes, they rose in terraces on a range of clouds, in the distance. Our skyline was marked out with beacons as permanent and free-flowing as fireworks on July 14th. We observed how on the long line of the horizon, missiles erupted in multicoloured bunches. Reds, greens, half notes which expressed themselves in French or in German above the continuous eruptions of volcanoes. In front of us, to the right, to the left, from everywhere, invisible cannons dropped broadsides of fire. We were still much too far from their lines to see the bright barkings of 75s. But the noise of the Somme rang like the links of a giant chain being shaken in the sky.[22]

As the hour of the attack came closer, the men of this engineer unit made their final preparations:

> Our watches show us we have only minutes to wait ... Before the acceleration of their fire, Demange confides of sympathy for our artillerymen. The imminence of the storm bedaubs the landscape. It is now time to adjust the chin straps of helmets, to fasten packs, to prepare the ladders. The preparation is coming to its end. Each Lebel rifle, model 1886 updated in '93, carries a bayonet. Our 75s signal H hour by rolling the barrage onto Sailly-Saillisel, the château and its park. I cannot believe that in the centre of the battlefield I hear only the roar of the 15–2 as it leaves the earth. Perhaps, in my case, I hear only as far as one is able to see: for it is autumn. But it is impossible that those who had eyes to see it in 1916 never heard the roar of the 15–2. Especially on this day when, according to our timetable, the tempest moved on to attack Sailly-Saillisel.

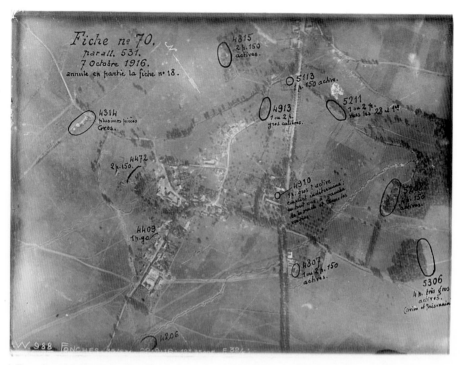

A French aerial photograph marked up to show the locations of enemy guns; this would then be used to direct artillery fire on to them.

After that swirling wind, in the birthplace of the attacking waves of the 15–2, continual silence now penetrates the ears of those men not having lived through the Somme …

Even before the roar of the 15–2 runs out of breath, German SOS beacons are marked out by red fires. The bright naivety of these spectres describes a semicircle, in an ugly sky. One saw all of this. One saw missiles coming into sight from in front of us and along the road to Bapaume, far too many missiles. And even before the red flares go out, machine-gun bullets draw a curtain where they touch the earth … Maulin will never rejoin the cavalry. A shell exploded on the ground close to the positions of the 150th [Regiment]. He got up again for a short time only to receive, a little later, a final blow so violent that his helmet burst. I was sorry for calling yesterday's tempest poor! What should I say of this hurricane? If there is a distinction, it is that this is more of a percussive nature. The curious thing is that some people and not others are taken in the net of the hodgepodge trajectories of the shells.[23]

Soon afterwards, the French left wing would take the heights of Sailly Saillisel, and gain a footing on the ridges running north from Peronne. South of the Somme the French would close within range of its southern approaches, and shortly after began to threaten the road from St Quentin. To the north the Germans were attempting to hold the ridges to the west of Le Transloy, as the British and Canadians continued to press them relentlessly. German officer Hauptman Cordt von Brandis, serving with *Infanterie Regiment Nr 24*, was in the line for three weeks here in early October, facing Gueudecourt. For his men also it was a matter of endurance, of hanging on through the grimmest of conditions, facing the full intensity of a British barrage which blew in their dugouts and made it impossible to extract the wounded:

Hauptmann Cordt von Brandis. He held a low opinion of the British soldier in the First World War.

> In a break in the afternoon I jumped along the line to check on my other groups. Three dugouts were still intact. In the first one sat a dead person on the uppermost step, with crossed arms, chin on the breast, a gaping hole in the steel helmet, [and] below lay badly wounded the vice sergeant. 'How are you doing, Melzow?' He smiled. 'Quite well, thanks!' Everywhere the same expression in the faces, a combination of unconscious fury and defiance. These shining men tried through jokes to make easier for themselves the fight between the desire for self-preservation which says: 'Get out from this hell', get out by any means, and the sense of duty which peremptorily demands: Endure. You are positioned here, you must hold on through the fire, until you are dead or are relieved.

> Often rifles were no longer intact. Where is my gas mask? Is the machine gun still working? Does the flare pistol still function? The hours crept on further. The neighbouring company sent a dispatch runner, 'Dear B.' read the message card. 'How does it look to you? To me it seems bad, if the bastards come, please hold the flank of my company!' Now, one had to go back to the battalion behind the Luisenhof and ask them to support us with extra machine guns, as soon as red flares were sent up. It was just as well that we could count so certainly on the protection of our artillery barrage! Relentlessly, continually it howled and gargled.

> A dying man had drunk the last remnants of coffee and cried for drinking water. Three times we had tried to carry him away, but he could not go. His voice became more quiet, 'Herr Leutnant, Herr Oberleutnant!' When we did not answer immediately, his voice became threatening in his delirium. 'My men, my men. The dogs! Shoot them!' The field before us remained desolate and deadly, no Englishman appeared.

> Oh, it would have been terrible for them, we would have torn them up in our intense, pent-up fury. The British knew this, yet we had been only four days in the ditch, and they needed ten days to grind down German soldiers. Nevertheless, to their wretched rabble … must come only the hour of the repayment; it must be so if we do not wish to become disloyal to ourselves, and our dead; the amassed fury of the long defensive battles will be discharged like a storm about you, the British, in a terrible retribution![24]

Von Brandis despised the British, stating that they would not fight honestly and that they would only attack when half-drunk. He called them 'Kitchener's Mercenaries'. Yet this was an injustice to men who, despite having seen the appalling nature of warfare on the Somme, continued into the autumn to remain committed to the ideals which had led them to take up this fight in the first place. Even Mark Plowman, returning to the Somme for his second stint under fire that October, remained committed to the British cause, despite the fact that he was not naturally predisposed towards being a soldier:

A German sentry keeps a lonely vigil in a muddy trench on the Somme, autumn 1916. Note the entrance to the dugout at his feet.

I suppose I am depressed by the weather, but quite possibly by the fact that we are on our way to that place of desolation again. I wonder how, in God's name, we do go on with this life! Looked at from an individual standpoint it is the very insanity of slavery. This endless hideous life of the automaton – I shall never get used to it. I am too old. Perhaps if I were seventeen I shouldn't mind. I should know so little that was different, and this would only seem a perpetual, rather unpleasant boarding-school. I should have less memory and be less inclined to reflect. I shouldn't be carrying about a heart that's fixed: it might easily be the bladder on a fool's stick. But now sometimes the thought that I may never again know any other life than this affects me like a madness. My God! I understand desertion. A man distraught determines that the last act of his life shall at least be one of his own volition; and who can say that what is commonly regarded as the limit of cowardice is not then heroic? But the job out here's not done. The Germans are still in France. While that is so, who can talk of peace? Truly there's nothing I'd sooner be doing than helping to push the Germans out of France. Why can't the devils go of their own accord? It would settle everything. If they only retired to their own frontier, for my part the war would be over tomorrow. But they don't; so all the loathsomeness of this life is swallowed up in the consideration that the work is fundamentally good to anyone who is fit for it. I am fit. I shall go on, even gladly. But it is hell.[25]

The worsening weather, with continual rain which turned the battlefield into a morass, made Plowman's spell in the line between Gueudecourt and Les Boeufs an ordeal of almost unimaginable proportions. He writes of trenches knee-deep in mud, or sometimes flooded completely, so that movement had to be undertaken along the top, rendering him and his comrades vulnerable to snipers. Despite his best efforts to ensure that his men had changes of socks, it was impossible to keep their feet dry in conditions like this, and cases of trench foot, as well as exhaustion among ration parties making the arduous journey up to the front line, were an increasing problem.

Alexander McLintock of the 87th Canadian Battalion (Canadian Grenadier Guards) went into the line on 17 October. His battalion was part of the 4th Canadian Division and had just arrived on the Somme from Belgium. An interesting character, McLintock was born in Lexington, Kentucky, and had seen service as a United States Naval Cadet at Kentucky State University. He writes candidly of the reality of warfare on the Somme battlefield after three-and-a-half months of continuous fighting:

On the Somme, we were constantly preparing for a new advance, and we were only temporarily established on ground which we had but recently taken, after long drumming with big guns. The trenches were merely shell-holes connected by ditches. Our old and ubiquitous and useful friend, the sand bag, was not present in any capacity, and, therefore, we had no parapets or dug-outs. The communication trenches were all blown in and everything had to come to us overland, with the result that we never were quite sure when we should get ammunition, rations or relief forces. The most awful thing was that the soil all about us was filled with freshly buried men. If we undertook to cut a trench or enlarge a funk hole, our spades struck into human flesh, and the explosion of a big shell along our line sent decomposed and dismembered and sickening mementoes of an earlier fight showering amongst us. We lived in the muck and stench of 'glorious' war; those of us who lived.[26]

McLintock's battalion was about to make another attack on Regina Trench, which after several postponements eventually took place on 21 October:

It seemed almost certain death to start over in broad daylight, yet, as it turned out, the crossing of 'No Man's Land' was accomplished rather more easily than in our night raids. Our battalion was on the extreme right of the line, and that added

Private Percy Odell MM, 6th Battalion Oxford and Bucks Light Infantry, who was killed on 9 October. After the war his body was found by exhumation parties roughly halfway between Gueudecourt and Beaulencourt.

RIFLEMAN E. S. GARD,
(London Rifle Brigade).

DIED FROM WOUNDS RECEIVED IN ACTION
ON OCTOBER 19TH, 1916.

" They are not dead whose lives lift ours on high:
To live in lives we leave behind is not to die."

A memorial card for Rifleman Ernest Gard, London Rifle Brigade. Mortally wounded on 8 October 1916, he died at the base hospital at Etaples.

The wreckage of a German artillery battery caught by shell fire at Les Boeufs, October 1916.

materially to our difficulties, first by compelling us to advance through mud so deep that some of our men sank to their hips in it and, second, by giving us the hottest little spot in France to hold later.

    I was in charge of the second 'wave' or assault line. This is called the 'mopping up' wave, because the business of the men composing it is thoroughly to bomb out a position crossed by the first wave, to capture or kill all of the enemy remaining, and to put the trench in a condition to be defended against a counter-attack by reversing the fire steps and throwing up parapets.[27]

McLintock goes on to give an insightful account of his own experience in going over the top, and how he struggled – successfully – to control his own natural reaction to the stress and fear of combat. In his modesty he plays down his bravery in continuing to advance, despite having received what might well have been a 'blighty' wound, sufficient to entitle him to return back at least as far as a regimental aid post, if not a casualty clearing station:

That day on the Somme, our artillery had given the Germans such a battering and the curtain fire which our guns dropped just thirty to forty yards ahead of us was so powerful that we lost comparatively few men going over – only those who were knocked down by shells which the Germans landed among us through our barrage. They never caught us with their machine guns sweeping until we neared their trenches. Then a good many of our men began to drop, but we were in their front trench before they could cut us up anywhere near completely. Going over, I was struck by shell fragments on the hand and leg, but the wounds were not severe enough to stop me. In fact, I did not know that I had been wounded until I felt blood running into my shoe. Then I discovered the cut in my leg, but saw that it was quite shallow, and that no artery of importance had been damaged. So I went on. I had the familiar feeling of nervousness and physical shrinking and nausea at the beginning of this fight, but, by the time we were half way across 'No Man's Land,' I had my nerve back. After I had been hit, I remember feeling relieved that I hadn't been hurt enough to keep me from going on with the men. I'm not trying to make myself out a hero. I'm just trying to tell you how an ordinary man's mind works under the stress of fighting and the danger of sudden death. There are some queer things in the psychology of battle. For instance, when we had got into the German trench and were holding it against the most vigorous counter-attacks, the thought which was persistently uppermost in my mind was that I had lost the address of a girl in London along with some papers which I had thrown away, just before we started over, and which I should certainly never be able to find again.[28]

Also among the Canadians here was Private William Callister, serving with the 102nd Battalion, which attacked alongside McLintock's men on 21 October. He was understandably jubilant about his battalion's role in the capture of Regina Trench. His letter cannot be dismissed purely as bravado, and shows that resolve to carry on the fight remained strong, even as casualties mounted and the autumn weather added to the misery of the men in the front line:

We made our first bayonet charge two days ago, and gained our objective, and hold it still. Everyone is talking of the feat, the trench we took having been taken before by three different divisions, but they were always driven out. So you see the honour it is for our green battalion to take and hold it after standing for 48 hours up to our waists in freezing mud. We were a terrible sight when we came out ... We had a good many casualties, and I certainly never expected to get out of it. I was buried half a dozen times, and three 'whizz bangs' burst over my head in succession, but I was never hit ... I walked on dead men all the way out – men who have fallen through numerous battles in the same place, and it was a horrible sight. But the charge was glorious. All hardships were forgotten when the signal came to get over the top, and we were on the top of Fritz before he realized what was happening ... a chum of mine was killed at my side. He was such a nice fellow, and I felt quite sick when we buried him where he lay. Don't think by what I have written that we are downhearted; in fact it is the other extreme, as we are too proud for our boots now that our blades have been wetted.[29]

A French officer, Major Pierre Louis Breant, serving with an infantry regiment, was posted to the Somme front around this time. His regiment was stationed in front of the wood of St Pierre-Vaast, which he records that the Germans had fortified with strongholds; indeed, he was probably facing the positions held by Hauptman Mentze, whom the reader met earlier. The corps commander briefed the newly arrived French officers on the differences between this front and the Verdun sector (where they had been stationed previously). Here, they were told, it was not necessary to resist at all costs; the enemy no longer held the initiative. There were, however, certain difficulties which arose as a result of the French success on the Somme battlefield thus far: they occupied a landscape which had been devastated by earlier fighting, where there remained only shell holes and ruins. The roads were destroyed, communications were precarious, and rations and supplies unpredictable. Setting out from Maricourt on 26 October, Breant was ordered to familiarise himself with the front-line positions:

Reconnoitring forward, we finally picked up the line running parallel to Bukovine Trench. This is serious! Our troops will arrive, at God knows what time, exhausted:

what effort is involved in a relief! Soon it will become apparent. In Leusse Wood, we dismount and we pass through amidst the dreadful eruptions of the big English guns, positioned without shelter, close by the road.

A sap: a new conference with the general commanding the —— division, which we are relieving, and which is going to move to the left. We depart towards Frégicourt, leaving Combles on the right hand side, and Morval on the left. Guillemont, soon reached, was nothing but a blasted wilderness, without a wall standing. Combles, in the bottom of a ravine, still looks like a village; but not one house is undamaged. And now that we leave the rabble of the rear areas, and advance towards the front lines, we are walking through a desert. There is nothing but shell craters, the edges of which meet each other.

It is necessary to go down into them, but to get out again, one must pull one's feet free of the cloying mud. Telephone wires run across the ground, which is covered with rubbish of all kinds, the debris of the clash of two armies. Here is Frégicourt trench. A new sap is clogged by staff officers. There we see the colonel of the regiment which we are to relieve. Another conference, with explanation of plans. And we leave again. The colonel wants to explain the situation and comes with me. Our direction is towards the crest between Sailly-Saillisel and Morval, north of Tripot wood … We arrive at a place called La Carrière, where a road from Morval towards Sailly passes. It is one of the most dangerous places; shells fall everywhere; but fortunately it is getting dark. La Carrière is nevertheless crowded with detachments from several regiments. We go on, with a new guide. It is always necessary to keep moving, but one does not place two footsteps together on flat soil; there are only shell holes. My heart is pounding, and I am short of breath; even though we have almost arrived, it is necessary that I pause to catch my breath.

The guide says to us that we should not stop, because of the barrage there. Too bad! I stretch out in a shell hole. After some minutes, they come back searching for me. I set off again and right away I am at the edge of a trench. An acrid and hot breath comes out of the hole. This is the place which I am going to share with T—— and where I shall stay for six nights and five days. This incomplete sap consists of only two dug outs, linked up by a trench in which it is necessary to walk on all fours. I establish myself at the bottom of a dug out, T—— at the bottom of the other one; our battalion signallers are crammed into the steps, where they can neither stand, nor breathe.[30]

The euphemistic 'hot acrid breath' of the trench mentioned here was more than likely the stench which accrued from a position occupied by men who had no proper facilities for performing their natural bodily functions – indeed, where the threat posed by enemy snipers made it too dangerous in all probability even to use an adjacent shell hole for this purpose. The awful nature of trench warfare in the memory of

Francisque-Joseph Mazeron, adjutant of the French *98e Régiment d'Infanterie*, killed in action at Chaulnes on 28 October 1916. At the front since the beginning of the war, he had previously been cited in corps orders for his steadfastness under bombardment.

Ein Unterstand a.d. Sommefront.

A German soldier finds what shelter he can in the remains of a trench on the Somme, October 1916.

veterans is often assumed to be associated with the arbitrary and sudden death or wounding of the occupants, but at a more basic level it also stemmed from the degradation of human beings forced to live, sleep and eat surrounded by their own filth and urine. It was an experience common to both sides, for those of their men who fought on the ground.

Those in the air services, as previously noted, still enjoyed the benefits of dry billets and warm food when not actually in combat. One of these men was Bert Hall, an American pilot who flew with the French *Lafayette Escadrille*, which arrived on the Somme in October. That autumn the German air service tried hard to regain aerial dominance over the Somme battlefield; new twin-gun aircraft, which the Germans had rushed through development in order to meet the allied threat, now began to reach the front-line squadrons. Hall and his comrades were flying Spads, also newly introduced, and far superior to the types they had flown previously. However, it was not just new machinery which the Germans would employ in the air, and the aerial ability of the Spad would be of little consequence as the Germans developed a new tactic of attempting to destroy their enemy on the ground.

Hall wrote of these events:

One night the Germans dropped bombs on our quarters about 2 o'clock in the morning. One of the mechanics was killed and many men wounded. The old shack was full of holes. A hangar containing seven machines was burned, and the Boche put about sixteen others out of commission; afterwards we got these planes in shape to use again. On another night we got hit again good and plenty. The Boche did it with one well-placed bomb, too. This bomb was dropped on an ammunition depot where 100,000 shells were stored.

The shells exploded for ten hours afterwards, which was rather peculiar, only a few exploding at a time. They certainly made quite a little noise. Amiens was bombed at night, killing a large number of women and children. These bombing raids at night were a feature of the fighting all that fall at the Somme. Of course we retaliated, going out after the Boche. It proved to be some of the most difficult work we had. It is almost impossible to see another machine at night unless you happen on it at very close range. Then it is very likely to be one of your own comrades. The risk to both pilot and machine is great – to the latter because landing is very difficult with a fast machine at night.

Otherwise our life at the Somme front was very agreeable. There were more than one hundred flyers of the fighting groups all on the same field. The formations here were called groups and consisted of four squadrons or escadrilles. Each one was made up of twelve flyers, four officers including the commanding officer and eight non-commissioned officers. Thus one group consisted of forty-eight machines. Each group was commanded by a major who fixed the hours and issued all orders. We had a regular routine of work, flying by patrol between fixed points, two hours and thirty minutes to each patrol. We went out once a day and were at alert for two hours and thirty minutes also.[31]

Hall also made a direct reference to the battle fatigue to which combat pilots were particularly susceptible, and gave an indication of its primary cause:

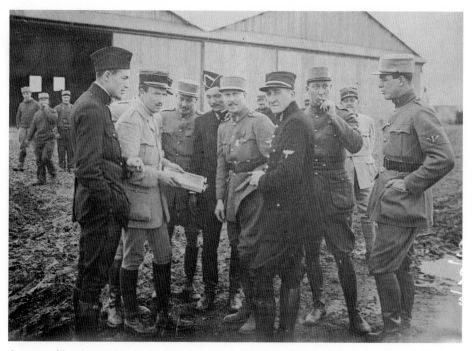

A group of American pilots in the French air service, 1916. Bert Hall stands at the centre, half turned toward the camera, wearing a dark uniform.

A great many men have nervous breakdowns or heart troubles and are sent to a separate hospital where they are treated by specialists and well rested before they are sent back. The life of an aviator at the front is very short. No one knows the exact figures, but I have heard it put at about seventeen hours of actual flying.[32]

For airmen as well as ground troops, Germans as well as British or French, regular leave was an important aspect of maintaining morale. For one particularly lucky German officer, a spell of home leave was followed almost immediately by a brief return to Germany to enable his artillery battery to refit in advance of a tour of duty on the southern part of the Somme front. This officer, Robert Hess, in writing to the newspaper of his Heidelberg University fraternity, described his sojourn in Berlin before recounting his journey to the Somme. Apart from the detail of his experiences in the French sector of the battlefield that autumn, he also, by way of an intriguing aside, casts light on the growing anti-Semitism within the German army at this time. This is widely supposed to have begun with Hitler in the 1930s, but in fact as early as 1915 a census of Jewish officers had been conducted, as it was perceived within the German army that Jews were not pulling their weight. Hess tells us that:

Gefreiter Josef Manzinger, Bavarian *Infanterie Regiment Nr 24*, who was killed in action on 4 November 1916.

The tale of my stay in this exciting city is marred by slight dysentery, which I had brought with me from the swampy forest, and by the sight of the many 'complaining' Berlin Jewish boys which did nothing to offset this evil, however, a respectable burgundy in the Kempinski hotel and the Kaiserkeller prevented it from getting worse. Shortly after my return to the battery came the command to change position. 'Do not move to the Somme, my son, mark my words,' sang a comrade ominously. The direction was right – St Quentin. There, suddenly, the command: the battery will be loaded for Cologne. Oh the joy of our fellows!

In Cologne, it was nice. We received new guns with fresh recoil springs and covers, we partook of the theatre, coffee houses, confectionery and all other worldly pleasures, and then after ten days, on 4 October we went to Cambrai – on the Somme. When we were posted here, although the peak of the great battle was already passed, after all, still we were greeted by heavy artillery fire from the west. It was hardly gratifying that during the march into quarters, at a railroad crossing one of our baggage wagons was destroyed and three horses were killed. Our location, Liéramont, was crowded with troops, so that men and horses had to bivouac in the dirt, and when we then finally received documents necessary to obtain houses, the enemy fired into our quarters, killing and wounding some of our people; the billeting problem was finally resolved in that our quarters were removed to Lempire about twenty miles behind the front. Our self-built dog-cart is used to take us to the firing line. This is in the area east of Bouchavesnes, and was very soon located by the enemy; we had therefore to endure some hostile fire. But two meter deep approach trenches and tunnels with 5–6 meters of cover protect against the worst damage. In this sector it was rather lively until mid–November. Trenches, batteries and rear area communications were under heavy fire, but it did not come to an attack. It was different in the adjacent northern sector, St Pierre-Vaast, Sailly. Instead there were almost daily small-scale attacks here, under fierce artillery activity; my battery supported the neighbouring sector with their long-range guns. It was serious on 5 November, when we lost a line of trenches between Sailly and the northern edge of St Pierre-Vaast Wood, however, after a solid artillery preparation, on 15 November it was taken back once again by Fusilier Regiment Nr 73.

Since that time it has all become a lot quieter and one has the impression that the Somme battle has ended. But the winter consists of rain, cold, snow and mud. From service in the firing position and observation, these are now replaced with walks and explorations in the trenches and shell holes of the infantry. With the classically shaped steel helmet on the head, and thigh boots on the legs, one wades through the waterlogged positions, filled with compassion and admiration for the brave men who have to endure here, and comes back looking like a lump of clay into quarters.[33]

Even as autumn was drawing into winter, the offensive still ground on. Perhaps surprisingly given the conditions, morale among the British remained generally high. The Fifth Army under General Gough was now given the task of capturing a number of objectives on either side of the River Ancre in the northern part of the British front. This would have the effect of clearing the Germans from the remaining portion of the Thiepval Ridge, and also bringing pressure to bear on parts of the German line which had not been subjected to a major attack since 1 July. It was hoped that after several months of fighting, the garrisons might now have been sufficiently weakened to enable these objectives to be taken, and a bombardment considerably heavier than that which preceded the attacks of 1 July fell upon Beaumont Hamel and the trench systems to the north and south.

The 51st Highland Division, a territorial unit regarded as one of the best in the BEF, was given the objective of Beaumont Hamel itself, whilst the 63rd (Royal Naval) Division was allotted the task of attacking Beaucourt sur Ancre to the southeast. The morning of 9 November found its battalions bivouacking in tents in cold and wet conditions; they had been reduced in number by illness, and there had been little sleep to be had in the days leading up to the attack. None the less, the RND had a sense of esprit de corps all of its own, as the adjutant of Hawke Battalion, Douglas Jerrold, confirmed. In speaking of the officers of his own battalion, he recorded:

We ourselves had few expectations [yet] officers left out of the attack bombarded me with bitter complaints, and one at least came up the line and led his company, in direct defiance of orders ... And yet we knew, as a matter of certainty, that most of us (all of us, it turned out) would be dead or wounded in the next twenty four hours.[34]

Jerrold wrote perceptively that in those days he and his brother officers were motivated by the idea (which as Jerrold saw it, later turned out to be an illusion) that youth held in its hands the fortunes of the world. The veterans of the Somme sometimes looked back with a cynical view of the battle, but this is to belie the very real idealism which existed at the time. As he waited in No Man's Land to follow up the successful attack of 13 November, Jerrold had a grandstand view of the battle:

> Every variety of shell was dropping, but we only saw the lines of infantry, first of our own men, then of the Nelson Battalion, disappearing into the mist in perfect order and sequence. Any barrack square in Christendom would have been dignified by such an exhibition of precision. Here, for hundreds of simple and Christian men, was their hour of opportunity. Here all grievances were forgotten and all enmity healed. 'They went like Kings in a pageant to the imminent death.' I shall never see a sight more noble. I was, you see, in the front row of the stalls. Eight lines of men passed me so closely that I could see every expression on their faces as they faded into the mist, and among all those men walking resolutely to wounding or death, I saw not one expression of fear or regret, or even of surprise.[35]

Moving forward fifteen minutes later, Jerrold discovered that the Hawke Battalion had been more or less destroyed, after being pinned down by a German strongpoint which had not been identified in the mist. Jerrold himself shortly afterwards lost an arm to a nearby shell burst, and after treatment from a medical orderly spent the remainder of the day and night in a shell hole.

Sidney Howard meanwhile served with the Honourable Artillery Company in the action at Beaucourt on 13 November, his duty being to carry Mills bombs. He wrote afterwards:

A German 17cm Minenwerfer trench mortar, captured at Beaucourt sur Ancre in November 1916. (*National Library of Scotland*)

On our right, across the Ancre, things appeared to have gone well. Snipers' bullets were heard occasionally, and now and then we crouched as a shell crashed on the road. Beyond the redoubt shone the fire of a burning dug out, evidently set alight by our bombers with incendiary grenades. But I had no time to stop and survey the scene. We passed by scores of British dead. I clambered past one man who had been shot through the head. He had collapsed in a sitting posture. The bullet had taken the top of his head off. His brains were hanging over one side of his face like a dreadful cap, but it was not that which affected me. His arms were stretched out horizontally in front of his body … as though he were holding his arms out to welcome a child running towards him.[36]

After delivering his supplies, Howard was asked by an officer to attend to a number of dead men from his battalion who had fallen in the attack:

It was the custom among us to try to ensure that the personal effects of a dead man should be retrieved with all possible speed and sent to relatives. Many of us wrote a letter to the one who meant most to us. We carried that letter in our paybooks. If a man was killed, his comrade took that letter from the dead and forwarded it. I did what our custom required for these six men.[37]

Returning from one journey late in the day, Howard came upon a line of men lying by the side of the road. He assumed they were dead, and only when he came closer did he realise that these were other bearers, who had fallen asleep in the mud despite the bitter cold, so exhausted were they. The following day brought more carrying work, until the day was drawing to a close:

[Then] we began our last task – to bury twelve of our comrades in the crater made by a monster shell. 'Huggie' was among the dead. I looked down upon his face and recalled how I had ragged him about the length of his hair … It was not good for men to bury their own like that … It is bad enough when you do not know them, but when you have been a man's comrade for weary months of war, when you have glimpsed the wonder of his soul, and then you look upon the lifeless husk of that bright spirit … Silently, we turned away.[38]

Private Roland Marsden, 2nd Royal Marine Battalion, who was killed in action on 13 November at Beaucourt.

Another eyewitness to this action was Geoffrey Sparrow, a Royal Naval surgeon and medical officer. He recounted the extraordinary bravery of individuals under fire:

Numerous unrecorded incidents of that advance are still fresh in my mind. To see Sergeant Meatyard of the Marines unconcernedly following behind the attacking companies, unrolling his coil of telephone wire as he advanced, was an incident typical of the coolness displayed by all ranks. It was entirely due to his initiative that telephone communication with Brigade Headquarters was kept up during the attack. The mending of this wire, when it was once established, was a matter of no small difficulty, and all of us who reached the bank on the far side of the Station Road remember the very gallant and successful attempts made to reopen our only method of communication with the rear. Sergeant Meatyard was eventually severely wounded, and later received a very well-deserved Military Medal.[39]

Sparrow continued with a description of the way in which by sheer force of personality a commanding officer could inspire his men to continue through the most trying of conditions:

When I reached the Station Road, above which the remains of the two Marine and Anson Battalions were digging themselves in, the only officers left in those three battalions were Lieutenant-Colonels Hutchison and Cartwright of the Royal Marines, Lieutenant-Commander Ellis and Captain Gowney of the Anson, Lieutenant van Praag and myself. All the remainder were killed or wounded, but there was no time for vain regrets. Colonel Hutchison took charge of this mixed body of men, and by his coolness, bravery, and wonderful personality, kept them cheerful and hard at work improving their position during the following two days and nights.[40]

Finally there was a reminder that after many months of fighting against Germans in improvised field positions as they were steadily pushed back across the battlefield, here they were in the original front line, prepared and strengthened during the almost two years of 'peace' on the Somme front before the battle began. The achievement of the British soldiers here in overcoming these carefully prepared defences was thus all the greater:

We were able to take over a large German dug-out along with a Boche medical officer, who rendered us great assistance until we were finally forced to send him back to the prisoners' cage. This dug-out was the most sumptuous I had ever seen. It was three storeys deep, and fitted with wire mattresses for over three hundred men. There were entrances from 'No Man's Land', from the first, second, and third line trenches, and also one facing the Station Road, up to which a light railway had been laid. It consisted of innumerable small rooms, offices, kitchens, messes and store-rooms, all of which were scattered with clothing, food, equipment and other material which had been hurriedly abandoned. One room was fitted up as an aid post, and was a model of its kind. It was lined with red canvas, lit with electric light, and replete with innumerable splints, bandages, instruments and drugs. Opening out of this was a ward containing twelve beds where the sick could be made very comfortable. In another part was what had been apparently an officers' mess, lined with a tasteful red wallpaper and adorned with pictures, a large gilt mirror, a mahogany table, and comfortable red plush chairs. Not far distant was a well-filled wine cellar and a luxurious kitchen. In this palatial dug-out we stored our casualties until the field ambulance stretcher-bearers arrived to evacuate them. On the afternoon of November 15th we were relieved, and wended our weary way back to Englebelmer, our numbers sadly depleted, but every man very cheery at the thought that the Royal Naval Division had advanced further, and taken more prisoners, than any other division engaged in the attack.[41]

British stretcher-bearers pick up a casualty on the flooded banks of the Ancre.

Another medical officer at work during this action was Colonel David Rorie, in command of the 1st/2nd Highland Field Ambulance, which was part of the 51st Highland Division. He wrote of the important work of the stretcher bearers in the aftermath of this battle, and indeed of the participation of German prisoners of war in this vital task:

> At 5.30 on November 13 our furious barrage started, and by 7am a steady stream of wounded was flowing in, which lasted all day; but evacuation went on well and steadily, with no congestion at the various posts. At 11am and 2.45pm Auchonvillers was vigorously shelled; and we had, for the time being, to carry all the cases lying in the farmyard, awaiting dressing or removal, inside our already crowded dressing-room. By the middle of the forenoon German prisoners began passing in large numbers, and a

hundred fit men were held up to help clear the field of their own wounded. These men were fed and treated like our own bearers, and worked willingly and well, being docile to a degree; any number up to fifteen at a time going off in charge of one RAMC man.[42]

Two days later Rorie was part of a group which went out in the biting cold and drizzling rain, searching shattered trenches and dugouts for any wounded men who might have been overlooked in the actual battle. It was a grim and unenviable task, and Rorie recalls one incident in particular:

This dug-out was typical of the many with which Beaumont Hamel was honeycombed. On descending about forty steps one was in a large floored and timbered chamber some fifty feet long; and at the farther end a second set of steps led to a similar chamber, one side of each being lined with a double layer of bunks filled with dead and wounded Germans, the majority of whom had become casualties early on the morning of the 13th. The place was, of course, in utter darkness; and when we flashed our lights on and the wounded saw our escort with rifles ready, there was an outbreak of 'kamerade!' while a big bevy of rats squeaked and scuttled away from their feast on the dead bodies on the floor. The stench was indescribably abominable, for many of the cases were gas gangrenous.

Any food or drink they possessed was used up, and our water bottles were soon emptied amongst them. After we had gone over the upper chamber and separated the living from the dead, we went to the lower one where the gas curtain was let down and fastened. Tearing it aside and going through with a light, I got a momentary jump when I caught a glimpse in the upper bunk of a man, naked to the waist and with his right hand raised above his head. But the poor beggar was far past mischief – stark and stiff with a smashed pelvis. Some twenty other dead Germans lay about at the disposal of the rat hordes. The romance of war had worn somewhat thin here.[43]

Joseph Smith also took part in the battle for Beaumont Hamel as part of the 51st Highland Division. He was yet another American serving with a British unit, this time as an officer with the Royal Scots. Even after the battle, there was no respite for these weary men:

The night of the fifteenth [November] we were relieved to go behind the lines and reorganize. About three o'clock the next morning we arrived in billets, dead tired but very happy. I had been reported killed and my valise, with a change of clothing and my bed, had been sent down the line. Dempsey was equal to the occasion, however, and produced a bed – from

Private George Sturman of the Cambridgeshire Regiment, who was killed in action near Beaumont Hamel on 13 November 1916.

where shall always remain a mystery. Things went bad in the line and at six o'clock that evening, a considerably battered bunch of men, we marched away to brigade reserve behind the lines. The men were still pretty much exhausted from their previous three days and roundly cursed the troops in the front, but up they went. On the night of the seventeenth we were ordered to relieve a knocked-about battalion in a new part of the line a little further south. Considering that I had one other officer and sixty-seven effectives by that time in my company, it struck us as a rather ghastly joke.

Eventually we reached the new line, if you can call it that, since there were no trenches. Only a couple of dugouts could be found. I divided the company into two parts, half in each dugout. The rest of the night I spent getting our bearings, with Dempsey's help, while the men stocked up the shelters with rations and water. At five o'clock in the morning all the men with me turned into our shelter – one of the kind known as a 'tube'. If you took half a subway car, stuck it in the ground and covered the top with two or three feet of earth, you would have a 'tube' dugout. Inside are seats as in the subway, and through the center runs a rudely constructed table.

Instantly the seats were crowded with 'Jocks', full fighting kit on, dog tired, and trying to rest. In the center of the table I placed some rations. Just outside, two sentries were posted while inside we slept. Six o'clock came, and with it merry hell! The Canadians just south of us were launching an attack and the Germans had put a barrage on our lines. I went outside to see my sentries. It was just breaking day and a light snow was falling. The shelling was heavy and was being aided by machine-gun fire. I turned to go in and rout out the men, as I thought we were to be attacked. Just as I stepped in, a shell lit at the door, seriously wounding the two sentries. We dragged them inside and the shelling increased to such violence there was no use putting other sentries out. I held a candle while the Red Cross men bandaged the wounded, both with bad thigh wounds. The candle was blown out time and time again by the concussion of the shells and the place reeked with burnt powder and blood.

All day this fire continued. The entrance to our dugout was blown in twice so that we had to dig it out to get fresh air. One man crept through the opening for a moment. We never found him. The rear corner was blown off and some of the men were made violently ill by the fumes, but still we sat there, waiting for the crash that would hurl us into eternity. It never came, though, and a little after ten that night it grew quiet enough for us to risk leaving our shelter. We had two badly wounded men to get to the dressing station and water and rations to locate, but the relief to the nerves after that day of hell was so great that the men went out on their parties softly singing. Exhaustion could not stop them. The rest of the night and the next day were comparatively quiet and that evening we were relieved.[44]

Even as the middle of November came and went, fresh attacks were still being made by the British, though by now it was very much a case of diminishing returns. Roy Corlett, who served as a second lieutenant with the King's Own Yorkshire Light Infantry, was wounded and captured on the Somme in November 1916. His battalion had been allotted the task of capturing Munich Trench and it attacked before dawn in driving sleet and rain. Visibility was practically nil, and the objectives, already hard to discern, were soon covered in snow. Corlett's official statement of the circumstances of his capture, which he was required to make to the War Office upon eventual repatriation, is matter of fact and to the point, and for the most part draws a veil over the detail of what must have been an awful business. Part of his statement runs as follows:

> My unit, the 2nd Battalion KOYLI attacked at 6.10 near Serre, on November 18th 1916. My orders were to take the third line of enemy trenches with my platoon. We reached the first line, and proceeded as quickly as possible up a communication trench towards the second line. We cleared this trench. I shot two of the enemy with my revolver; the remainder were disposed of by rifle fire. We sent a few prisoners back to the first line ... This communication trench ended at the second line, so I decided to go over the open to the third line. We came under fire, and a number of us were hit. I was hit by a ricochet rifle bullet in the knee. A corporal put on a tourniquet and bandaged my knee. I tried to proceed with this corporal's help, but found my wounded leg perfectly useless; so I sent him on. I crawled towards the third line, but could only proceed very slowly, as I had to pull myself along with my hands ... before I reached the third line, the enemy ... sent out a party of about twenty under an officer. I was captured by these people, who gave me a German Red Cross man and an English private wounded in the arm to carry me down a dugout.[45]

This was part of the final offensive operation of the battle, at least as far as the BEF was concerned. If there is one criticism of the British high command during the Somme battle that can be justified, then it must surely be that military operations were continued far too late into autumn to stand any real chance of success. Guns could not be brought up through the mud to new firing positions, and even if they could, ammunition could not easily be carried to them over a battlefield which had been devastated. For men who had in many cases already seen a great deal of combat, even reaching the front now in deep slush and mud was time-consuming and exhausting in its own right. Ashley Gibson, serving as a subaltern with the 20th Battalion Royal Fusiliers, wrote of such experiences afterwards:

> The mud got no solider. It was dashed cold, but wouldn't freeze. We went in again, back at Lesboeufs, and came out with my company seventy greatcoats short. There was an awful row, but how can a man drag half a hundredweight of dripping, slime-sodden felt on top of his arms, ammunition and equipment, through three miles of morass under shell-fire? They saved their gas-masks, which was something. Helping me re-adjust my pack before starting, my batman rested his own on what looked like a solid sandbag. When

Corporal Clement Anchant, 7th Battalion Royal West Kent Regiment. He was wounded and taken prisoner on 18 November 1916, in the last British action on the Somme.

he turned around it was gone, swallowed up clean. Napoo. Stragglers got hopelessly bogged. There were lives lost that way.

D Company were detailed for a small show on their own. The line, such as it was, wanted straightening, up beyond Dewdrop and Summer trenches, so-called optimistically in the new maps. The lie of the ground was again unfavourable. In supports we heard Fritz start up with his machine-guns, and knew exactly what was happening. One officer brought them back. My excellent batman and I had crawled forward in the middle of the operation to see if the supports could do anything, but what had to be done was, apparently, already accomplished.

Wylie's grey and ravaged countenance (our oldest, he was forty-three, and now looked sixty) peered over the wet sandbags, and his dull eyes, opaque like those of a dead man, moved stiffly in their sockets. 'No thanks,' he said. 'But have you got your brandy flask? Mine's empty.'

War's main horror was something different down here. It wasn't the smell any longer, the universal, ever-present, trenchy odour of mortality plus chloride of lime that had tainted every moment of existence in earlier days of campaigning. The air at least was cleaner here; one could breathe it without that perpetual inclination to vomit. What wore and jangled us was the everlasting deprivation of sleep. We never had more than two hours off duty, for week after week. Short of officers as we were, we knew this demand upon us was unavoidable. But it made old men of us before our time.[46]

Even as offensive operations drew to a close, the steady drain of men through the attrition of trench warfare continued. Jean Julien Weber, a French priest who had joined the colours as an officer upon the outbreak of war, rejoined his unit, the *21e Regiment d'Infanterie* on the Somme after a spell in hospital in late October 1916. On 19 November his unit was in the front line near Ablaincourt when an arbitrary and sudden incident caused devastation:

On the 19th [November] at 11 hours, I had to inspect my saps when the bombardment became more violent. I decided to take shelter in my old command post. At the moment I set foot on the first step, a tremendous explosion took place and my helmet rolled off into the hole. Some grenades exploded. I thought it was a German attack and rushed outside. In fact, it was the ammunition store which had exploded, blocking the trench, and engulfing twenty-eight occupants in the shelter which was below it. It was now nothing more than a smoking funnel. The Germans fired more shots accurately onto the scene of the accident. I met on my journey Legangneux the lieutenant of the 5th company who came to my command post during my visit to the saps. I was lucky to have this brave young officer. With some men, under fire, he began to dig. He managed to find an entrance that had collapsed, but not completely. It was therefore possible to save some men: twenty came out on their own, telling of the horror that had seized them, the second such anxiety they had experienced. Some were very ill. There were still eight men left, a man named Guillaume Gauthier told me. I wanted to see for myself.

An officer of the brigade who had come to see the progress of saps had now arrived at the scene. I quickly showed him, and then equipped with my holy oil I tried to climb into the shelter. It was in vain: the hole was too narrow. I took off my jacket and I could enter, not, however, without tearing my braces. Sergeant Ringard, brave, tall and thin, accompanied me. We descended without noticing that we had crawled over the corpse of stretcher bearer Fiolet. There was a candle to illuminate us. It died. The only match we had left failed. I appealed to the rest for a flashlight. We then saw the corpse of Fiolet. At the other exit of the shelter, Corporal Gindre was smothered by the earth which had been erupted. A soldier named Fouquet was delirious, sitting and waving his arms wide. Sergeant Comptour lay, quietly groaning. Two others lay one on top of the other. Everything was in a state of chaos indicating panic. But the shelter had not collapsed. I extracted those I could reach: we hoped to save just four.[47]

These men met their fate not in going over the top, but instead suffering the horror of being buried alive in the apparent safety of their dugout. Even the simple task of survival on a battlefield laid waste by months of shelling was a challenge as autumn gave way to winter. Charles Carrington, at the time an officer with the Royal Warwickshire Regiment, reflected upon this phase of the battle in 1974:

We did six weeks at Le Sars on the Albert to Bapaume road, the road that runs right through the battlefield. This I think was the hardest physical experience that we ever went through and we lost a third of our strength simply through illness. Through trench diseases, trench foot and trench fever. We were simply never warm. Always cold, never dry, always with wet feet and coming out of the line for what was called a rest there was nowhere to go because you were in the middle of this vast devastated area of Somme battlefield which had been completely deprived of its inhabitants where there wasn't a single house standing. Hardly a tree standing, a landscape entirely composed of mud, and one camped in very rough huts or tents in the greatest misery in the mud. I

An aerial photograph showing the Albert–Bapaume road at Le Sars, November 1916. The white chalk indicates the site of thousands of shell bursts.

don't know that I can say much more of this except that it went on and on and seemed as if it was never coming to an end.[48]

Thus the battle ground to a halt amid the chill and mists of autumn; there was already some snow on the ground in October – the winter of 1916/17 would be one of the coldest in living memory and it had started early. What had been achieved in the preceding four-and-a-half months? There is no doubt that the British in particular had moved from being junior partners in the western entente to now holding the initiative. Sir Douglas Haig had once told Lord Kitchener that he did not command an army in France, more a collection of untrained divisions. Now those divisions had learned their trade in the hardest school of all. Co-operation between infantry, artillery and, of course, tanks were all new skills, but these had been learned or were being learned and would be applied in the following year. The cost of this learning curve had been appallingly high.

General Erich Ludendorff. He knew that the German army could not withstand another experience like the Battle of the Somme.

The casualty return is disputed, but one source gives total allied casualties for the Battle of the Somme as 490,000, as against German losses of 520,000.

Controversy will for ever surround the Somme offensive, particularly over whether this price had to be so high, and if it was worth paying. Perhaps one answer to this is provided by the Germans. There can be no doubt that the German army had been severely damaged by the Battle of the Somme. Their withdrawal to the Hindenburg Line <u>before it was even finished</u> can be seen as little else but an admission of defeat. Ludendorff told his political masters that it was imperative that the German army be spared another Somme battle, and in his memoirs he stated that by the end of 1916 his infantry had been fought to a standstill and were utterly worn out. If one accepts that there could be no conclusion to the First World War which was politically acceptable to Britain and France without the German army being first destroyed or at least seriously reduced in strength and morale, then the Battle of the Somme must be seen as a necessary, if costly, step towards this outcome.

Chapter Seven

Epilogue

T he Battle of the Somme made its indelible mark both upon the landscape over which it was fought, and upon those who lived through it. The battlefields themselves were left, in the months which followed, as a shattered wilderness. In many places not a single structure remained above ground, beyond a few huts and tents. In the early spring of 1917 the Germans had fallen back to the Hindenburg Line, and in doing so abandoned many of the positions which they had fought so hard to defend the previous year. Strongpoints which battalion after battalion of men had flung themselves at were now captured almost without a shot being fired. In the north, at Gommecourt, the 1st/4th Leicesters, who had been in reserve on 1 July, walked across No Man's Land the following February and occupied the positions opposite without sustaining a single casualty. The regimental historian observes ruefully that as they did so they passed the remains of those who had been killed in the original attack on Gommecourt eight months earlier, still lying exactly where they had fallen in No Man's Land. The tide of war had receded from the Somme and left its debris behind like driftwood on a beach. Not all of the debris, however, was inanimate – some of it still lived and breathed. Ardern Beaman was a captain in the Indian Army attached to the 4th Hussars. In *The Squadroon* he writes of an incident in early 1917 in which he led a party in search of a group of escaped German prisoners of war:

> Soon we got into the old front system of the Somme, the wildest part of it that I had ever seen. At one bound the war had rolled on from there to the Hindenburg Line. The armies of France had swept over it and on, leaving it behind them, and it was still as they had left it. Here and there were hideously disembowelled factories and machinery, all overgrown with grass. Food, stores, ammunition and unburied dead, still lay plentifully around. At Fresnes on the borders of this horrid desolation, we met a Salvage Company at work. They told us that we were the first people they had seen since they had been there, and they laughed at our mission. That warren of trenches and dug-outs extended for untold miles, and we might as well look for a needle in a haystack. They warned us, if we insisted on going further in, not to let any men go singly, but only in strong parties, as the Golgotha was peopled with wild men, British, French, Australian, German deserters, who lived there underground, like ghouls among the mouldering dead, and who came out at nights to plunder and to kill. In the night, an officer said, mingled with the snarling of carrion dogs, they often heard inhuman cries and rifle shots coming from that awful wilderness, as though the bestial denizens were fighting among themselves; and none of the Salvage Company ever ventured beyond the confines of their camp after the sun had set. Once they had put out, as a trap, a basket containing food, tobacco, and a bottle of whisky. But the following morning they found the bait untouched, and a note in the basket, 'Nothing doing!'[1]

A contemporary card showing the original Australian memorial at Pozières, erected around 1918.

Even two years later, as the war was drawing to a close, the devastated landscape had still not recovered. British officer Alban F. Bacon, writing in October 1918, observed:

> On our way we passed over the Somme battlefield, that scene of, perhaps, the bloodiest fighting in the whole war; and never have I seen a more terrible sight, with overthrown tanks, like antediluvian monsters, brooding over the desolate, shell-pitted scene. Had the Devil wished to create a dreary waste of a fair land he could have done no better than did the Hun with smiling Picardy. It was a scene calculated to sink the cheeriest soul into the profoundest gloom.[2]

The English journalist and poet William Arthur Dunkerley (who wrote under the name 'John Oxenham') managed to arrange for a tour of the battlefields almost as soon as hostilities had ceased. For him, the Somme battlefield had almost a holy quality, for in his eyes the ground had been consecrated by so much British blood spilled upon it. He wrote:

> Next day we started early for the battlefields of the Somme. A long run through living country, where the villages still stood upright and were occupied; where children still trotted to school, and priests in long soutanes and shovel-hats lent an air to the proceedings; where there were cattle in the pastures and tractor ploughs on the corn-lands, – till, bit by bit, these were all left behind and we were in the dead-lands once more, – the lands swept bare by the fiery tide of war, and we came at last, after a look round Gommecourt, to Beaumont Hamel. Captain L. had fought here and knew all the ground like a book. He took us over our own lines and the German lines, into dug-outs and trenches, along duck-boards through the gardens of the chateau all cratered with shell-holes, and out over No Man's Land on to the grim desolated wastes where the fighting had been bitter and bloody. And often he stood and looked round on specially remembered spots with eyes full of knowledge and painful reminiscence.
>
> The salvage men had carried off almost everything worth saving, even to the boardings of the trenches and dug-outs. The trenches were still well defined but much fallen in, and seemed small compared with the work they had had to do. Their narrow proportions brought home to one the difficulties of passage for gear-laden men or stretcher-bearers. The dug-outs were mostly dilapidated. But one we went down some sixteen steps into, cut out of the solid chalk, was in good condition and still contained a very decent bedstead strewn with hay, and had possibly been used by some of our salvage men. It had a gallery running perhaps a hundred yards to another outlet. An industrious mole is the Boche, but full of venomous guile. When the owner of the chateau heard

that the Germans had been driven back, she exclaimed with joy, 'Now I can go back home!' But by that time nothing was left of the chateau but the front gate-posts and a handful of tumbled stones and many great holes. As we stood by the great mine-crater which crossed the German trenches, looking out over the scored and pitted wastes of the countryside towards the flooded Ancre, and Grandcourt and Petit Miraumont on the opposite bank, every inch of which was won by our men at such terrible cost, a friend at my side said quietly, 'It reminds me of a Scottish moor. But a Scottish moor is full of life, and here there is nothing but death, death, death.'

And again – and overwhelmingly – there came upon us the thought that, but for the good providence of God and the mighty valour of those men who had held the ways, this which we were looking at might well have been our lot at home. Suffolk and Essex, Kent and Surrey might have been – nay, assuredly would have been – blasted desolations like these, if by any means the evil powers could have compassed it, and – unless the fleet had managed to stop it.[3]

In the months and years after the war, the villagers of the Somme would return and reclaim their farms, their homes and their former lives. They were assisted at first in the British sector by the army, which provided huts and temporary accommodation. Gradually nature, and human effort, restored the lush and fertile fields to much the same appearance as they had had before the war, superficially at any rate. Stephen Graham, visiting the battlefield in 1920 wrote:

Ten years ago the whole land was a fair pleasaunce. Ten years hence it will doubtless be tamed again if not so fair. The *sinistrés* of the Somme are doing a marvellous work already, filling in the pits, levelling with their spades, and ploughing up the whole with their little petrol-ploughs. The shell-splashed approaches to the line can with industry be recovered. And the Frenchman when working for himself has what seems a slavish love of toil. He does his real worship bending over *la France* and he will work on to the end. He has to do a hundred times what he has already done – and he will do it. A hundredth part of the battle area of the Somme has been recovered, and on the ninety-nine parts grow all that naturally would arise if man died out upon this fertile world.[4]

But the evidence of what had taken place here would never be far away. Yves Foucat, a young Frenchman growing up around Pozières in the 1930s, was fond of hunting rabbits. He had no need of a gun, for each time he set off on an expedition he would simply retrieve a rifle from a ditch. If it was broken, he threw it away and a hundred yards or so further on would find another. This young man would go on to become a gardener for the Imperial (later Commonwealth) War Graves Commission. The cemeteries built for the fallen (of whatever nationality) would in due course become the most visible reminders of what had taken place here. Stephen Graham again:

Near Bernafay … the crosses of the dead lie spread out like rows of pins, memorial crosses where there is no body, crosses for the unknown, more surely for the unknown British soldier than for the known. So also it will be with them. The babies are rising, the younger men are growing, growing to hide all and everything. The nakedness of reality which we see to-day will be hidden in the shade by and by. These brand-new cemeteries, looking often so fresh and rich in their masses of brown-stained wood, will pass. They will first be re-set up in stone. 1921 will see them rolling out in new stone crosses, at first startlingly pallid and virginal, but as the months go on, getting gradually greyened and darkened, rain-washed, wind-blown, then falling a little from the straight … Meanwhile look reverently at the graves of the men of the 32nd A.I.F., with little rising suns adorning the centre-posts of their crosses! See where lies Capt. Claude with his high memorial, or Private Harry who carried out an equal sacrifice with him. Rusty old cans on ten-foot poles mark the limits of the burial-ground, and a notice says 'Cemetery closed' as one might read outside a theatre at night – 'Pit full' 'Gallery full' 'Stalls full'. On the hillside above sounds the laughter of men and the clatter of spades where a new acre of God is being dug, the foundations of a new theatre being laid. Here French Negroes, Flemings, and French peasants are at work under the guidance of British soldiers. Occasionally a car rushes up through the dust and a couple of British officers come forward to see how things are going on.[5]

After the war the Imperial War Graves Commission (IWGC) took over from the army the task of searching for and exhuming bodies for reburial in war cemeteries. The process went on well into the 1920s, with some areas searched six times. Experience was vital in knowing where to dig. Indeed, the IWGC preferred experienced men such as former soldiers for this work. Clues to the location of remains included rifles or stakes protruding from the ground, bearing helmets or equipment, and partial remains or equipment on the surface or protruding from the ground. Rat holes were a clue – often small bones or pieces of equipment would be brought to the surface by the rats. Discoloration of grass was another sign – often it was a vivid bluish-green with broader blades where bodies

A sketch made by a fellow officer of the battlefield grave of Captain Lionel Crouch, killed in action on 21 July 1916, as it appeared at the end of the war. His body was later exhumed and moved to Pozières British Cemetery.

were buried. Sticks pushed into the ground would sink in more easily where a body was located. Once found, the remains were placed on cresol-soaked canvas. For identification purposes, a careful examination of pockets, the neck, wrists and braces for identity discs was required. Personal effects such as watches were forwarded to base, and in the case of an unidentified casualty a record was kept of features such as rank pips, regimental buttons, or distinctive dental work. An officer might also be distinguished by privately made boots.

Louis Perret, whose remains were reinterred in the French National Cemetery at Bouchavesnes after the war.

Similar work was undertaken on the French parts of the Somme battlefield as bodies were exhumed and brought into the large National Cemeteries which were created for the French dead. Brigadier Louis Perret was killed by a bullet to the forehead near Bouchavesnes on 25 September 1916. With the coming of peace, and the beginning of the concentration of isolated graves, family members were summoned to assist with his identification. His mother could not face the prospect but his father and a younger brother made the journey. Led by the reburial team, they went to a group of three isolated graves marked by a single cross, the brother later recalling:

> But with the first turn of the pitchfork rust-coloured bones were brought to the light of day and the exhumers, quickly noting the disorder of the skeletons, gently invited my father to identify amongst them those which belonged to his son. 'According to the teeth,' they said, 'or the size of the long bones.' He nodded, looked questioningly at me, and replied gently with words to the effect of: 'Just do your best', which was meant not just out of modesty, but also of kindness.[6]

The gravediggers divided the bones into three lots that were then hastily placed in labelled bags and transported to the cemetery under construction at Bouchavesnes.

Between the wars many ex-servicemen and the families of the deceased made the pilgrimage to the Somme to find the last resting-place of a loved one or comrade. Indeed, so popular were these pilgrimages among the British that the Michelin series of guides to the battlefields were published to cater for the demand for accurate maps. In 1932 the Thiepval memorial was completed, memorialising those who have no known grave. The monument stands on the approximate site of Thiepval chateau, which was never rebuilt. The choice of the high ground at Thiepval was a good one, for the monument, designed by Sir Edwin Lutyens, can be seen from most parts of the battlefield. Other memorials included the Ulster Tower, also at Thiepval, and the South African monument at Delville Wood.

The mother and brother of a British officer killed on 1 July 1916 visit his grave at Fricourt in July 1920.

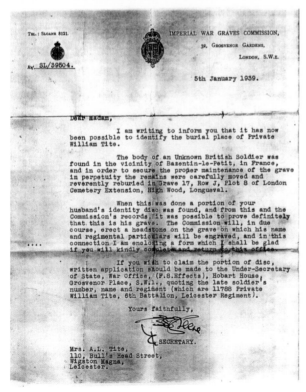

TEL.: SLOANE 8121.

Ref. SL/39504.

IMPERIAL WAR GRAVES COMMISSION,
32, GROSVENOR GARDENS,
LONDON, S.W.I.

5th January 1939.

Dear Madam,

    I am writing to inform you that it has now been possible to identify the burial place of Private William Tite.

    The body of an Unknown British Soldier was found in the vicinity of Bazentin-le-Petit, in France, and in order to secure the proper maintenance of the grave in perpetuity the remains were carefully moved and reverently reburied in Grave 17, Row J, Plot 8 of London Cemetery Extension, High Wood, Longueval.

    When this was done a portion of your husband's identity disc was found, and from this and the Commission's records, it was possible to prove definitely that this is his grave. The Commission will, in due course, erect a headstone on the grave on which his name and regimental particulars will be engraved, and in this connection I am enclosing a form which I shall be glad if you will kindly complete and return to this office.

    If you wish to claim the portion of disc, written application should be made to the Under-Secretary of State, War Office, (F.S.Effects), Hobart House, Grosvenor Place, S.W.1., quoting the late soldier's number, name and regiment (which are 11788 Private William Tite, 6th Battalion, Leicester Regiment).

Yours faithfully,

SECRETARY.

Mrs. A.L. Tite,
110, Bull's Head Street,
Wigston Magna,
Leicester.

The Somme battlefield continued to give up its dead, year by year, as this letter to the widow of a soldier killed in 1916 testifies.

During the Second World War German tanks rolled down the Albert–Bapaume road, and there was briefly fighting here once again. For the next four years the Somme was quiet, garrisoned by German soldiers who left swastika graffiti on the Ulster Tower and on some of the British headstones. After the Second World War visits from bereaved parents more or less ceased as they were now too old to make the journey, but ex-soldiers continued to return, albeit in steadily decreasing numbers. Former French soldier Pierre Jolly, writing in the 1950s, was still haunted by his experiences on the Somme; describing a recent pilgrimage in which he had walked across the former battlefield, he stated:

> We did not need [our guide] to persuade ourselves of a certainty which fills our lungs. This is the smell of death, French, German and British. Morval is not so far from the dead of yesterday, and of the day before yesterday. On this old road, buried at such great depth under the loose stones of the tarmac of another postwar era, I gasped for breath just as I had done in 1916. Afterwards, everything seemed as though I was the victim of a hallucination. During that autumn night I believed I saw the gathering of the dead.[7]

Jolly remarked that although the French government had sought to pigeonhole away the dead in order to allow life to return to normal in the area after the war, for him at least the spirits of the fallen were ever-present:

> In order to clean up the battlefield, the authorities thought that it would be sufficient, after having sorted them out according to their nationality, to park them, free, in the cemeteries. They made their escape well before the rust began to make the gates squeak. Placed in lines as straight as a die by the employees of the contractors, having no more

The summer of '66. British veterans of the Somme enjoy an impromptu game of football at a ceremony at Thiepval to mark the fiftieth anniversary of the battle, in the year England hosted the World Cup. (*Liddle Collection, University of Leeds*)

reasons to fight, speaking, moreover, the universal language of the deceased, the dead are grouped in a crowd 'huge, impossible to count' and their presence dominates these now-fertile lands. Perhaps it will be so until the disappearance of the last survivor of the Somme.[8]

Whilst the effects of the battle upon the landscape were obvious to anyone who cared to look, its impact upon those who lived through it is far less easy to discern. Popular British historiography would have it that the battle was indecisive, unnecessary and futile, and that as a result it bred both resentment and disillusion among those on the British side who had lived through it. The chief exponent of this view was perhaps the historian A.J.P. Taylor. Yet the impact of the Somme on the civilian population at the time, and upon the fighting men, is far from easy to quantify or pigeonhole, and certainly cannot be encapsulated by simple words like 'disillusion'. Among those who had lost a dearly beloved husband, brother or son, emotion ranged widely. If there was sometimes resentment, then there was also an enormous amount of quiet pride. One man who lost his son, killed in action with the Black Watch on the Somme in August 1916, wrote shortly afterwards:

It is nearly an impossibility for a man to be long in this war without being wounded or killed. And after the continual suspense it seems that even the dread news of 'killed in action' brings to overstrained human nature a sense of relief and relaxation. This may be strange but it is true. Our greatest agony I believe was giving him up at first ... the motive power of his going was the sense that his country called him and his was no craven coward spirit – to put personal safety before the call of duty which in his case was clearly the call of God ... but we also had a sacrifice to make, and we did not falter either, and we know what it is to give our only begotten son ... in our deep sorrow we have been helped by the rivers of sympathy which have flowed to us from hosts of good people ... I thank God that in his infinite mercy he ... gave to Emily and me the tremendous honour of possessing (if only for a short time) such a true, brave, honest & affectionate son as Gordon whose memory we honour & revere.[9]

The reverence with which bronze memorial plaques were framed and hung in front rooms across Britain in the 1920s and 1930s is further evidence that brothers and sons who had been killed were not perceived to have died in vain. There is also ample testimony from British and Commonwealth soldiers at the time and afterwards, who certainly believed that the battle had been a clear British victory. One of them, a Canadian stretcher-bearer, wrote to his wife:

I wonder if you at all realize what an amazing, wonderful thing this move is, realize that the Germans with all their so-called thoroughness and their thorough understanding of war according to their own rules made by themselves, having for eighteen months prepared a position, we have gone and walked right over it – manufactured machinery and trained the men to do it. Remember not one mistake has been made, not one. Have you ever thought, supposing all our carefully thought-out plans, our reliance on the morale of our new troops: any one tiny thing had gone wrong, all the world today would be saying that we were gone coons; that we could not beat the Germans at their own game; that the sooner we quit and got the best peace terms we could, the better. Instead, not one thing has gone wrong. Our amateur soldiers have proved as good as trained men, brought up to breathe the very idea of a victorious war. Our machinery has stunned the enemy. All the German ideas of artillery have been outdone. In the air we have absolute supremacy, our men even coming down to fire on troops with their machine guns.[10]

It would probably be fair to say as well that a certain degree of naivety had been lost by those who had lived through it. They had, after all, gazed through the gates of Hell and witnessed sights that few of us alive today are ever likely to see. How could that not affect any individual? One German officer, out of the battle and in a rest area, wrote of the way the Somme and his experiences in the battle had changed him as a soldier. For one thing, it had hardened his outlook:

> The poetry of the trenches is a thing of the past. The spirit of adventure is dead. We are now oppressed by the reflection that we have seen what a battle is like and shall see it again. We have become wise, serious and professional. Stern duty has taken the place of a keenness sometimes amounting to passion – a frigid, mechanical doing of one's duty.
>   When one has seen how brutal, how degrading war can be, any idyllic interval comes like a reprieve from the gallows ... I sometimes feel so wintry inside. The war which began as a fresh youth is ending as a made-up, boring, antiquated actor. Death is the only conqueror. We are all disillusioned, at least as regards what is called world philosophy.[11]

In the years which followed, there was much debate about the purpose of the battle, its conduct by the generals (particularly on the British side) and its outcomes. It became fashionable in the 1960s to deride the generals as 'donkeys', unimaginative and thoughtless, but these were the views of later generations, who subsequently tried to project them back upon the men who had lived through the Somme. In fact, the evidence suggests that the 1914–18 generation perceived the battle as a necessary evil, and that those who sought to deride their erstwhile commanders lacked an appreciation of the difficulties facing them – difficulties of logistics, of communications and of terrain. Charles Douie, who served as a subaltern at the Battle of the Somme, wrote perceptively afterwards of it, summing up the strategic conundrum facing the allies thus:

> Of the conduct of the war by the higher command I have no qualification to speak. But in reading much of the criticism which has been levelled against the 'war of attrition' and the 'wearing out battle', and the brilliant expedients which in the opinion of the critics might have re-established a war of manoeuvre and evaded the need of frontal attack, I have sometimes wondered whether anything short of a breakdown in German morale would ever have taken us to the Rhine, and whether that breakdown could have been accomplished by any other means than the hard pounding which the German army always expected, and obtained, in their battles against the British Army, however small the territory gained.[12]

Could anything positive be said about this dreadful experience? Surely not? In fact, Douie went on also to describe the way that the battle sometimes brought out the best in the characters of the men who fought in it:

> ... and while it is well that we should remember the material horror and carnage of the Somme, it is not well that we should forget that many men there found their

In 1987 Donald Price, a veteran of the 20th Battalion Royal Fusiliers, planted an English oak tree on the edge of High Wood, in memory of those of his comrades who had died there in July 1916.

manhood, there first knew the triumph of the spirit over fear and fatigue, there enjoyed a comradeship which was in itself a sufficient recompense for all things forfeited.[13]

These are perhaps difficult words for us to accept now, looking back from the vantage point of the twenty-first century, but Douie's was not an isolated example. The celebrated author Charles Carrington, who also served as an officer on the Somme, remained convinced that Britain's involvement in the war was just, that there was no alternative to persevering until victory was won, and that Britain had reason to be proud of her army's achievement. The distinguished academic Guy Chapman, who served with the Royal Fusiliers in the battle, held similar views.

The battlefield of the Somme exercised a strange hold over those who had fought on it, and many veterans returned again and again. The experience often caused these men to become reflective. Donald Price was one such ex-serviceman, even though, as he admitted, he was unsure why he was drawn back to a place of such devastation. Looking back on his experiences, he added:

When I look at the lovely countryside of the Somme ... I ask myself 'Did it really happen, or was it a dream? Was I really there? Yet, I have the scars of two wounds to show.' That was no dream. How was it that a sensitive boy like me (I was only sixteen when I enlisted) was able to stand the indescribable strain? Did my mind become so callous that death became commonplace? More often than not, pity and sorrow didn't seem to exist ... There is no doubt in my mind that the extraordinary comradeship that existed in those awful days helped to sustain one's sanity. I wasn't a particularly brave lad, but thoroughly disciplined, and when going into an attack certainly had an intense 'wind up'. One tried to hide one's fears, but the look in one's eyes betrayed the true feelings. What was my attitude to death at this time? I really don't know. What I did consciously fear was the fact of being seriously wounded, lying out there all alone, with the possibility of not being rescued. After an attack, and during roll-call discussing casualties, little grief was shown. Remarks such as 'so and so got shot through his bloody helmet' and 'so and so was blown to bloody-hell' were common. It seemed so ordinary and pitiless. Pity seemed to have vanished, and my mind had become oblivious to death.[14]

For many in their 70s and 80s, it became literally a pilgrimage: a journey they felt they must make before they died. Former private Jack Horner, who was wounded at Bazentin in July 1916, first made the journey back in May 1980. Writing after visiting Mametz and Flat Iron Copse Cemetery, he stated:

The cries of the wounded are muted, and the dead in regal solitude lie in peace, in these most beautiful and lonely surroundings, and nature in her most gracious mood has covered the woods and fields in emerald green, leaving it a most lovely sight. Beyond Mametz Wood, the green fields, the battlefields of long ago where these men fell, and with many others gave their all, leaving their blood to enrich the soil of France, their names written in the Book of Remembrance. In the little cemetery by the cart track and beneath the crested stones they sleep in peace … Maudlin sentimentality? Maybe so, but these are the men who would, and did, share their last drop of water, and think it right that they should do so. These are the men who gave their all, and asked for nothing in return, so that you should walk tall and free …[15]

It seems that, for Horner, the sacrifice made in 1916 was still valid, even after nearly seventy years. But what of those who perhaps paid the heaviest of prices for the Allied advance on the Somme? – those who were permanently maimed or blinded. What were their views? In most cases there is strong evidence that men made the best of their situation. The same determination to overcome adversity in the trenches saw them through obstacles and difficulties in civilian life. Reginald Davis, writing shortly after receiving a wound that would have life-changing consequences, remarked:

The Hun has put me completely out of action, and I hope within a few months to be amongst you all again for good, and certainly in time for the autumn session. The sight of my right eye has completely gone out, but as long as the left one keeps as it is I shall not be seriously handicapped. My glass eye will be an acceptable ornament. The left hand will mend in time; when healed, it will be pushed and squeezed into its original shape. Apart from the wounds I feel very well, and my rapid recovery has surprised all.[16]

Even allowing for the fact that this particular soldier might be 'putting a brave face on it', there is still evidence, from the 1930s and later, that the wounded would not allow themselves to be pitied, nor would they look back upon their war service with anything but pride. Gilbert Nobbs, blinded on the Somme, wrote after the war:

I do not deplore the loss of my sight, for I can say in all sincerity that I was never happier in my life than I am to-day.[17]

Ian Fraser, who also lost his sight in the battle, experienced an initial maelstrom of emotions, before settling down to get on with the business of leading as normal a life as possible. One night alone in his room he experimented with a bulb to see if he could detect any light at all:

> I should have looked such a fool if anyone had come in and seen me. Looking a fool! That was the worst part of blindness, or so it seemed to me then. And they would be sorry for me. The kindest people would be sorry for me. And I was sorry for myself. My God, what a sacrifice I had made, so light-heartedly, so cheerfully! ... And here I was ... Not only out of the war, but out of life. That was a dreadful thought.[18]

Fraser spent many weeks in bitterness and turmoil before a letter arrived inviting him to St Dunstan's, Sir Arthur Pearson's establishment for the retraining of blind officers and men:

Ian Fraser in the 1930s. He was blinded on the Somme, but the pioneering work of St Dunstan's gave him a new direction in life.

> I accepted the invitation, and entered a new world ... I went to St Dunstan's, and a marvellous change came over me ... The attainment of a measure of independence in reading to myself and typewriting and getting about alone, and looking after my own personal needs, began to dispel some part of my despair. There were intervals of cheerfulness when the clouds would be dispelled and the sun would shine through, and one would forget the darkness. And there were times when irritation at the restrictions of blindness gave way to interest in the overcoming of them. The process was slow, and though a superficial happiness pervaded my mind, it was some time before contentment and peace of mind came to me. But looking back now on the early months of blindness I think more of agreeable companions and jokes and new experiences than of despair or loneliness.[19]

The Siegfried Sassoon poem 'Does it Matter' portrays the maimed and blinded of the First World War as despondent and hopeless, their war service discredited and their sacrifice forgotten. In contrast, one British soldier, also blinded on the Somme, composed his own little-known verse to describe his position. George Eames, an ex-sergeant of the Cheshire Regiment from Port Sunlight, composed 'After All', a poem in which he remains strikingly positive about his war service:

> We got our order sharp and short and with the boys I went,
> over the top as you term it, 'til every shell was spent.
> We fought like tigers, hard we fought, when in less than a glance,
> a bursting shell, a loud report, blotted out my sight of France.
> Then next the shore of England, the cliffs of Dover white,

ah friends 'twas then I felt the strain of having lost my sight.
But people, though my sight has gone, I'm glad I played the man,
and often smile when others say 'You've done your bit, old man.'
I've done my bit, well others have, God bless them one and all,
my blindness seems with friends like you, a curtain after all.[20]

In regard to those who suffered permanent disability, such as the loss of a limb, it is also perhaps surprisingly difficult to find any evidence of post-war bitterness in relation to their involvement in the war in general, or the Battle of the Somme in particular. Undoubtedly there was sometimes anger over post-war unemployment, or the parsimony of a 1930s pension, but not a direct rejection of the values which had led men to serve their country in 1916. Ex-Royal Fusilier Daniel Faragher lost his leg on the Somme; he nevertheless lived to be 81. Prior to the war he had been a painter and decorator. He could not return to his pre-war occupation, as with one leg he was unable to climb ladders, and so he retrained as a boot repairer. His father's greenhouse at the rear of the family home became his first workshop. His daughter later recalled that in spite of his disability, her father remained cheerful all his life, only becoming occasionally unhappy when his stump caused him pain. She particularly recalled an incident around 1970 when he attended hospital in Liverpool, where children suffering from Thalidomide disabilities were fitted for artificial limbs. He said on that occasion that people who complained about their lot should see how those children got on with life with a smile. Only one illustration, yes, but it exemplifies the determination of the war generation not to be pitied.

For the Germans, the battle was just one of a series of nails in the coffin of the cohesion and morale of their fighting forces. Others included Verdun, and the Third Battle of Ypres the following year. The fact that Germany lost her best officers and men on the Somme in 1916 is an oft-stated truism. But the effects of the fighting of 1916 (at Verdun as well as on the Somme) ran much deeper than this, and its consequences were far more pervasive than many observers have realised. Prior to the war the German army was a deeply conservative institution. Its officer class was dominated by the aristocracy, and it drew its recruits in the main from agricultural labourers, avoiding as far as possible the urban working class whose members were more likely to be influenced by socialist ideas. Up until 1915 it had largely managed to maintain this character, but the inevitable result of the battles of 1916 was the dilution of the officer corps by bourgeois middle-class members, and of the ranks by socialist-minded soldiers from the cities. This

Sergeant George Eames was also blinded on the Somme. In 1921, after rehabilitation at St Dunstan's, Eames was chosen to unveil the Port Sunlight war memorial, erected by Lever Brothers, his former employers. He later carved out a career as a singer.

marked a change in the army's character away from the disciplined, cohesive formation which it had been at the start of the war; descriptions of the German army as merely a militia were already current by the winter of 1916/17. German officer Rudolf Binding arrived on the Somme from the Eastern Front around this time, and in his letters home he has some interesting observations to make:

> The battle here is the epitome of everything which the War represents to-day, that is to say, constantly repeated destruction, constant putting forth of effort, development of power and means, employment of masses of men and material, constant physical and mental strain.[21]

He confirms the decline in the quality of the German army, writing shortly after this:

Daniel Faragher and his wife at his eightieth birthday party. Faragher lost a leg while serving on the Somme with the Royal Fusiliers.

> Far away we hear the rumble of troop trains carrying the latest drafts, which, although they are the last, will yet by a touch of magic become the best. For handfuls of men are being picked out from every company and battery, to be specially trained for new formations – all those who have proved their worth at the Front and distinguished themselves for bravery and usefulness, the 'Old Guard' of the war, not the latest drafts from home.[22]

The new formations of which he speaks were the storm troop units, being developed at this time, and it is apparent from the fact that the high command was drawing for these upon the last of its pre-1916 troops that the new arrivals were not of the same quality. Binding is disparaging about Haig in his letters, accusing him of a lack of imagination during the Somme battle, but he is equally despairing about Germany's own position, stating that her generals are no better. Finally, after the withdrawal to the Hindenburg Line, he adds tellingly of his own men in St Pierre-Vaast Wood:

> Although we can flatter ourselves on the helplessness of the English, our own becomes now unpleasantly apparent. Our troops have had no successes; everybody wanted to get away as quick as possible; they were not going to risk fighting.[23]

As Winston Churchill was to observe a generation later, wars are not won by withdrawals, and the German departure from the Somme front in the spring of 1917 can only be read one way, in that it was an admission by the high command that they had suffered badly on the Somme. Both materially and in terms of morale, the British had bested them. The Somme had been the schoolroom of the British army and, although some of the tactical lessons it had learned there had been harsh ones, it would apply them with more and more success over the coming two years. Ironically, for the French the Battle of the Somme had been a successful operation, at least on the surface, but it was not enough to paper over the widening cracks in French army morale, which were appearing as a result of more than two years of continuous fighting, the most severe of which had been at Verdun. These cracks would in turn develop into open mutiny the following year. Nevertheless, most historians now agree that on the Somme were sown the seeds which would eventually flower into allied victory in 1918.

Notes

Chapter 1

1. G.C.N. Webb, unpublished letter, 31 July 1915, Liddle Collection, University of Leeds.
2. R. Archer-Houblon, unpublished recollections, Liddle Collection, University of Leeds.
3. Charles Barton, undated letter, courtesy of John Davies.
4. George F. Campbell, *A Soldier of the Sky*, Chicago, 1918, p. 176.
5. Georg Paul Neumann, *Die deutschen Luftstreitkräfte im Weltkriege*, Berlin, 1920, p. 470.
6. Marcel Étévé, *Lettres d'un Combattant*, Paris, 1917, p. 213.
7. *Ibid.*, p. 214.
8. Robert Whitney Imbrie, *Behind the Wheel of a War Ambulance*, New York, 1918, p. 77.
9. William Yorke Stevenson, *At the Front in a Flivver*, Boston MA, 1917, p. 87.
10. *Ibid.*, p. 95.
11. Charlotte Alice Hamilton Osborne Maxwell, *Frank Maxwell; a Memoir and Some Letters*, London, 1921, p. 139.
12. Charles Douie, *The Weary Road – Recollections of a Subaltern of Infantry*, London, 1929, p. 164.
13. A.V. Ratcliffe, letter, *The Microcosm*, 2 May 1916.
14. Stephen H. Hewitt, *A Scholar's Letters from the Front*, London, 1918, p. 107.
15. Ashley McGain, unpublished letter, Manx National Heritage.
16. W.A.D. Goodwin, unpublished letter, Liddle Collection, University of Leeds.
17. Alan Seeger, *Letters and Diary of Alan Seeger*, New York, 1917, p. 211.
18. Mrs Denis O'Sullivan (ed.), *Harry Butters, R.F.A., 'An American Citizen'; Life and War Letters*, New York, 1918, p. 272.
19. M.A. De Wolfe Howe (ed.), *The Harvard Volunteers in Europe; Personal Records of Experience in Military, Ambulance, and Hospital Service*, Cambridge MA, 1916, p. 170.
20. Douie, *The Weary Road*, p. 168.
21. Campbell, *A Soldier of the Sky*, p. 176.
22. Arthur Guy Empey, *Over the Top*, New York, 1917, p. 256.
23. Gerhard Siegert, *Bis Zum Bitteren Ende. Vier Jahre Stellungskrieg*, Leipzig, 1930, p. 156.
24. *Ibid.*, p. 158.
25. Edward G. Liveing, *Attack; an Infantry Subaltern's Impressions of July 1st, 1916*, New York, 1918, p. 39.
26. Richard Vincent Sutton, *Richard Vincent Sutton: A Record of His Life Together With Extracts From His Private Papers*, London, 1922, p. 125.
27. Brigadier F.P. Roe, unpublished tape-recorded recollections, Liddle Collection, University of Leeds.
28. Liveing, *Attack*, p. 54.
29. Arthur Mack, *Shellproof Mack, an American's Fighting Story*, Boston, *sd*, p. 40.

Chapter 2

1. Liveing, *Attack*, p. 59.
2. *Ibid*, p. 65.
3. Sir John Ernest Hodder-Williams, *One Young Man*, London, 1917, p. 119.
4. Empey, *Over The Top*, p. 259.

5. Mack, *Shellproof Mack*, p. 41.
6. Aubrey Moore, unpublished memoir, author's collection.
7. George Ramshaw, unpublished tape-recorded recollections, Liddle Collection, University of Leeds.
8. Otto Lais, *Erlebnisse badischer Frontsoldaten, Band 1: Maschinengewehre im Eisernen Regiment (8. Badisches Infanterie-Regiment Nr 169)*, Karlsruhe, 1935. Translation from http://www.pals.org.uk/lais_e.htm, courtesy of Andrew Jackson.
9. *Ibid.*
10. Franz Seldte, *Front-Erlebnis*, Leipzig, 1929, p. 606.
11. Charles Barton, undated letter, courtesy of John Davies.
12. Geoffrey H. Malins, *How I Filmed the War*, London, 1920, p. 161.
13. *Ibid.*
14. Edward Packe, unpublished memoir.
15. Olive Dent, *A V.A.D. in France*, London, 1917, p. 329.
16. J.W. Shannon report, WO 161/96/10, The National Archives, London.
17. F.P. Crozier in Sir John Hammerton (ed.), *The Great War … I Was There!*, London, *sd*, p. 659.
18. *Ibid.*
19. *Ibid.*
20. George A. Birmingham, *A Padre in France*, London, 1918, p. 210.
21. John Terraine, *General Jack's Diary 1914–1918*, London, 1964, p. 147.
22. B. Gordon, unpublished account, Liddle Collection, University of Leeds.
23. *Ibid.*
24. *Ibid.*
25. Oliver Elmer, unpublished letter, Liddle Collection, University of Leeds.
26. T.R. Price, unpublished tape-recorded recollections, Liddle Collection, University of Leeds.
27. *Isle of Man Examiner*, 29 July 1916.
28. Emil Goebelbecker, unpublished account, Liddle Collection, University of Leeds.
29. *The Advertiser* [Adelaide, South Australia], 11 September 1916.
30. Georges Lafond, *Covered with Mud and Glory: a Machine Gun Company in Action*, Boston MA, 1918, p. 227.
31. Siegert, *Bis Zum Bitteren Ende*, p. 170.
32. Adolf Köster, *Wandernde erde: Kriegsberichte aus dem Westen*, München, 1917, p. 103.
33. *Ibid.*
34. John Morris, *Hired to Kill*, London, 1960, p. 44.

Chapter 3
1. Seeger, *Letters and Diary*, p. 212.
2. Paul Ayres Rockwell, *American Fighters in the Foreign Legion, 1914–1918*, Boston MA, 1930, p. 203.
3. Harry Davis Trounce, *Fighting the Bouche Underground*, New York, 1918, p. 118.
4. Lionel William Crouch, *Duty and Service: Letters From the Front*, London, 1917, p. 117.
5. Paul Ettighoffer, *Wo Bist du Kamerad? der Frontsoldat im Reichssender Köln*, Essen, 1938, p. 216.
6. D.G. Gregory, unpublished account, Liddle Collection, University of Leeds.
7. R.H. Hutchings, unpublished account, Liddle Collection, University of Leeds.
8. Llewellyn Wynn-Jones in Sir John Hammerton (ed.), *The Great War … I Was There!*, p. 662.
9. Augustin Cochin, *Le Capitaine Augustin Cochin. Quelques Lettres de Guerre*, Paris, 1917, p. 55.

10. *Ibid*, p. 57.
11. Ettighoffer, *Wo Bist du Kamerad?*, p. 144.
12. M. Dutrèb, *Nos Sénégalais pendant la Grande Guerre*, Metz, 1922, p. 48.
13. *Ibid*, p. 49.
14. Max Plowman, *A Subaltern on the Somme*, New York, 1928, p. 54.
15. William Strang, unpublished manuscript diary, Liddle Collection, University of Leeds.
16. Maxwell, *Frank Maxwell*, p. 154.
17. *Ibid*, p. 155.
18. Anon, *Erinnerungsblätter der 178er*, Dresden, 1917, p. 177.
19. I.L. Read, *Of Those We Loved*, Bishop Auckland, 1994, p. 143.
20. *Ibid*, p. 149.
21. Alexander de Lisle, unpublished account. Courtesy of Squire de Lisle.
22. *Ibid*.
23. Read, *Of Those We Loved*, p. 159.
24. A.F. Wedd, *German Students' War Letters Translated and Arranged from the Original Edition of Dr Philip Witkop*, London, 1929, p. 227.
25. Graham Seton Hutchison in Sir John Hammerton (ed.), *The Great War … I Was There!*, p. 726.
26. *The Canadian* magazine, vol. 47 (1916), p. 421.
27. B.U.S. Cripps, unpublished tape-recorded recollections, Liddle Collection, University of Leeds.
28. Nicholas Vlok, in *South Africa* magazine (quoted in Ian Uys, *Rollcall*, Uys Publishers, Germiston, South Africa, 1991, p. 60).
29. G.A. Lawson in Sir John Hammerton (ed.), *The Great War … I Was There!*, p. 739.
30. Köster, *Wandernde erde*, p. 94.
31. Hope Bagenal, *Fields and Battlefields*, New York, 1918, p. 204.
32. *Ibid*, p. 206.
33. *Ibid*, p. 207.
34. H.J. Brooks, unpublished diary, 15 July 1916, Liddle Collection, University of Leeds.
35. Cecil Lewis in Sir John Hammerton (ed.), *The Great War … I Was There!*, p. 753.
36. R.H.M.S. Saundby, *Flying Colours*, London, 1919.
37. *Ibid*.
38. *Ibid*.
39. Oswald Boelcke (trans. Robert Reynold Hirsch), *An Aviator's Field Book*, New York, 1917, p. 139.
40. Manfred von Richthofen (trans. J. Ellis Barker), *The Red Battle Flyer*, New York, 1918, p. 114.
41. Max Zeidelhack, *Bayerische Flieger im Weltkrieg; Ein Buch der Taten und Erinnerungen*, München, 1919, p. 80.
42. Étévé, *Lettres d'un Combattant*, p. 243.
43. *Ibid*, p. 247.
44. Etienne Derville, *Correspondances et notes Aout 1914–Juin 1918*, Tourcoing, 1921, p. 293.
45. C.M. Murray, unpublished diary, Liddle Collection, University of Leeds.
46. *Ibid*, 21 July 1916.
47. Donald Price, unpublished account, Liddle Collection, University of Leeds.
48. Frank Richards, *Old Soldiers Never Die*, London, 1933, p. 190.
49. *Ibid*.
50. Dominic Devas, *From Cloister to Camp, Being Reminiscences of a Priest in France 1915 to 1918*, London, 1919, p. 46.
51. Ian Fraser, *Whereas I Was Blind*, London, 1942, p. 75.
52. *Ibid*, p. 4.

53. John Robertson Hawke, letter 29 July 1916, D55/053, University of Wollongong.
54. Ron Austin, *Cobbers in Khaki*, McCrae, Australia, 1997, p. 122.
55. *Ibid*, p. 122.
56. Ron Austin, *Forward Undeterred*, McCrae, Australia, 1998, p. 86.

Chapter 4
 1. Rudolf Hoffmann, *Der Deutsche Soldat – Briefe aus dem Weltkrieg*, München, 1937, p. 254.
 2. Patrick Terrence McCoy, *Kiltie McCoy, an American Boy with an Irish Name Fighting in France as a Scotch Soldier*, Indianapolis, 1918, p. 215.
 3. *Ibid*, p. 215.
 4. *Ibid*, p. 224.
 5. *Ramsey Courier*, 18 August 1916.
 6. George Coppard, *With a Machine Gun to Cambrai*, London, 1980, p. 92.
 7. Rockwell, *American Fighters*, p. 203.
 8. Wedd, *German Students' War Letters*, p. 322.
 9. Roger Cadot, *Souvenirs d'un Combattant*, [sl], 2010, p. 404.
10. Louis Mairet, *Carnet d'un Combattant*, Paris, 1919, p. 174.
11. *Ibid*, p. 202.
12. Anon, *Wissen und Wehr*, vol. 3, Berlin, 1922, p. 328.
13. Wedd, *German Student's War Letters*, p. 289.
14. *Ibid*, p. 289.
15. *Isle of Man Times*, 9 September 1916.
16. Andrew R. Buxton, *Andrew R. Buxton, the Rifle Brigade, a Memoir*, London, 1918, p. 208.
17. *Ibid*.
18. O'Sullivan (ed.), *Harry Butters*, p. 285.
19. Ernst Junger in Sir John Hammerton (ed.), *The Great War ... I Was There!*, p. 771.
20. E.J. Rule in Sir John Hammerton (ed.), *The Great War ... I Was There!*, p. 779.
21. *Ibid*, p. 780.
22. Theodore Drexel, *Einundzwanzig tage im trommelfeuer an der Somme, august–september 1916*, Kaiserslautern, 1917, pp. 13–14.
23. *Ibid*.
24. Mairet, *Carnet d'un Combattant*, p. 212.
25. Wedd, *German Students' War Letters*, p. 315.
26. Eduard Heyck (ed.), *Briefe einer Heidelberger Burschenschaft 1914–1918. Zu Ehren studentischer deutscher Gesinnung hrsg. von Ed. Heyck*, Lahr i. Baden, 1919, p. 133.
27. *Ibid*.
28. *Ibid*.
29. Heinrich Stegemann, *Infanterie-Regiment Bremen im Felde 1914–1918*, Bremen, 1919, p. 41.
30. Nar Diouf, oral history interview. Archive of Professor Joe Lunn. By courtesy of Joe Lunn.
31. Mairet, *Carnet d'un Combattant*, p. 224.
32. Pierre Mac Orlan, *Les Poissons Morts; la Lorraine-l'Artois-Verdun-la Somme*, Paris, 1917, p. 217.
33. Adela Marion Adam, *Arthur Innes Adam, 1894–1916. A Record Founded on his Letters*, Cambridge, 1920, p. 289.
34. *Ibid*, p. 242.
35. Laurence Housman, *War Letters of Fallen Englishmen*, New York, 1930, p. 168.
36. *Ibid*, p. 311.
37. Gilbert Nobbs in Sir John Hammerton (ed.), *The Great War ... I Was There!*, p. 786.
38. Paul Dubrulle, *Mon Régiment: dans la Fournaise de Verdun et dans la Bataille de la Somme. Impressions de Guerre d'un Prêtre Soldat*, Paris, 1917, p. 208.

39. *Ibid.*
40. G.B. Horridge papers, Liddle Collection, University of Leeds.
41. Louis Botti, *Avec Les Zouaves – Journal d'un Mitrailleur*, [sl] 1922, p. 274.
42. F. Fonsagrive, *En Batterie! Verdun (1916)–La Somme–L'Aisne*, Paris, 1919, p. 153.
43. *Ibid.*

Chapter 5
1. Hardiman Scott, *Many a Summer*, Thwaite, 1991, p. 86.
2. *Ibid*, p. 81.
3. Robert Tate, unpublished tape-recorded recollections, Liddle Collection, University of Leeds.
4. G.P.A. Fildes, *Iron Times with the Guards*, London, 1918, p. 246.
5. Robert Derby Holmes, *A Yankee in the Trenches*, Boston MA, 1918, p. 127.
6. *Ibid.*
7. Leonard Wilkinson, unpublished typescript diary, author's collection.
8. *Ibid.*
9. R.L. Bradley, unpublished letter, 22 September 1916, Liddle Collection, University of Leeds.
10. C.H. Weston, *Three Years with the New Zealanders*, London, 1918, p. 97.
11. *Isle of Man Weekly Times*, 30 September 1916.
12. Friedrich Frerk, *Die Sommeschlacht*, Leipzig, 1916, p. 67.
13. *Ibid.*
14. Valentine Williams, *The Adventures of an Ensign*, Edinburgh and London, 1917, p. 247.
15. *Ibid.*
16. *Ibid*, p. 249.
17. Joseph Smith, *Over There and Back in Three Uniforms, Being the Experiences of an American Boy in the Canadian, British and American Armies at the Front and Through No Man's Land*, New York, (sd), p. 168.
18. Frederick Thomas Rowland Howard, *On Three Battle Fronts*, New York, 1918, p. 105.
19. Armine Norris, *Mainly for Mother*, Toronto, (sd), p. 105.
20. *Ibid*, p. 106.
21. Wilhelm Bruns in Paul Hildebrandt (ed.), *Das deutsche Schwert; Kriegserlebnisse deutscher Oberlehrer 2. folge*, Leipzig, 1918, p. 32.
22. Arthur Hunt Chute, *The Real Front*, New York, 1918, p. 136.
23. Adrien Henry, *Un Meusien au Coeur des Deux Guerres*, Louviers, 2011, p. 70.
24. Jacques Civray, *Journal d'un Officier de Liaison (la Marne–la Somme–l'Yser)*, Paris, 1917, p. 109.
25. Alan Bott, *An Airman's Outings*, London, 1917, p. 41.
26. *Ibid*, p. 42.
27. Boelcke, *An Aviator's Field Book*, p. 192.
28. Frank T. Courtney, *Flight Path – My Fifty Years of Aviation*, London, 1972, p. 95.
29. John Glubb, *Into Battle – A Soldier's Diary of the Great War*, London, 1978, p. 66.
30. *Ibid*, p. 67.
31. Alice Fitzgerald, *The Edith Cavell Nurse From Massachusetts: a Record*, Boston MA, 1917, p. 26.

Chapter 6
1. Hoffmann, *Der Deutsche Soldat*, p. 269.
2. Read, *Of Those We Loved*, p. 199.
3. Neumann, *Die deutschen Luftstreitkräfte*, p. 575.
4. Wedd, *German Students' War Letters*, p. 372.

5. Housman, *War Letters of Fallen Englishmen*, p. 259.
6. *Ibid*, p. 260.
7. *Ibid*, p. 261.
8. Bernard Newman, *Speaking From Memory*, London, 1960, p. 28.
9. Alfred Ihne, *50 Fahrten mit dem Lazarettzuge nach der Westfront*, Darmstadt, 1917, p. 79.
10. Coningsby Dawson, *Carry on: Letters in Wartime*, New York, 1917, p. 57.
11. *Ibid*, p. 59.
12. Ettighoffer, *Wo Bist du Kamerad?*, p. 229.
13. Jules Émile Henches, *À l'École de la Guerre; Lettres d'un Artilleur, Août 1914–Octobre 1916*, Paris, 1918, p. 205.
14. *Ibid*, p. 208.
15. Adolf Hitler, *Mein Kampf*, London, 1939, p. 247.
16. *Ibid*.
17. Hoffmann, *Der Deutsche Soldat*, p. 278.
18. *Ibid*, p. 281.
19. Henry, *Un Meusien au Coeur des Deux Guerres*, p. 72.
20. *Ibid*.
21. *Ibid*.
22. Pierre Jolly, *Les Survivants Vont Mourir*, Paris, 1954, p. 75.
23. *Ibid*, p. 135.
24. Cordt von Brandis, *Die Stürmer von Douaumont; Kriegserlebnisse eines Kompagnieführers*, Berlin, 1917, p. 126.
25. Plowman, *A Subaltern on the Somme*, p. 114.
26. Alexander McLintock, *Best o' Luck; How a Fighting Kentuckian Won the Thanks of Britain's King*, New York, 1917, p. 114.
27. *Ibid*, p. 121.
28. *Ibid*, p. 129.
29. *Isle of Man Weekly Times*, 11 November 1916.
30. Pierre Louis Georges Bréant, *De l'Alsace à la Somme; Souvenirs du Front (Août 1914–Janvier 1917)*, Paris, 1917, p. 205.
31. Bert Hall, *En L'Air! Three Years On and Above Three Fronts*, New York, 1918, p. 91.
32. *Ibid*, p. 94.
33. Heyck (ed.), *Briefe einer Heidelberger Burschenschaft 1914–1918*, p. 147.
34. Douglas Jerrold in Sir John Hammerton (ed.), *The Great War … I Was There!*, p. 887.
35. *Ibid*, p. 888.
36. Sidney Howard in Sir John Hammerton (ed.), *The Great War … I Was There!*, p. 891.
37. *Ibid*, p. 892.
38. *Ibid*.
39. Geoffrey Sparrow & J.N. Macbean Ross, *On Four Fronts with the Royal Naval Division*, London, 1918, p. 175.
40. *Ibid*, p. 177.
41. *Ibid*, p. 180.
42. David Rorie in Sir John Hammerton (ed.), *The Great War … I Was There!*, p. 900.
43. *Ibid*, p. 901.
44. Smith, *Over There and Back in Three Uniforms*, p. 200.
45. Roy Corlett, officer's service papers, Manx National Heritage, MS 10987.
46. Ashley Gibson, *Postscript to Adventure*, London and Toronto, 1930, p. 155.
47. Jean Julien Weber, *Sur les Pentes du Golgotha – Un Prêtre dans les Tranchées*, Strasbourg, 2001, p. 153.
48. Charles Carrington, unpublished tape-recorded recollections, Liddle Collection, University of Leeds.

Epilogue

1. Ardern Beaman, *The Squadroon*, London, 1920, p. 187.
2. Alban F. Bacon, *The Wanderings of a Temporary Warrior: a Territorial Officer's Narrative of Service (and Sport) in Three Continents*, London, 1922, p. 195.
3. John Oxenham, *High Altars; The Battle-fields of France and Flanders as I Saw Them*, New York, 1918, p. 28.
4. Stephen Graham, *The Challenge of the Dead*, London, 1921, p. 98.
5. *Ibid*.
6. J. Perret, *Raisons de Famille. Souvenirs II*, Paris, 1976, p. 357.
7. Jolly, *Les Survivants Vont Mourir*, p. 105.
8. *Ibid*.
9. Quayle papers, Manx National Heritage, MS 13070.
10. Anna Chapin Ray, *Letters of a Canadian Stretcher Bearer*, Boston MA, 1918, p. 82.
11. Wedd, *German Students' War Letters*, p. 325.
12. Douie, *The Weary Road*, p. 74.
13. *Ibid*, p. 164.
14. David A. Clark, *Great War Memories*, Blackburn, 1987, p. 52.
15. Jack Horner, unpublished typescript memoir (author's collection).
16. Hodder-Williams, *One Young Man*, p. 124.
17. Gilbert Nobbs, *On The Right of the British Line*, New York, 1918, *preface*.
18. Fraser, *Whereas I Was Blind*, p. 2.
19. *Ibid*, p. 5.
20. Quoted on: www.liverpoolmuseums.org.uk/podcasts/transcripts/over_by_christmas.aspx.
21. Rudolf Binding, *A Fatalist At War*, New York, 1929, p. 140.
22. *Ibid*, p. 144.
23. *Ibid*, p. 154.

Bibliography

Adam, Adela Marion, *Arthur Innes Adam, 1894–1916. A Record Founded on his Letters*, Cambridge, 1920.

Adams, John Bernard, *Nothing of Importance*, New York, 1918.

Anon, *Erinnerungsblätter der 178er*, Dresden, 1917.

Anon, *Wissen und Wehr*, vol. 3, Berlin, 1922.

Austin, Ron, *Cobbers in Khaki*, McCrae, Australia, 1997.

Austin, Ron, *Forward Undeterred*, McCrae, Australia, 1998.

Bacon, Alban F., *The Wanderings of a Temporary Warrior: a Territorial Officer's Narrative of Service (and Sport) in Three Continents*, London, 1922.

Bagenal, Hope, *Fields and Battlefields*, New York, 1918.

Beaman, Ardern, *The Squadroon*, London, 1920.

Binding, Rudolf, *A Fatalist At War*, New York, 1929.

Binet-Valmer, Gustave, *Mémoires d'un Engagé Volontaire*, Paris, 1918.

Birmingham, George A. (pseud. of James Owen Hannay), *A Padre in France*, London, 1918.

Boelcke, Oswald (trans. Hirsch, Robert Reynold), *An Aviator's Field Book*, New York, 1917.

Bott, Alan, *An Airman's Outings*, London, 1917.

Botti, Louis, *Avec Les Zouaves – Journal d'un Mitrailleur*, (sl), 1922.

Bréant, Pierre Louis Georges, *De l'Alsace à la Somme; Souvenirs du Front (Août 1914–Janvier 1917)*, Paris, 1917.

Buxton, Andrew R., *Andrew R. Buxton, the Rifle Brigade, a Memoir*, London, 1918.

Cadot, Roger, *Souvenirs d'un Combattant*, (sl), 2010.

Campbell, George F., *A Soldier of the Sky*, Chicago, 1918.

Chute, Arthur Hunt, *The Real Front*, New York, 1918.

Civray, Jacques (pseud. of Capitaine Plieux de Diusse), *Journal d'un Officier de Liaison (la Marne–la Somme–l'Yser)*, Paris, 1917.

Clark, David A., *Great War Memories*, Blackburn, 1987.

Cochin, Augustin, *Le Capitaine Augustin Cochin. Quelques Lettres de Guerre*, Paris, 1917.

Coppard, George, *With a Machine Gun to Cambrai*, London, 1980.

Courtney, Frank T., *Flight Path – My Fifty Years of Aviation*, London, 1972.

Crouch, Lionel William, *Duty and Service: Letters From the Front*, London, 1917.

Dawson, A.J., *Somme Battle Stories*, London, 1916.

Dawson, Coningsby, *Carry on: Letters in Wartime*, New York, 1917.

Dawson, N.P., *The Good Soldier, a Selection of Soldiers' Letters, 1914–18*, (sl), 1918.

De Lévis-Mirepoix, Antoine, *Les Campagnes Ardentes; Impressions de Guerre*, Paris, 1917.

Dent, Olive, *A V.A.D. in France*, London, 1917.

Derville, Etienne, *Correspondances et notes Aout 1914–Juin 1918*, Tourcoing, 1921.

Devas, Dominic, *From Cloister to Camp, Being Reminiscences of a Priest in France 1915 to 1918*, London, 1919.

Dinning, Hector William, *By-ways on Service; Notes from an Australian Journal*, London, 1918.

Douie, Charles, *The Weary Road – Recollections of a Subaltern of Infantry*, London, 1929.

Drake, Vivian, *Above the Battle*, New York/London, 1918.

Drexel, Theodore, *Einundzwanzig tage im trommelfeuer an der Somme, august–september 1916*, Kaiserslautern, 1917.

Dubrulle, Paul, *Mon Régiment: dans la Fournaise de Verdun et dans la Bataille de la Somme. Impressions de Guerre d'un Prêtre Soldat*, Paris, 1917.

Dutrèb, M., *Nos Sénégalais pendant la Grande Guerre*, Metz, 1922.

Eckhardt, Curt, *An alle Frontsoldaten*, Berlin, 1919.

Empey, Arthur Guy, *Over the Top*, New York, 1917.

Étévé, Marcel, *Lettres d'un Combattant*, Paris, 1917.

Ettighoffer, Paul, *Wo Bist du Kamerad? Der Frontsoldat im Reichssender Köln*, Essen, 1938.

Fallon, David, *The Big Fight (Gallipoli to the Somme)*, New York, (sd).

Farrer, Reginald, *The Void of War; Letters from the Three Fronts*, Boston MA, 1918.

Fernand-Laurent, Camille Jean, *Chez nos Alliés Britanniques (With our British Allies in the Field); Notes et Souvenirs d'un Interprète*, (sl), 1917.

Fildes, G.P.A., *Iron Times with the Guards*, London, 1918.

Fitzgerald, Alice, *The Edith Cavell Nurse From Massachusetts: a Record*, Boston MA, 1917.

Fonsagrive, Lieutenant F., *En Batterie! Verdun (1916)–La Somme–L'Aisne*, Paris, 1919.

Fraser, Ian, *Whereas I Was Blind*, London, 1942.

Frerk, Friedrich Willy, *Die Sommeschlacht*, Leipzig, 1916.

Fryer, E.R.M., *Reminiscences of a Grenadier*, London, 1919.

Gibson, Ashley, *Postscript to Adventure*, London and Toronto, 1930.

Glubb, John, *Into Battle – A Soldier's Diary of the Great War*, London, 1978.

Graham, Stephen, *The Challenge of the Dead*, London, 1921.

Hall, Bert, *En L'Air! Three Years On and Above Three Fronts*, New York, 1918.

Hammerton, Sir John (ed.), *The Great War … I Was There!*, London, *sd*.

Henches, Jules Émile, *À l'École de la Guerre; Lettres d'un Artilleur, Août 1914–Octobre 1916*, Paris, 1918.

Henry, Adrien, *Un Meusien au Coeur des Deux Guerres*, Louviers, 2011.

Hewitt, Stephen H., *A Scholar's Letters from the Front*, London, 1918.

Heyck, Eduard (ed.), *Briefe einer Heidelberger Burschenschaft 1914–1918. Zu Ehren studentischer deutscher Gesinnung hrsg. von Ed. Heyck*, Lahr i. Baden, 1919.

Hildebrandt, Paul (ed.), *Das deutsche Schwert; Kriegserlebnisse deutscher Oberlehrer 2. Folge*, Leipzig, 1918.

Hitler, Adolf, *Mein Kampf*, London, 1939.

Hodder-Williams, Sir John Ernest, *One Young Man: the Simple and True Story of a Clerk Who Enlisted in 1914, Who Fought on the Western Front For Nearly Two Years, Was Severely Wounded at the Battle of the Somme, and is Now on His Way Back to His Desk*, London, 1917.

Hoffmann, Rudolf, *Der Deutsche Soldat – Briefe aus dem Weltkrieg*, München, 1937.

Holmes, Robert Derby, *A Yankee in the Trenches*, Boston MA, 1918.

Housman, Laurence, *War Letters of Fallen Englishmen*, New York, 1930.

Howard, Frederick Thomas Rowland, *On Three Battle Fronts*, New York, 1918.

Howcroft, Gilbert Burdett, *The First World War Remembered By a Yorkshire Territorial*, Oldham, 1986.

Howe, M.A. De Wolfe (ed.), *The Harvard Volunteers in Europe; Personal Records of Experience in Military, Ambulance, and Hospital Service*, Cambridge MA, 1916.

Ihne, Alfred, *50 Fahrten mit dem Lazarettzuge nach der Westfront*, Darmstadt, 1917.

Imbrie, Robert Whitney, *Behind the Wheel of a War Ambulance*, New York, 1918.

Jolly, Pierre, *Les Survivants Vont Mourir*, Paris, 1954.

Kingsley, Ronald, *Fighting Fritz; A True Narrative of the Experiences Gained in Five Months of Furious Fighting on the Somme and at Ypres*, Detroit, 1917.

Knyvett, R. Hugh, *'Over there' with the Australians*, New York, 1918.

Köster, Adolf, *Wandernde erde; Kriegsberichte aus dem Western*, München, 1917.

Lafond, Georges, *Covered with Mud and Glory: a Machine Gun Company in Action*, Boston MA, 1918.

Lais, Otto, *Erlebnisse badischer Frontsoldaten, Band 1: Maschinengewehre im Eisernen Regiment (8. Badisches Infanterie-Regiment Nr 169)*, Karlsruhe, 1935.

Liveing, Edward G., *Attack; an Infantry Subaltern's Impressions of July 1st, 1916*, New York, 1918.

McBride, Herbert W., *The Emma Gees*, Indianapolis, 1918.

McCoy, Patrick Terrence, *Kiltie McCoy, an American boy with an Irish Name Fighting in France as a Scotch Soldier*, Indianapolis, 1918.

McLintock, Alexander, *Best o' Luck; How a Fighting Kentuckian Won the Thanks of Britain's King*, New York, 1917.

Mac Orlan, Pierre, *Les Poissons Morts; la Lorraine–l'Artois–Verdun–la Somme*, Paris, 1917.

Mack, Arthur, *Shellproof Mack, an American's Fighting Story*, Boston MA, (sd).

Mairet, Louis, *Carnet d'un Combattant*, Paris, 1919.

Malins, Geoffrey H., *How I Filmed the War*, London, 1920.

'Mark VII' (pseud. of Max Plowman), *A Subaltern on the Somme*, New York 1928.

Maxwell, Charlotte Alice Hamilton Osborne, *Frank Maxwell; A Memoir and Some Letters*, London, 1921.

Morris, John, *Hired to Kill*, London, 1960.

Neumann, Georg Paul, *Die deutschen Luftstreitkräfte im Weltkriege*, Berlin, 1920.

Newman, Bernard, *Speaking From Memory*, London, 1960.

Nobbs, Gilbert, *On The Right of the British Line*, New York, 1918.

Norris, Armine, *Mainly for Mother*, Toronto, (sd).

O'Sullivan, Mrs Denis (ed.), *Harry Butters, R.F.A., 'An American Citizen'; Life and War Letters*, New York, 1918.

Oxenham, John, *High Altars; The Battle-fields of France and Flanders as I Saw Them*, New York, 1918.

Palmer, Frederick *With the New Army on the Somme: My Second Year of the War*, London, 1917.

Pellissier, Robert, *Letters from a Chasseur à Pied*, (sl), 1917.

Perret, J., *Raisons de Famille. Souvenirs II*, Paris, 1976.

Plowman, Max (alias 'Mark VII'), *A Subaltern on the Somme*, New York, 1928.

Purdom, C.B., *Everyman at War*, London, 1930.

Ray, Anna Chapin, *Letters of a Canadian Stretcher Bearer*, Boston MA, 1918.

Read, I.L., *Of Those We Loved*, Pentland Press, Bishop Auckland, 1994.

Richards, Frank, *Old Soldiers Never Die*, London, 1933.

Riebicke, Otto, *Ringen an der Somme und im Herzen*, Magdeburg, 1918.

Rockwell, Paul Ayres, *American Fighters in the Foreign Legion, 1914–1918*, Boston MA, 1930.

Saundby, R.H.M.S., *Flying Colours*, London, 1919.

Scott, Frederick George, *The Great War As I Saw It*, Toronto, 1922.

Scott, Hardiman, *Many a Summer*, Thwaite, 1991.

Seeger, Alan, *Letters and Diary of Alan Seeger*, New York, 1917.

Seldte, Franz, *Front-Erlebnis*, Leipzig, 1929.

Siegert, Gerhard, *Bis Zum Bitteren Ende. Vier Jahre Stellungskrieg*, Leipzig, 1930.

Smith, Joseph, *Over There and Back in Three Uniforms, Being the Experiences of an American Boy in the Canadian, British and American Armies at the Front and Through No Man's Land*, New York, (sd).

Sparrow, Geoffrey and Macbean Ross, J.N., *On Four Fronts with the Royal Naval Division*, London, 1918.

Stegemann, Heinrich, *Infanterie-Regiment Bremen im Felde 1914–1918*, Bremen, 1919.

Stevenson, William Yorke, *At the Front in a Flivver*, Boston MA, 1917.

Sutton, Richard Vincent, *Richard Vincent Sutton: a Record of His Life Together With Extracts From His Private Papers*, London, 1922.

Terraine, John, *General Jack's Diary, 1914–1918*, London, 1964.

Trounce, Harry Davis, *Fighting the Bouche Underground*, New York, 1918.

Uys, Ian, *Rollcall*, Uys Publishers, Germiston, South Africa, 1991.

Von Brandis, Cordt, *Die Stürmer von Douaumont; Kriegserlebnisse eines Kompagnieführers*, Berlin, 1917.

Von Richthofen, Manfred (trans. Barker, J. Ellis), *The Red Battle Flyer*, New York, 1918.

Weber, Jean Julien, *Sur les Pentes du Golgotha – Un Prêtre dans les Tranchées*, Strasbourg, 2001.

Wedd, A.F., *German Students' War Letters Translated and Arranged from the Orginal Edition of Dr Philip Witkop*, London, 1929.

Wells, Clifford Almon, *From Montreal to Vimy Ridge and Beyond; the Correspondence of Lieut. Clifford Almon Wells, B.A., of the 8th battalion, Canadians, B.E.F., November, 1915–April, 1917*, Toronto, 1917.

Weston, C.H., *Three years with the New Zealanders*, London, 1918.

Williams, Valentine, *The Adventures of an Ensign*, Edinburgh and London, 1917.

Witkop, Phillip, *Kriegsbriefe gefallener Studenten*, Leipzig, 1918.

Zeidelhack, Max, *Bayerische Flieger im Weltkrieg; ein Buch der Taten und Erinnerungen*, München, 1919.

Index